PHILOSOPHY OF MIND

Imaginative cases, or what might be called puzzles and other thought experiments, play a central role in philosophy of mind. The real world also furnishes philosophers with an ample supply of such puzzles.

This volume collects 50 of the most important historical and contemporary cases in philosophy of mind and describes their significance. The authors divide them into five sections: consciousness and dualism; physicalist theories and the metaphysics of mind; content, intentionality, and representation; perception, imagination, and attention; and persons, personal identity, and the self. Each chapter provides background, describes a central case or cases, discusses the relevant literature, and suggests further readings. *Philosophy of Mind: 50 Puzzles, Paradoxes, and Thought Experiments* promises to be a useful teaching tool as well as a handy resource for anyone interested in the area.

Key Features:

- Offers stand-alone chapters, each presented in an identical format:
  - Background
  - The Case
  - Discussion
  - Recommended Reading
- Each chapter is self-contained, allowing students to quickly understand an issue and giving instructors flexibility in assigning readings to match the themes of the course.
- Additional pedagogical features include a general volume introduction as well as smaller introductions to each of the five sections and a glossary at the end of the book.

Torin Alter is Professor of Philosophy at the University of Alabama, USA. Most of his publications concern consciousness and the mind–body problem, including *The Matter of Consciousness: From the Knowledge Argument to Russellian Monism* (Oxford UP, 2023) and *A Dialogue on Consciousness* (Oxford UP, 2009; co-written with Robert J. Howell).

Robert J. Howell is Yasser El-Sayed Chair of Philosophy at Rice University, USA. He has published extensively in the philosophy of mind, and is the author of *Self-Awareness and the Elusive Subject* (Oxford UP, 2023) and *Consciousness and the Limits of Objectivity* (Oxford UP, 2013). With Torin Alter, he has co-authored *A Dialogue on Consciousness* (Oxford UP, 2009) and *The God Dialogues* (Oxford UP, 2011).

Amy Kind is the Russell K. Pitzer Professor of Philosophy at Claremont McKenna College, USA. She has published extensively in the philosophy of mind, with much of her work taking up issues relating to imagination. She has also authored and edited numerous books, including *Philosophy of Mind: The Basics* (Routledge, 2020).

PUZZLES, PARADOXES, AND THOUGHT EXPERIMENTS IN PHILOSOPHY

Imaginative cases—or what might be called puzzles, paradoxes, and other thought experiments—play a central role in philosophy. This series offers students and researchers a wide range of such imaginative cases, with each volume devoted to fifty such cases in a major subfield of philosophy. Every book in the series includes: some initial background information on each case, a clear and detailed description of the case, and an explanation of the issue(s) to which the case is relevant. Key responses to the case and suggested readings lists are also included.

Recently published volumes:

EPISTEMOLOGY
KEVIN MCCAIN

FREE WILL AND HUMAN AGENCY
GARRETT PENDERGRAFT

PHILOSOPHY OF LANGUAGE
MICHAEL P. WOLF

AESTHETICS
MICHEL-ANTOINE XHIGNESSE

PHILOSOPHY OF MIND
TORIN ALTER, ROBERT J. HOWELL, AND AMY KIND

BIOETHICS
SEAN AAS, COLLIN O'NEIL, AND CHIARA LEPORA

FORTHCOMING VOLUMES:

ETHICS
SARAH STROUD AND DANIEL MUÑOZ

METAPHYSICS
SAM COWLING, WESLEY D. CRAY, AND KELLY TROGDON

For a full list of published volumes in Puzzles, Paradoxes, and Thought Experiments in Philosophy, please visit www.routledge.com/Puzzles, Paradoxes, andThoughtExperimentsinPhilosophy/book-series/PPTEP

PHILOSOPHY OF MIND
50 Puzzles, Paradoxes, and Thought Experiments

Torin Alter, Robert J. Howell, and Amy Kind

NEW YORK AND LONDON

Designed cover image: Greyscale version of an image
by Adrien Converse from Unsplash.

First published 2024
by Routledge
605 Third Avenue, New York, NY 10158

and by Routledge
4 Park Square, Milton Park, Abingdon, Oxon, OX14 4RN

Routledge is an imprint of the Taylor & Francis Group, an informa business

© 2024 Torin Alter, Robert J. Howell, and Amy Kind

The right of Torin Alter, Robert J. Howell, and Amy Kind to be identified as authors of this work has been asserted in accordance with sections 77 and 78 of the Copyright, Designs and Patents Act 1988.

All rights reserved. No part of this book may be reprinted or reproduced or utilised in any form or by any electronic, mechanical, or other means, now known or hereafter invented, including photocopying and recording, or in any information storage or retrieval system, without permission in writing from the publishers.

Trademark notice: Product or corporate names may be trademarks or registered trademarks, and are used only for identification and explanation without intent to infringe.

ISBN: 978-1-032-01585-9 (hbk)
ISBN: 978-1-032-01584-2 (pbk)
ISBN: 978-1-003-17919-1 (ebk)

DOI: 10.4324/9781003179191

Typeset in Bembo
by codeMantra

CONTENTS

Acknowledgements   xi

General Introduction   1

Part I: Consciousness and Dualism   3
    Introduction   3

1. The Floating Man   5
2. Leibniz's Mill   9
3. The Disembodied Pain   13
4. The Hard Problem of Consciousness   18
5. What it's Like to be a Bat   26
6. Mary and the Black-and-White Room   31
7. Zombies   38
8. Yogis   44
9. The Coffee Tasters   49

10 The Hornswoggle Problem	55
11 The Slugs and the Tiles	61

Part II: Physicalist Theories and the Metaphysics of Mind — 67
Introduction — 67

12 The Exclusion Problem	70
13 The Puzzle of the Special Sciences	77
14 The Super-Spartans	82
15 Mad Pain and Martian Pain	87
16 The Blockhead	92
17 The Imitation Game	98
18 The Chinese Room	104
19 Eloise and the Tree	110
20 Inverted Qualia	115
21 Hempel's Dilemma	122
22 Brains within Brains	128

Part III: Content, Intentionality, and Representation — 135
Introduction — 135

23 Rabbits and Rabbit Stages	139
24 Swampman	146
25 Twin Earth and Arthritis Man	153
26 Otto's Notebook	161
27 The Brain in a Vat	167
28 Puzzling Pierre	173
29 The Shopping List	178

Part IV: Perception, Imagination, and Attention — 183
    Introduction — 183

30 Molyneux's Problem — 185
31 The Missing Shade of Blue — 190
32 Imagining Chiliagons — 195
33 Color Swatches and Speckled Hens — 200
34 The Skywalk — 206
35 Pine Trees and Cyrillic Text — 212
36 Synesthesia — 217
37 Change Blindness — 224
38 Blindsight, Distracted Driving, and Pneumatic Drills — 230

Part V: Persons, Personal Identity, and the Self — 237
    Introduction — 237

39 The Prince and the Cobbler — 240
40 The Chariot and the Candle — 247
41 The Body-Swap Puzzle — 254
42 Mind Uploading — 260
43 The Puzzle of Too Many Minds — 267
44 Split Brains and the Unity Puzzle — 272
45 Sharing Feelings, Combining Minds — 279
46 The Elusive Self — 285
47 The Essential Indexical — 290
48 The Queen and the Gametes — 295
49 The Trekkie, Mr. Oreo, and Narrative Conceptions of the Self — 301
50 The Puzzle of Transformative Choice — 307

Glossary — 315
Index — 325

ACKNOWLEDGEMENTS

When this project began, Chase Wrenn was a co-author. He co-wrote the book proposal and helped compile the initial list of chapters, and he contributed other ideas as well. We are grateful to him for his contributions. We also thank Andrew (AJ) Holzer for helpful suggestions on the chapters in Part I. Finally, we thank two anonymous referees for Routledge for helpful suggestions.

GENERAL INTRODUCTION

Even if there were no sentient creatures around, the world would be a puzzling place. Where did it come from? What is the nature of space and time? Why do those spinning orbs we call "planets" spin? But things get a lot more interesting when minds enter the picture— especially when those minds are the reasonably complicated sort possessed by humans. Mentality introduces a host of new puzzles into philosophy. One sort involves knowledge: how do minds know about the world? Can we know anything about other minds? These topics belong to *epistemology*, the part of philosophy that concerns knowledge. The existence of minds raises other sorts of questions, though. What is the nature of minds? Are they related to or even identical with souls? They obviously relate to bodies and brains, but how? What is the nature of consciousness? How does consciousness relate to the brain and other physical stuff? What, if anything, makes you the same person at 50 as you were at 15? These topics belong to the field of *metaphysics*, the part of philosophy that concerns existence and identity. Philosophy of mind takes up both these epistemological topics and metaphysical topics. It is concerned with questions about selves, minds, and their interactions with bodies. If you're like us, you'll find these topics gripping precisely because they are about persons and what sorts of things they are. Puzzles about minds and persons have an existential pull that is sometimes missing from abstract philosophy.

DOI: 10.4324/9781003179191-1

There are many ways to dive into the philosophy of mind. You could study the history of theories about the mind or read biographies of the major contributors to the discipline. There's nothing wrong with those approaches; but we find it much more compelling to start with a set of puzzles or problems. A good philosophical puzzle focuses on a concept or thought we tend to take for granted and shows that, on closer observation, it might not be as coherent or straightforward as it first seemed. Sometimes the puzzle begins with a *thought experiment*: a situation conjured up in imagination; other times it begins with what we learn from science, and still other times it begins with drawing out consequences of apparently unrelated commonsense. Whichever way it proceeds, if the puzzle is good, we will likely find ourselves troubled by what before seemed unproblematic. It's from this seed that some of the most promising theories bloom.

In this book we consider 50 such puzzles, divided into five sections. The puzzles in Part I concern mind–body dualism, the nature of consciousness, and the relationship between consciousness and the physical world. Those in Part II concern *physicalist* theories, according to which mentality is a physical phenomenon, such as a brain state. Those in Part III concern mental content, thought, and how the mind represents things. The puzzles in Part IV concern perception, imagination, and attention, and those in Part V concern the self and personal identity over time. Although we have tried to keep each chapter relatively self-contained, so that they can be read independently of the others, at the start of each section we provide a brief introduction to the general issues raised therein. For those who wish to pursue the topics further, each chapter includes a bibliographic guide to canonical presentations, overview articles, and other important contributions to the area. While we've attempted to keep jargon to a minimum, it's hard to avoid some technical terms that are widely used by philosophers of mind, so we've also included a brief glossary.

Although this brief introduction has provided only a quick glimpse of the topics covered in this book, we hope your interest has been piqued. Rather than taking more time on preliminary matters, we'll stop here so that you can dive into the puzzles and see what grabs you!

PART I

CONSCIOUSNESS AND DUALISM
Introduction

How should we understand the relationship between the mental and the physical? That is a way of stating a central problem in the philosophy of mind known as *the mind–body problem*. In Western philosophy, contemporary discussions of the mind–body problem trace to René Descartes' 17th-century writings. He argued for a sort of dualist view on which the mind is an immaterial thing that is importantly distinct from the body. Defining *body* in terms of extension and *mind* in terms of thought and consciousness, Descartes reasoned that he could clearly and distinctly conceive of his mind without his body and of his body without his mind. He went on to infer that his mind and body can exist without each other, and thus are what he termed "really distinct." In other words, the mind and the body are fundamentally distinct substances. This position is known as *substance dualism*.

Descartes' discussion did not arise out of nowhere. Centuries earlier, Ibn Sina (commonly known as Avicenna) drew similar conclusions based on his "floating man" thought experiment. He imagined a man floating through the air without any awareness of his body or the physical environment, but nonetheless knowing that he exists. Chapter 1 discusses that case. Chapter 2 concerns another historical case: Leibniz's mill, a thought experiment devised by Gottfried Wilhelm

Leibniz. Like Avicenna and Descartes, Leibniz rejected physicalism—a view on which the mind is a physical phenomenon. He imagined a physical system (such as a brain, perhaps) enlarged to a size where we can walk inside it and observe its parts, just as we can walk into a grain mill and observe the rotation of the wheel and grindstones. According to Leibniz, such observations would not reveal the existence of mental phenomena such as "perceptions."

The other chapters in Part I also concern the debate between dualism and physicalism, but they describe more recent ideas from 20th- and 21st-century philosophy. In those chapters, the focus is no longer on *mind* generally or on *minds* in the sense of subjects of experience (that is, things that have experience). Instead, the focus narrows to conscious experience. Though there are many different varieties of consciousness (for example, awakeness and awareness), these chapters focus on an experiential variety of consciousness—the variety of consciousness picked out when we talk about what it's like to undergo a particular experience at a particular time (see Chapters 4 and 5). For example, Chapter 3 focuses on the experience of pain. There is something it is like to feel pain, as anyone who has felt pain knows. How does conscious experience (in the "what it's like" sense) relate to the brain? Using reasoning reminiscent of Descartes' argument for mind–body dualism, Brie Gertler argues that we can imagine a specific pain experience being disembodied—and that, when we do this, we grasp everything that is essential to that experience. She goes on to infer that physicalism is mistaken, at least when it comes to the nature of particular pain experiences. Her position is not *substance* dualism but rather *property* dualism: mental properties, such as the property of *being painful*, are distinct from physical properties, such as the sorts of properties discovered by neuroscience. The other eight chapters in this section also concern the question of whether physicalism falters when it comes to consciousness. Chapters 4–7 focus on arguments for answering that question in the affirmative, while Chapters 8–11 focus on arguments for answering in the negative.

THE FLOATING MAN

BACKGROUND

In *Phaedo*, Plato (c. 425–357 BCE) argued that the soul was separable from the body. Aristotle left the issue a little less clear. By defining the soul as the "perfection" or "form" of the body, it could seem as though the soul exists only as a modification of the body, and thus that its essence—that which makes it what it is, and that it cannot exist without—includes the body. Avicenna (a Latinization of Ibn Sina, 980–1037) argued otherwise using his Floating Man argument. Though the soul can be attached to a body, it need not be. The argument is often seen as an anticipation of Descartes' (1596–1650) *Sixth Meditation* argument for the separability of the mind and the body—which is also based on a thought experiment involving conceiving of oneself (or one's mind or soul) as existing disembodied.

THE CASE

Imagine that God created you, suddenly and fully formed, floating in the sky. You have no sight, and none of your limbs are in contact with one another. You do not see or feel your body. Additionally, suppose that you do not feel the air against your skin. In that oddly suspended state, though you would have no awareness of your body, you could be confident that you existed. You would not only know you exist; you would fully grasp your essence without even thinking that you occupied space. Since you are able to grasp your essence without thinking of yourself as spatial or embodied, your essence, and thus your soul, is immaterial and distinct from the body.

DISCUSSION

The most natural response to the Floating Man argument is to claim that it illicitly moves from an epistemological premise—about what the floating man would know or be aware of—to a metaphysical conclusion—about the floating man's essence and the immateriality of the soul. (Kaukua 2014, p. 37; Sebti 2000, p. 121; Black 2008, p. 65). Consider an analogy. I might know that I have a cold without understanding that it is a virus, and could thus imagine having the cold in a world where there were no viruses. Really, though, my imagination is misleading because I don't know all the relevant facts. Similarly, the soul might in fact be bodily, but the awareness the floating man has of the soul simply doesn't reveal that fact.

Avicenna will respond that, unlike the case of my virus confusion, the floating man fully grasps his own essence. If he can have a complete grasp of his essence without needing to think of himself as embodied, his essence does not include embodiment. This, though, only raises the question of why we should think the floating man fully grasps his own essence (Adamson and Benevich 2018, pp. 158, 160). It could be that, in his peculiar situation, the floating man is given only a superficial grasp of his own nature and that a more complete grasp would show that he must be embodied.

Some philosophers in the latter half of the 13th century (e.g. Matthew of Aquasparta and Vital du Four) backed off of Avicenna's metaphysical conclusion, and instead argued that the case of the floating man revealed something special about self-awareness. Even if one must in fact be embodied, one can be aware of oneself without being aware of the body and without having any sensory experience whatsoever (Toivanen 2015, pp. 80–86). But even that epistemological conclusion could be challenged. One could maintain in response that the floating man *is* aware of his body; he just isn't aware of it *as* his body. If the soul is material, by being aware of the soul one is aware of one's material body. Nevertheless, it is plausible that something of the epistemological point remains—that the floating man thought experiment might establish an interesting epistemological conclusion. If the thought experiment is coherent, and it seems to be, it does suggest that self-awareness does not depend on a sensory awareness of the body.

Some interpreters see the floating man argument as being more concerned with other special features of self-awareness (Alwishah 2013). It might be concluded, for example, that every case of awareness is a case of self-awareness. Though the floating man doesn't perceive himself in any obvious way—by vision, taste, smell, etc.—he is still aware that he exists. This self-awareness is immediate, in the sense that it requires no intermediary awareness—no awareness of something else by which one becomes aware of the self, in the way that I become aware of the dog in the yard by hearing its bark. One can be aware of the self without being aware of anything else. Avicenna arguably goes further, claiming that self-awareness doesn't even require the activity of thought—self and self-awareness are in some sense identical (Alwishah 2013, pp. 62–3). However, it is difficult to see how either of these claims of immediacy follows from the floating man thought experiment, at least directly. After all, the floating man is presumably engaging in conscious thought and is aware of those thoughts. If the floating man is no longer engaging in any intellectual activity at all, it is no longer obvious that he is self-aware.

Though the debate about the possibility of disembodied existence has medieval origins, the discussion remains alive and well today, as evidenced by the "disembodied pain" thought experiment to be discussed in Chapter 3. Not only is there active debate about the soundness of floating man-type arguments—which is echoed in discussions of zombies (see Chapter 7)—there is live debate of the role of bodily awareness in self-awareness, with some philosophers (such as Gertler 2011, esp. Chapter 7, and Howell 2023) siding with Avicenna that one can be self-aware without being bodily aware, and with others (such as Bermúdez 1998) insisting otherwise.

RECOMMENDED READING

CANONICAL PRESENTATION

Avicenna. 1959. "On the Soul." In Fazlur Rahman (ed.), *Avicenna's De Anima: Being the Psychological Part of Kitab al Shifa*. London: Oxford University Press.

OVERVIEWS

Adamson, Peter, and Benevich, Fedor. 2018. "The Thought Experimental Method: Avicenna's Flying Man Argument." *Journal of the American Philosophical Association* 4 (2): 147–64.

Alwishah, Ahmed. 2013. "Ibn Sīnā on Floating Man Arguments." *Journal of Islamic Philosophy* 9: 32–53.

Kaukua, Jari. 2014. *Self-Awareness in Islamic Philosophy: Avicenna and Beyond*. Cambridge: Cambridge University Press.

ADDITIONAL DISCUSSIONS

Black, Deborah. 2008. "Avicenna on Self-Awareness and Knowing that One Knows." In S. Rahman, T. Street, and H. Tahiri (eds) *The Unity of Science in the Arabic Tradition*. Dordrecht: Springer: 63–87.

Marmura, Michael. 1986. "Avicenna's 'Flying Man' in Context." *The Monist* 69 (3): 383–95.

Sebti, Meryem. 2000. *Avicenne: L'âme humain*. Paris: Presses universitaires de France.

Sorabji, Richard. 2006. *Self: Ancient and Modern Insights about Individuality, Life, and Death*. Chicago: University of Chicago Press.

Toivanen, Juhana. 2015. "Fate of the Flying Man: Medieval Reception of Avicenna's Thought Experiment." *Oxford Studies in Medieval Philosophy* 3: 64–98.

OTHER REFERENCES

Bermúdez, José Luis. 1998. *The Paradox of Self-Consciousness: Representation and Mind*. Cambridge, MA: MIT Press.

Cottingham, John (ed.). 1996. *Descartes: Meditations on First Philosophy: With Selections from the Objections and Replies*. Cambridge: Cambridge University Press.

Gertler, Brie. 2011. *Self-Knowledge*. Abingdon, UK: Routledge.

Howell, Robert J. 2023. *Self-Awareness and the Elusive Subject*. Oxford: Oxford University Press.

Plato. 1948. *The Portable Plato: Protagoras, Symposium, Phaedo, and the Republic: Complete, in the English Translation of Benjamin Jowett*. New York: Penguin.

LEIBNIZ'S MILL

BACKGROUND

By the time Gottfried Wilhelm Leibniz wrote his *Monadology* in the 18th century, several philosophers—such as Thomas Hobbes, Damaris Masham, and John Locke—were flirting with, if not explicitly endorsing, *materialism* (or *physicalism*) about minds: the theory that all mental phenomena are fundamentally physical. Leibniz found materialism, with what he took to be its mechanistic underpinnings, inadequate to explain perception and thought. Some of his reasons had to do with his other philosophical commitments. But the thought experiment of the mill appears to be an attempt to independently motivate the rejection of materialism. Leibniz's argument can be seen as a precursor to more contemporary arguments that structure and dynamics cannot explain phenomenal consciousness (see Chapter 4), as well as to Searle's Chinese Room argument (see Chapter 18).

THE CASE

According to the materialist, the mind is ultimately a physical machine. Thinking, perception, and consciousness are just results of the machine's operation. Imagine such a machine—perhaps the brain—being enlarged to the point that we could walk inside it and see the movements of the parts, just as we can walk into a mill and see the rotations of the wheel and grindstones. Although we can easily see how these movements produce other movements or generate physical activity, nothing about the workings of a machine would suggest the existence of thoughts or perceptions. No matter how much we analyze the movements of the mill's inner parts, and no matter how much we understand about the physics of the situation, there would be no reason to think there were things like thoughts or perceptions. Their existence would seem to be something beyond what we can conclude from our understanding of the material workings of the mill. Thoughts and perceptions thus cannot be explained by material operations alone.

DISCUSSION

Although it has been influential, many philosophers find the thought experiment of the mill and Leibniz's subsequent argument to be unconvincing. Part of the reason, though, is that it's not entirely clear what the argument is, or even what it is meant to prove (Lodge and Bobro 1998, Duncan 2012). If the idea is that when walking in the machine we wouldn't see thoughts or perceptions, the argument seems unsuccessful. Watching the parts of a thing work might reveal some of its properties, but there is no reason to believe we would visually apprehend all of the properties or capacities of the whole (Rorty 1979, p. 26; Churchland 1995, pp. 191–2). From the premise that we can't "see" thoughts or perceptions in the mill, it does not follow that the mill contains no thoughts or perceptions.

There are more charitable interpretations of Leibniz's argument. For example, instead of arguing directly that we can't "see" perceptions in the machine, so they must not be there, he might be arguing as follows: If materialism were true, then what we would see in the movements of the parts would *explain why* or *provide evidence that* the machine had thoughts or perceptions. But none of what we would see in the movements of the parts would do either of those things. Therefore, materialism is false. That interpretation of Leibniz's argument might improve upon the one stated in the last paragraph. But it's not clear that it avoids the problem. Here again, it seems entirely possible that focus on the parts wouldn't show the properties of the whole—looking only at the movements of the parts might well obscure the purpose and potential of the whole. If one shrank down to the atomic level and wandered around a heart, it's doubtful one would know it was an organ, that it pumped blood, or even that it was biological. Those features of the heart just wouldn't be apparent on that level. Perhaps the same is true of the brain (Searle 1983, pp. 267–8).

Leibniz could be making an even stronger claim, though: it is *inconceivable* that something like the pushing and pulling of gears, or anything else mechanical, could explain something like thought or perception. This brings the argument closer in some ways to more contemporary conceivability arguments, such as the zombie argument discussed in Chapter 7. But it could again be objected that we simply don't have a sufficient grasp of how the activity of material things generates thoughts or perceptions. If we knew more, either about the way the movements of the parts generated properties in the whole or about thought itself or perception itself, we wouldn't have such difficulty conceiving of material minds.

Still, defenders of Leibniz's argument will insist that there is a difference in kind between material movements and thoughts and perceptions, at least when thoughts and perceptions are *conscious*. Material movements concern how things operate in space and time, while consciousness is about how things feel—what it's like for the being that has conscious experiences. It's not clear why, no matter how complicated the movement, material operations should feel like anything. It's important to remember that the question isn't whether material operations could give rise to thoughts or perceptions—with the addition of laws, connecting thoughts to movements in space, they certainly could. But that would involve *adding* something to the machine. If something must be added, the machine isn't all there is.

RECOMMENDED READING

CANONICAL PRESENTATION

Leibniz, G. W. 1989. *Monadology*. In Roger Ariew and Daniel Garber (eds.) *Philosophical Essays*. Indianapolis: Hackett: Section 17.

OVERVIEWS

Duncan, Stewart. 2012. "Leibniz's Mill Arguments against Materialism." *Philosophical Quarterly* 62 (247): 250–72.

Landesman, Charles. 2011. *Leibniz's Mill: A Challenge to Materialism*. Notre Dame, IN: University of Notre Dame Press.

Lodge, Paul, and Bobro, Marc. 1998. "Stepping Back Inside Leibniz's Mill." *The Monist* 81 (4): 553–72.

ADDITIONAL DISCUSSIONS

Churchland, Paul M. (1995). *The Engine of Reason, the Seat of the Soul: A Philosophical Journey into the Brain*. Cambridge, MA: MIT Press.

Lodge, Paul (2014). "Leibniz's Mill Argument against Mechanical Materialism Revisited." *Ergo: An Open Access Journal of Philosophy* 1. https://doi.org/10.3998/ergo.12405314.0001.003.

Rorty, Richard. 1979. *Philosophy and the Mirror of Nature*. Princeton: Princeton University Press.

Rozemond, Marleen. 2014. "Mills Can't Think: Leibniz's Approach to the Mind–Body Problem." *Res Philosophica* 91 (1): 1–28.

Searle, John R. 1983. *Intentionality: An Essay in the Philosophy of Mind*. Cambridge: Cambridge University Press.

Wilson, Margaret D. 1974. "Leibniz and Materialism." *Canadian Journal of Philosophy* 3 (4): 495–513.

THE DISEMBODIED PAIN

BACKGROUND

In the 17th century, French philosopher René Descartes developed and defended dualism in works such as *Meditations on First Philosophy*. In the *Sixth Meditation*, Descartes argues that we could conceive of the mind existing apart from the body and, since God can bring about whatever we can conceive, it is possible for the mind to exist apart from the body. For two things to be independent substances, all that's needed is that it be possible for them to exist apart. Thus, Descartes concludes that the mind and body are independent substances, and that dualism must be true. More recently, taking inspiration from this Cartesian discussion, Brie Gertler has put forth a thought experiment about disembodied pain that aims to support a dualist view. Unlike Descartes, Gertler does not rely on the existence of God to support dualism. Her argument is wholly secular.

THE CASE

Most thought experiments begin directly with contemplation of a proposed scenario; but the one we consider in this chapter requires a brief prelude—and, unfortunately, the prelude involves a bit of pain. Pinch yourself, say, on the underside of your left arm. You don't have to pinch very hard, but you should pinch forcefully enough that you

DOI: 10.4324/9781003179191-5

can focus on the pain you're feeling. Once you have that pain in focus, the thought experiment itself can begin. Imagine that you are feeling the very same pain you are feeling right now, even though you are completely disembodied. In this state, you experience the very same pain you are feeling right now, and it feels to you that the pain is on the underside of your left arm; but you don't have a left arm. Not only do you not have a left arm, but you also don't have a right arm. You have no bodily parts whatsoever.

By successfully engaging in this thought experiment, you conceive of a case of disembodied pain. According to a long philosophical tradition, whatever is conceivable is possible. Granted, we can conceive of things that are *physically* impossible (or at least improbable), as when I conceive of dropping a tennis ball and having it float unsupported rather than falling to the ground. But the sense of possibility intended is not *physical possibility* but, rather, something stronger—sometimes put in terms of *metaphysical possibility* and sometimes put in terms of *logical possibility*. Even if it is not physically possible for the ball to float unsupported, it is logically possible. In contrast, it is not logically possible for the ball to be at the same time both wholly spherical and wholly cubical. Moreover, if you were to try to conceive of this, you would fail. (Try it!)

Given that you can conceive of a case of disembodied pain, it is (logically) possible for the particular pain under consideration to occur in a disembodied being. It can occur in the complete absence of any brain states, and, indeed, of any physical states altogether. If this is possible, then the particular pain under consideration cannot itself be a physical state. Contrary to what the physicalist claims, the pain is an irreducibly mental state. In saying that it is irreducible, Gertler means that it does not reduce to physical states. For comparison, consider a glass of water. Arguably, the water in that glass is nothing more than a collection of H_2O molecules. In other words, the water reduces to H_2O, and H_2O itself reduces to bonded hydrogen and oxygen atoms. By contrast, according to Gertler, pain does not reduce to any physical state.

DISCUSSION

A related scenario has also been posed by W. D. Hart (1988); though, unlike Gertler, he does not focus on pain. Rather, he focuses on visualizing oneself disembodied (see also Chapter 1). Hart moves us slowly in imagination from embodiment to disembodiment. You're asked to imagine waking up in your usual embodied state. Before you open your eyes, you carefully walk over to the mirror. In front of the mirror, when you raise your eyelids, you see empty eye sockets. You then peel back the top of your skull, and you can see that your entire skull is empty. There is no brain inside. As you stare into the mirror, the rest of your body slowly seems to melt away. By visualizing what you would see in the mirror once the entirety of your body has disappeared, you are able to conceive of yourself in a completely disembodied state. Again, on the assumption that whatever is conceivable is possible, we get to the conclusion that physicalism must be false and that dualism must be true.

Arguments that rely on this assumption—that whatever is conceivable is possible—are often referred to as *conceivability arguments*. Many arguments concerning the mind–body problem and the nature of consciousness take this basic form: that is, they begin with a claim about what is conceivable and move to a claim about what is possible. The disembodiment scenarios and the corresponding arguments proposed by Descartes, Gertler, and Hart attempt to establish the possibility of mental states existing without the physical states that typically correspond to them. Other conceivability arguments, such as the argument based on the Zombie thought experiment (see Chapter 7), attempt to establish the possibility of physical states without the corresponding mental states, in particular, without phenomenally conscious mental states—that is, without states that are conscious in the sense that there's something it's like to have them (see Chapter 5).

Conceivability arguments have long come in for criticism. One basic criticism dates back to an objection that Antoine Arnauld posed to Descartes. Someone without a deep understanding of geometry might think that they are conceiving of a right triangle for which the Pythagorean theorem does not hold. But the Pythagorean theorem holds for all right triangles, so the given scenario is not possible. Thus, it looks like conceivability does not entail possibility. (This objection can be found in the fourth set of replies in the "Selections from the Objections and Replies" in Descartes 1641/2017; see also the criticisms of Leibniz's mill argument in Chapter 2)

Descartes had attempted to guard against this type of objection by insisting that only when a conception is *clear and distinct* will conceivability entail possibility. When someone is ignorant of geometry, their attempts to conceive of right triangles will not be clear and distinct. Like Descartes, Gertler suggests that it is only when the concepts involved are *sufficiently comprehensive* that conceiving of a given scenario will entail that the scenario is possible. But when does a concept meet this standard? Though Gertler admits that this is a high standard, she does not give us a precise answer; instead, she provides some examples to help flesh out the notion. The introductory geometry student who learns that a right triangle is a three-sided closed figure with one 90-degree angle needs to learn more before their concept of right triangle will be of use in conceivability arguments, as they don't yet understand what other properties go along with a figure's having a right angle. Their concept is still incomplete. But now consider a simple and straightforward concept like *bachelor*. Once you know that the definition of "bachelor" is "unmarried man of eligible marrying age," that's all you need to know for your concept to be clear and complete—that is, to be sufficiently comprehensive for use in conceivability arguments.

Given that Gertler requires that a concept must be sufficiently comprehensive for it to be of use in conceivability arguments, her thought experiment will succeed in supporting dualism only if our concept of pain is sufficiently comprehensive. To defend this assertion about our concept of pain, Gertler contrasts the concept of pain with the concept of water. Someone might know how water feels and tastes, while being ignorant of its chemical composition. They might not know that water is H_2O. As Gertler puts the point, water has a *hidden essence*. This essence can be discovered only by way of scientific investigation. On her view, pain is unlike water in this respect: "Pain wears its essential nature on its sleeve, as it were" (Gertler 2007: 40). Because we conceptualize pain in terms of the way it feels—or, as it's often put, in terms of its *phenomenology*—it lacks a hidden essence. Though we do not come to know the essence of water in virtue of feeling it, we do come to know the essence of pain in virtue of feeling it. Thus, in Gertler's view, our concept of pain is sufficiently comprehensive to be used in an argument that moves from conceivability to possibility.

RECOMMENDED READING

CANONICAL PRESENTATIONS

Descartes, René. 1641/2017. *Meditations on First Philosophy with Selections from the Objections and Replies*, edited by John Cottingham. Cambridge: Cambridge University Press.

Gertler, Brie. 2007. "In Defense of Mind–Body Dualism." In Joel Feinberg and Russ Shafer-Landau (eds.) *Reason and Responsibility*. Belmont, CA: Wadsworth: 34–46.

Hart, W. D. 1988. *The Engines of the Soul*. Cambridge: Cambridge University Press.

OVERVIEWS

Kind, Amy. 2020. *Philosophy of Mind: The Basics*. Abingdon, UK: Routledge. (See especially pp. 26–31.)

Robinson, Howard. 2020. "Dualism." *The Stanford Encyclopedia of Philosophy* (Fall 2020 Edition), Edward N. Zalta (ed.), URL = <https://plato.stanford.edu/archives/fall2020/entries/dualism/> (See especially Section 4.3.)

ADDITIONAL DISCUSSIONS

Gendler, Tamar Szabo, and Hawthorne, John. 2002. "Introduction: Conceivability and Possibility." In Tamar Szabo Gendler and John Hawthorne (eds.) *Conceivability and Possibility*. Oxford: Oxford University Press: 1–70. (See especially pp. 13–26.)

Goff, Philip. 2010. "Ghosts and Sparse Properties: Why Physicalists Have More to Fear from Ghosts than Zombies." *Philosophy and Phenomenological Research* 81 (1): 119–39.

Kripke, Saul. 1980. *Naming and Necessity*. Cambridge, MA: Harvard University Press. (See especially Lecture 3.)

Tye, Michael. 1983. "On the Possibility of Disembodied Existence." *Australasian Journal of Philosophy* 61 (3): 275–82.

THE HARD PROBLEM OF CONSCIOUSNESS

BACKGROUND

Can consciousness be explained scientifically? If so, how? Historically, this question was often intermixed with others, including the more general question about the nature of the human mind and its relationship to the physical world. For over two centuries, many philosophers subscribed to views such as Cartesian dualism (Descartes 1641), according to which mind and body exist in separate realms. Such views waned in the 20th century as science developed, including especially science relating to our mental processes. Nowadays, cognitive science and neuroscience are progressing at ever-increasing rates. So much so that, though there remains much to learn, it might seem all but inevitable that a scientific explanation of consciousness is forthcoming. Former mysteries, including some about life itself, are mysteries no longer. Why should consciousness be any different? In fact, there may be a reason. Some argue that consciousness presents an especially perplexing difficulty, which David J. Chalmers (1995) calls *the hard problem of consciousness*. We use terms like "conscious" and "consciousness" in different ways. For example, sometimes we want to mark the distinction between being awake and being asleep, as in

"I lost consciousness the minute my head hit the pillow." Sometimes we want to indicate awareness, as in: "Yes, I am fully conscious that my socks have holes in them." And sometimes we mean subjective experience, such as the pain of arthritis, the visual experience of seeing a red rose, or the existential angst one might feel while contemplating Sartre's reflections on death. What unites such diverse states is that there is *something it's like* to have them (Nagel 1974; see Chapter 5). It is this last sort of consciousness—the "what-it's-like" sort, also known as *phenomenal consciousness*—that the hard problem concerns. In this chapter, we'll refer to that aspect of consciousness simply as "experience."

THE CASE

At the moment, my elbow hurts. We know from science that my pain experience, along with all of my other experiences, happens as a result of brain processes. For each of us, our brain creates a subjective inner life, rich with pains, pleasures, images, moods, etc. But how does that happen? Our brains are continuously processing information acquired from our senses. Why is this information processing accompanied by experiences? Why doesn't the brain's activity go on in the dark, so to speak? That, in a nutshell, is the hard problem of consciousness.

Standard methods in cognitive science can explain many features associated with consciousness. For example, consider *reportability*—the ability to produce verbal reports about one's inner states. Here the feature we want to explain is a cognitive ability, or the performance of a cognitive function. That is something the standard methods of cognitive science are especially good at: working out the computational and/or neural mechanisms that underlie the performance of cognitive functions (or the exercise of an ability). Once such mechanisms have been sufficiently detailed, there is nothing left to explain. When that is the case, we could describe a feature as being *functionally definable*. And the problem of explaining functionally definable features is what Chalmers calls an "easy" problem. The same explanatory model applies to almost all other features associated with the term "consciousness"—such as being awake rather than asleep and being able to focus one's attention on one's holey socks.

But there is a glaring exception: experience itself—that is, the what-it's-like aspect of consciousness. Here, the problem isn't about explaining the performance of a cognitive function. It's about why there's any experience there all. Suppose we have explained the performance of any cognitive function associated with consciousness. The question remains: why is the performance of that function accompanied by experience? And why the particular sort of experience that accompanies that performance, rather than one with a distinct experiential character? There would seem to be what Joseph Levine (1983) calls an *explanatory gap* between the performance of functions and experience. To bridge that gap, we will need more materials than the standard methods of cognitive science supply. This is the hard problem of consciousness.

To support that conclusion, David Chalmers considers some theories of consciousness that scientists have developed. One is Bernard Baars' (1988) global workspace theory of consciousness. In this theory, the cognitive system that our brains realize includes a sort of central processor—a global workspace that mediates communication between more specialized processors. Baars uses the model to explain contrasts between conscious and unconscious cognitive functions: information in the global workspace is conscious, while other information is not. Baars' theory is controversial. But, even if his theory is true, the hard problem isn't solved. The hard problem isn't about explaining cognitive functions. One might suppose that all and only conscious experiences (in the relevant what-it's-like sense) are contents of the global workspace. But the question remains: why are those contents experienced at all? Similar things can be said about other scientific theories of consciousness, such as the theory that certain 35–75 hertz neural oscillations in the cerebral cortex are the basis of consciousness (Crick and Koch 1990). Indeed, some such theories aim only to account for the neural correlates of consciousness—the neural processes that accompany all and only conscious experiences. And correlation is not explanation. (Perhaps red cars are more likely to be involved in accidents than non-red cars; that is, perhaps there is a correlation between being a red car and being especially likely to get in an accident. The question remains: why is there that correlation?)

The hard problem concerns scientific explanation. But it gives rise to a challenge to physicalism—the philosophical theory on which no aspect of the mind is over and above the physical. The challenge could be stated roughly as follows. The explanatory gap indicates that consciousness is independent of physical phenomena. Even if the brain generates experience, that is a mere contingent fact; everything about the brain might be just as it is, and yet no experience is generated. If so, then consciousness itself is wholly different from anything physical. To put it another way, since nothing *physical* can bridge the explanatory gap, we need to appeal to something *non-physical*. Otherwise, the connection between consciousness and the physical world will remain forever mysterious.

DISCUSSION

The hard problem has long been recognized. For example, Thomas Nagel's 1974 classic "What Is It Like to Be a Bat?" begins with the following sentence: "Consciousness is what makes the mind-body problem really intractable." And in 1866, T. H. Huxley wrote,

> How it is that anything so remarkable as a state of consciousness comes about as a result of initiating nerve tissue, is just as unaccountable as the appearance of the Djin, where Aladdin rubbed his lamp in the story.

Philosophers of earlier eras doubtless understood the problem no less acutely than Chalmers, Nagel, and Huxley do. Even so, work on it has intensified considerably since the publication of Chalmers's 1995 article, "Facing Up to the Hard Problem of Consciousness," and his influential 1996 book, *The Conscious Mind: In Search of a Fundamental Theory*.

Some regard the hard problem as insoluble. For example, according to Colin McGinn (1989), although there is a naturalistic solution, we humans are "cognitively closed" to it, due to limitations in our concept-forming abilities. In his view, we simply cannot form concepts that would enable us to see why, for example, undergoing a certain type of brain process *must* be felt as pain, even if pain were identical to that brain process. Daniel Stoljar (2005) also doubts that we are currently positioned to solve the problem; but, unlike McGinn,

Stoljar thinks that might change. In his view, there are probably unknown physical truths that provide the requisite explanatory bridge—truths that we may well one day discover.

Chalmers himself thinks we shouldn't conclude that the hard problem is insoluble, at least not yet. The nature of the problem places constraints on a solution: explaining the performance of cognitive functions will never suffice. But that does not entail that no scientific solution is possible. One option is to regard consciousness as a fundamental feature of the universe, alongside the basic posits of physics such as mass and charge. Assuming that mass, charge, etc. are, unlike consciousness, non-mental features; this results in what Chalmers calls *naturalistic dualism*. But Chalmers is open to other options as well, including a view he later dubs "Russellian monism" (1997), in reference to the English philosopher Bertrand Russell. According to Russellian monism, although there is again an "extra ingredient" to the universe—something that physical science, as we know it, fails to reveal—that extra ingredient need not be experiential. Instead, it might be "proto-experiential" (or "proto-phenomenal"). On Russellian monism, such proto-experiential properties underlie mass, charge, and the other basic properties physics describes (Alter and Pereboom 2023).

Other responses are critical of Chalmers's position. Some deny that there really is a hard problem in addition to the so-called easy problems. Others accept the existence of such an additional hard problem but maintain that it can be accommodated within a standard physicalist framework. Chalmers classifies philosophers who give those responses as *type-A materialists* and *type-B materialists*, respectively.

Some type-A materialists deny that there is a hard problem of consciousness on the grounds that consciousness does not exist: consciousness, in the sense that Chalmers intends, is a sort of cognitive illusion (Frankish 2016; and see Chapter 9). But that is a minority view. Type-A materialists more typically accept the existence of consciousness, but argue that it is a mistake to think that any problem regarding its existence or its nature will remain after the so-called easy problems have been solved. For example, Patricia Churchland (1996) argues that, insofar as we cannot imagine how that would work, this is attributable to our own limitations—and that we have good reason to expect that further scientific progress will overcome them. (We will return to Churchland's response to the hard problem in Chapter 10.)

In a similar vein, Daniel Dennett (1996) concludes that if we remove all functional features of our experience, there is nothing left to explain. He reaches that conclusion by taking a "third-person perspective" on his own experiences—viewing himself objectively, from the outside, so to speak (he refers to this method as *heterophenomenology*). Indeed, his conclusion might seem inevitable unless one considers consciousness subjectively, from the inside—that is, from the first-person perspective. One might regard taking information acquired from the first-person perspective as unscientific. But, if we are trying to understand consciousness, that attitude strikes many philosophers as overly restrictive.

Type-B materialists agree that the hard problem does not reduce to a bunch of easy problems. But they deny that this indicates that the universe itself must contain some extra non-physical ingredient. These philosophers often attribute the hard problem to how we *think* about conscious experience, rather than to conscious experience itself. In other words, they blame the hard problem on our *concepts* of consciousness. This approach is known as "the phenomenal concept strategy" (Stoljar 2005, Balog 2012).

Though popular, the phenomenal concept strategy faces serious challenges. For example, there is concern about the concepts themselves—that explaining *their* distinctive features might raise the same hard problem that arises in the first instance for the experiences they pick out (Chalmers 2007). Further, Chalmers argues that, even if type-B materialism is correct, the *explanation* of consciousness will be quite distinctive: "our explanation will always require explanatorily primitive principles to bridge the gap from the physical to the phenomenal" (2010, p. 118).

RECOMMENDED READING

CANONICAL PRESENTATION

Chalmers, David J. 1995. "Facing Up to the Hard Problem of Consciousness." *Journal of Consciousness Studies* 2: 200–219.

Descartes, René. 1641/2017. *Meditations on First Philosophy with Selections from the Objections and Replies*, edited by John Cottingham. Cambridge: Cambridge University Press.

OVERVIEWS

Howell, Robert. J., and Alter, Torin. 2009. "The Hard Problem of Consciousness." *Scholarpedia* 4 (6): 4948. http://www.scholarpedia.org/article/Hard_problem_of_consciousness.

Weisberg, Joshua. n.d. "The Hard Problem of Consciousness." *Internet Encyclopedia of Philosophy*. https://iep.utm.edu/hard-problem-of-conciousness/.

ADDITIONAL DISCUSSIONS

Alter, Torin, and Pereboom, Derk. 2023. "Russellian Monism." *The Stanford Encyclopedia of Philosophy* (Fall 2023 Edition), Edward N. Zalta and Uri Nodelman (eds.), URL = <https://plato.stanford.edu/archives/fall2019/entries/russellian-monism/>.

Baars, Bernard J. 1988. *A Cognitive Theory of Consciousness*. New York: Cambridge University Press.

Balog, Katalin. 2012. "A Defense of the Phenomenal Concept Strategy." *Philosophy and Phenomenological Research* 84: 1–23.

Chalmers David J. 1996. *The Conscious Mind: In Search of a Fundamental Theory*. New York: Oxford University Press.

Chalmers, David J. 1997. "Moving Forward on the Problem of Consciousness." *Journal of Consciousness Studies* 4: 3–46.

Chalmers, David J. 2007. "Phenomenal Concepts and the Explanatory Gap." In T. Alter and S. Walter (eds.) *Phenomenal Knowledge and Phenomenal Concepts: New Essays on Consciousness and Physicalism*. New York: Oxford University Press: 167–94.

Chalmers, David J. 2010. *The Character of Consciousness*. New York: Oxford University Press.

Churchland, Patricia S. 1996. "The Hornswoggle Problem." *Journal of Consciousness Studies* 3 (5–6): 402–8.

Crick, Francis, and Koch, Christof 1990. "Toward a Neurobiological Theory of Consciousness." *Seminars in the Neurosciences* 2: 263–75.

Dennett, Daniel C. 1996. "Facing Backwards on the Problem of Consciousness." *Journal of Consciousness Studies* 3 (1): 4–6.

Frankish, Keith. 2016. "Illusionism as a Theory of Consciousness." *Journal of Consciousness Studies* 23 (11–12): 11–39.

Hardcastle, Valerie. 1966. "The Why of Consciousness: A Non-Issue for Materialists." *Journal of Consciousness Studies* 3 (1): 7–13.

Howell, Robert J. 2013. *Consciousness and the Limits of Objectivity: The Case for Subjective Physicalism*. Oxford: Oxford University Press.

Huxley, Thomas H. 1866. *Lessons on Elementary Physiology*, 8th Edition. London: R. Clay, Son, and Taylor, Printers.
Levine, Joseph. 1983. "Materialism and Qualia: The Explanatory Gap." *Pacific Philosophical Quarterly* 64: 354–61.
McGinn, Colin. 1989. "Can We Solve the Mind–Body Problem?" *Mind* 98: 349–66.
Nagel, Thomas. 1974. "What Is It Like to Be a Bat?" *Philosophical Review* 83: 435–50.
Stoljar, Daniel. 2005. "Physicalism and Phenomenal Concepts." *Mind and Language* 20: 469–94.

WHAT IT'S LIKE TO BE A BAT

BACKGROUND

According to physicalism, consciousness is a physical phenomenon. This is widely taken to imply that the nature of any creature's conscious experience can be fully explained in objective, scientific terms. But that implication is hard to square with the apparent fact that experience (phenomenal consciousness) is subjective, in the sense that there is something it is like to have an experience. The difficulty can be brought out by considering experiences that differ considerably from those we humans have, such as bat echolocation experiences.

THE CASE

Many bats use echolocation to navigate their way through the world. Echolocation is a kind of natural sonar. Bats emit high-pitched chirping sounds, and the sound waves bounce off objects in their environment. That provides bats with information about where those objects are located. It seems reasonable to suppose that echolocation is a form of conscious perception. If so, there must be something it's like for a bat to echolocate, just as there's something it's like for humans to see red or to smell a rose. But *what* is it like? How does echolocating *feel* to bats?

According to Thomas Nagel (1974), bat echolocation illustrates a problem for physicalism. The problem begins with the claim that it seems to be impossible for humans to imagine what it's like to be an echolocating bat. Try it. There is no good reason to think it's much like anything with which you're familiar. So, it seems, you don't have the resources you need to do the imaginative work. Probably you can imagine yourself growing wings, flying, and even hunting mosquitos. But that's not enough to capture what it feels like *for bats* to echolocate. Since we can't experience what it's like to be a bat, and since we also can't imagine it, Nagel thinks we can't know what it's like for bats to echolocate.

So far, physicalism is unthreatened. After all, physicalism is a theory about what consciousness *is*, not a theory about what we can and cannot know or imagine. But a threat lurks nearby. If physicalism is true, then the nature of bat echolocation experiences is something that should be explicable in objective, scientific (e.g., neurophysiological) terms. So, to understand the nature of those experiences, we shouldn't *have* to adopt the bat's viewpoint. But there doesn't seem to be any alternative. Explaining the bat's experiences objectively, without imagining them accurately, wouldn't reveal what they're really like. Indeed, such an explanation would not, it seems, bring us any closer to understanding their distinctive nature. A human bat scientist—a chiropterologist—might know the complete neuroscientific truth about the bat's brain, and yet be no less mystified than other humans about what it's like *for the bat* to echolocate. The problem generalizes. Conscious experiences are subjective: there's something they're like for the experiencing subject. How, then, could they really be wholly explicable in objective terms, as physicalism seems to imply?

DISCUSSION

Importantly, Nagel does not take these considerations to show that physicalism is false. (This differentiates the bat argument from Frank Jackson's knowledge argument, which will we consider in Chapter 6.) Rather, he conceives of the problem for physicalism as concerning not so much whether physicalism is true but how we can understand its truth. In Nagel's view, based only on what is presently known, we can't understand how physicalism could be true.

What does that mean? Nagel explains by drawing an analogy. Imagine a current-day physicist time-travels to ancient Greece. She finds a philosopher there (Thales, say), and tells him that matter is energy—something that was discovered in the 20th century. Suppose Thales has good reason to believe the scientist, and that he therefore accepts her statement that matter is energy as the truth. But does he understand the truth that the statement expresses? Does he even understand how matter *could* be energy? No. Understanding how matter could be energy requires knowledge of the general theory of relativity, and this is knowledge that Thales lacks.

Nagel suggests that we're in a similar situation with respect to physicalism. Maybe we have enough evidence to conclude *that* physicalism is true—and that consciousness is a physical process of some kind. But, even if we do, we don't understand *how* physicalism could be true. At present, our theoretical understanding of the mental–physical relationship is so impoverished that understanding how physicalism could be true is beyond our ken. With respect to physicalism, we are in roughly the position that Thales is in with respect to the theory that matter is energy. We might believe, or even know, *that* it is true; we just don't have any sense of *how* it could be true.

But that might change. Nagel thinks we might one day be able to understand how physicalism could be true. He speculates that we might develop new theoretical concepts connecting the mental and the physical, thereby showing how an objective physical theory could reveal the true nature of conscious experiences. Some are less optimistic than Nagel is. They argue that it will always seem mysterious to us how a conscious experience could literally be a brain event or any other physical phenomenon (McGinn 1989). Our concept-forming capacities are simply not capable of forming the concepts needed for understanding how physicalism could be true. That more pessimistic conclusion is consistent with physicalism's truth, just as Nagel's more optimistic conclusion is. But some philosophers go further. They take our puzzlement to reflect an insight about the nature of consciousness: consciousness can't be explained physically—not because of something we don't understand, but because consciousness is not a physical phenomenon. These philosophers therefore develop non-physicalist theories, such as property dualism (Chalmers 1996).

Other philosophers try to defuse the threat to physicalism. Some invoke strategies similar to those used to defend physicalism from the knowledge argument (see Chapter 6). For example, some propose that knowing what it's like for bats to echolocate is really just possessing the ability to imagine such experiences—and that Nagel is wrong to infer anything about the *nature* of such experiences from inability to imagine them (Nemirow 1980). Other philosophers concede that Nagel's reflections undermine the claim that the nature of conscious experiences can be objectively explained—and then go on to detach physicalism from that claim (Howell 2013). Physicalism, they argue, is a metaphysical theory, about what experiences are, and it therefore need not imply the epistemological claim that the physical nature of experiences is objectively explicable. Whether such a detachment is defensible is controversial (Chalmers 1996, 2003).

Still others challenge assumptions they take to be implicit in Nagel's reasoning. For example, Kathleen Akins (1993) argues that Nagel errs in relying too much on the assumption that introspection (a process by which one can know about one's own mental life) is a reliable source of information. More specifically, she suggests that Nagel's reasoning concerns "pure phenomenal experience"—something entirely separate from other mental features, such as representing the world (see Chapters 23–27). But, Akins argues, introspection does not show that there is any such thing. In response, Nagel could deny that his reasoning concerns pure phenomenal experience; it is at least unclear why we should think it does.

There's also a question of whether bat echolocation experiences are really as different from human experiences as Nagel suggests. Blind people sometimes learn to echolocate, and most people use echolocation to some degree (Schwitzgebel and Gordon 2000). So, perhaps Nagel's example is not ideal for his purposes. But it's only an example. There might be better actual examples. Can someone who has been blind from birth understand what it is like to see (see Chapters 6 and 32)? Can we understand the electric eel's experience when it uses electricity to stun its prey? And, even if no actual example is perfect, it might be plausible to accept that a perfect example of some wholly alien experience could exist.

RECOMMENDED READING

CANONICAL PRESENTATION

Nagel, Thomas. 1974. "What Is It Like to Be a Bat?" *Philosophical Review* 83: 435–50.

OVERVIEWS

Chalmers, David J. 2003. "Consciousness and Its Place in Nature." In S. Stich and T. Warfield (eds.) *The Blackwell Guide to Philosophy of Mind*. Malden, MA: Blackwell: 102–42. Reprinted in D. J. Chalmers (ed.) *Philosophy of Mind: Classical and Contemporary Readings*, second edition. New York: Oxford University Press, 2021: 260–82.

Van Gulick, Robert. 2021. "Consciousness." *The Stanford Encyclopedia of Philosophy* (Winter 2021 Edition), Edward N. Zalta (ed.), URL = <https://plato.stanford.edu/archives/win2021/entries/consciousness/>.

ADDITIONAL DISCUSSIONS

Akins, Kathleen. 1993. "A Bat without Qualities." In M. Davies and G. Humphreys (eds.) *Consciousness*. Cambridge: Blackwell: 258–73.

Chalmers, David J. 1996. *The Conscious Mind: In Search of a Fundamental Theory*. New York: Oxford University Press.

Dennett, Daniel C. 1991. *Consciousness Explained*. Boston: Little, Brown.

Howell, Robert J. 2013. *Consciousness and the Limits of Objectivity: The Case for Subjective Physicalism*. Oxford: Oxford University Press.

Levin, Janet. 1986. "Could Love Be Like a Heatwave? Physicalism and the Subjective Character of Experience." *Philosophical Studies* 49: 245–61.

Lewis, David K. 1988. "What Experience Teaches." In *Proceedings of the Russellian Society*. Sydney: University of Sydney. Reprinted in P. Ludlow, D. Stoljar, and Y. Nagasawa (eds.) *There's Something about Mary: Essays on Phenomenal Consciousness and Frank Jackson's Knowledge Argument*. Cambridge, MA: MIT Press, 2004: 77–104.

McGinn, Colin. 1989. "Can We Solve the Mind–Body Problem?" *Mind* 98: 349–66.

Nagel, Thomas 1986. *The View from Nowhere*. New York: Oxford University Press.

Nagel, Thomas, 1998. "Conceiving the Impossible and the Mind–Body Problem." *Philosophy* 73 (285): 337–52.

Nemirow, Laurence. 1980. "Review of Thomas Nagel's *Mortal Questions*." *Philosophical Review* 89: 473–7.

Pereboom, Derk. 1994. "Bats, Brain Scientists, and the Limitations of Introspection." *Philosophy and Phenomenological Research* 54: 315–39.

Schwitzgebel, Eric, and Gordon, Michael S. 2000. "How Well Do We Know Our Own Conscious Experience? The Case of Human Echolocation." *Philosophical Topics* 28: 235–46.

Stoljar, Daniel. 2006. *Ignorance and Imagination: The Epistemic Origin of the Problem of Consciousness*. New York: Oxford University Press.

Yong, Ed. 2022. *An Immense World: How Animal Senses Reveal the Hidden Realms around Us*. New York: Random House.

MARY AND THE BLACK-AND-WHITE ROOM

BACKGROUND

If physicalism is true, then all information is physical information. What exactly "physical" means is a matter of dispute; but many agree on two things. First, physical information is information of the sort revealed by science. Second, information revealed by science is objective: understanding it requires intelligence but not specific sensory capacities. Thus, in principle, a colorblind person could understand any physical truth no less than a color-sighted person could, even if the physical truth in question concerns color perception. If all information is objective, physical information, then a complete physical description of the world would leave nothing out. Frank Jackson's knowledge argument suggests that such a description would leave out information about consciousness.

THE CASE

Imagine a time far in the future when the complete physical truth about the world has been discovered. Physics, chemistry, neuroscience, etc. have been completed. Now imagine Mary, a brilliant scientist,

DOI: 10.4324/9781003179191-8

who has never seen colors. She isn't colorblind. It's just that there were never any colors for her to see. She was raised in an entirely black-and-white room. Suppose her clothing is black and white too, that there aren't any mirrors, etc. Even so, Mary knows a lot about color vision. From a scientific perspective, she knows *everything* about it. Indeed, she knows the complete physical truth. She learns that truth by reading black-and-white books and watching lectures on a black-and-white television monitor. If that seems like a lot of information to master, well it is. But Mary is not just brilliant: she is a perfect reasoner. And she has plenty of time.

After learning the complete physical truth, Mary is released from her room. She sees colors for the first time. Does she learn anything new? Intuitively, she does. She already knew the complete science of how the human vision system processes information about colors, and so she doesn't learn anything more about that. Even so, she learns something that she didn't previously know—something that color-sighted people outside the room did know. She learns *what it's like* to see in color (see Chapters 4 and 5).

The Mary case causes trouble for physicalism. According to physicalism, all information is physical. That includes all information about color experiences. So, if physicalism is true, then, before leaving the room, Mary should know all there is to know about seeing in color. But she doesn't. At that point, she lacks information about what it's like to see in color. She doesn't acquire that information until she leaves. But that means the information she acquires cannot be physical information, since she has all that information in the room. And if her newly acquired information is not physical, then not all information is physical, and so physicalism is false. That is known as *the knowledge argument* against physicalism.

DISCUSSION

Some respond by accepting the knowledge argument and exploring non-physicalist theories of consciousness. That is what Jackson did when first presenting the argument in his 1982 article, "Epiphenomenal Qualia." There he defended a non-physicalist theory called *epiphenomenalist property dualism*. According to this theory, phenomenal properties—properties of experience such as those Mary learns about after leaving the black-and-white room—are non-physical properties that have physical causes but lack physical effects. Others develop different non-physicalist theories, such as *interactionist dualism*, on which there are non-physical phenomenal properties that have both physical causes and physical effects (Chalmers 1996).

But many reject the knowledge argument, for a variety of reasons. We'll mention four. First, some reject the set-up of the case by challenging the claim that Mary learns all physical information while still in the black-and-white room. These philosophers grant that she learns all information that can be expressed in objective, scientific language. But they deny that all physical information can be so expressed (Horgan 1984, Howell 2013). Physical information, they argue, is information about physical things. And some information that cannot be expressed in objective, scientific language might nonetheless be information about physical things. In response, knowledge argument proponents contend that such non-objective (or subjective) information cannot be reconciled with a core physicalist doctrine: that all information is ultimately based on the information revealed by fundamental physics (Chalmers 2010, Alter 2023).

Second, some challenge the claim that Mary learns anything when she leaves the black-and-white room (Dennett 1991). Daniel C. Dennett is skeptical about that claim. Suppose we play a trick on Mary. When she leaves the room, we hand her a banana that has been painted blue. Would she be fooled into thinking "Aha! That's what it's like to see yellow!"? Not necessarily. She's a brilliant scientist, and so, before rushing to judgment, she might check. For example, she could study the surface features of the blue banana, including all its microphysical properties, and deduce what frequency of electromagnetic radiation the banana would reflect, and how humans typically react when seeing that frequency. She'd thereby realize that this particular banana is blue—and thus that her experience of seeing it doesn't reveal to her what it's like to see yellow. In response, some knowledge argument proponents point out that Dennett's question about whether Mary is being fooled by the blue-banana trick misses the point. Seeing the banana would provide Mary with phenomenal information, regardless of whether that information is associated with bananas or the term "yellow"—information that she did not know before leaving the room. And that is all that is needed for the knowledge argument to go through (Nida-Rümelin 1995).

A third response relies on the distinction between different kinds of knowledge: *knowledge-that* (as when I know that riding a bike requires pedaling) and *know-how* (as when I know how to ride a bike). Philosophers offering this kind of response accept that Mary learns what it's like to see in color when she leaves the black-and-white room, but argue that she doesn't thereby gain information. They argue that to know what an experience is like is not to possess information (it's not knowledge-that). It's some other sort of knowledge (know-how), such as having the ability to imagine the experience (Lewis 1998, Nemirow 1990). And though physicalism might entail that, before leaving the room, Mary knows all *information* about color experiences, physicalism does *not* entail anything about what she can or can't imagine. In response, knowledge argument proponents argue that knowing what it's like can't plausibly be reduced to possessing abilities—or that if it can, then those abilities can't be possessed without possessing information (Conee 1994, Coleman 2009, Alter 2023).

Fourth, some argue that the Mary case shows something about our *concepts* of experience but nothing about the *nature* of experiences (Loar 1997, Balog 1999, Montero 2007; see Chapter 8). Seeing color doesn't give Mary any new information, but rather provides her with new conceptual resources. This is known as *the phenomenal concept strategy* (see Chapters 7 and 8). In response, knowledge argument proponents argue that the phenomenal concept strategy doesn't really solve the problem; it just moves the bump under the rug, so to speak. For example, consider Mary shortly after she leaves the room and has seen some red tomatoes. She knows what it's like to see red and green, and she possesses the associated phenomenal concepts. She might still wonder about other creatures' experiences. Even given a complete physical description of bats (or Martians), Mary might not be able to figure out if they have what she'd describe as red experiences or green experiences (Chalmers 2004).

In a historical twist, in the late 1990s, Jackson himself came to reject his knowledge argument and embrace physicalism. He now attributes the intuition that Mary gains information when she leaves the room primarily to a failure to recognize that to experience color is to *represent* the world in a distinctive way—a way that can be explained in entirely physical terms (Jackson 2003). He grants that Mary's pre-release knowledge of what it's like to see in color is incomplete. But, in his view, that is only because possessing such knowledge requires possessing certain abilities, such as the ability to visualize in color—a fact that is perfectly consistent with the physicalist claim that all information is physical information. (That last idea corresponds to the third kind of response above.)

Despite Jackson's change of mind, the debate his Mary case inspired continues to flourish. Indeed, the case has led to a plethora of issues that Jackson did not even hint at when he created Mary. And, in many instances, the issues have led others to vary the case. One of the earliest such variant is Martine Nida-Rümelin's (1995) Marianna case. Like Mary, Marianna has lived in a black-and-white environment without seeing colors. But instead of going outside and encountering a rose or a ripe tomato, which she knows are typically colored red, she is brought into another room that contains only artificial objects (walls, tables, etc.) of various colors. The Marianna case helps us distinguish between knowing what it's like to see red and knowing something about the reference of color terms.

Other variants of the Mary case serve other philosophical purposes. David J. Chalmers (2004, 2010) discusses Inverted Mary, who is just like Jackson's Mary except her color vision is red/green inverted (see Chapter 20), and Zombie Mary, who lacks consciousness entirely—despite saying upon leaving the room, "Aha! This is what it's like to see red!" (see Chapter 7). Daniel Soljar (2005) describes Experienced Mary, who is returned to her black-and-white room and forgets some truths she learned outside, such as which things (such as firetrucks and ripe tomatoes) cause people to see red. Dennett (2007) conjures up RoboMary, a robotic variation. He also discusses Swamp Mary, who is created by a cosmic accident and is physically just like Mary after she returns to the black-and-white room and is no longer experiencing colors (see Chapter 24). Jesse J. Prinz (2012) discusses four other variants: Subliminal Mary, who is exposed to color patches only very briefly; Inverse Mary, who knows nothing about the brain but knows a lot about color experience; and two others (Arid Mary and Clumsy Mary). Robert J. Howell (2019) imagines a Mary-like character, Rick, who knows everything physical about a type of human-like robot but doesn't learn that robots have selves until discovering that he himself is a robot of that type. And the list goes on.

RECOMMENDED READING

CANONICAL PRESENTATION

Jackson, Frank. 1982. "Epiphenomenal Qualia." *Philosophical Quarterly* 32: 127–36.

OVERVIEWS

Alter, Torin. 2017. "Physicalism and the Knowledge Argument." In M. Velmans and S. Schneider (eds.) *The Blackwell Companion to Consciousness*, second edition. Oxford: Blackwell: 404–14.
Alter, Torin, and Howell, Robert J. 2009. *A Dialogue on Consciousness*. New York: Oxford University Press.
Nida-Rümelin, Martine, and O Conaill, Donnchadh. 2021. "Qualia: The Knowledge Argument." *The Stanford Encyclopedia of Philosophy* (Summer 2021 Edition), Edward N. Zalta (ed.), URL = <https://plato.stanford.edu/archives/sum2021/entries/qualia-knowledge/>.
Stoljar, Daniel, and Nagasawa, Yujin. 2004. "Introduction." In P. Ludlow, D. Stoljar, and Y. Nagasawa (eds.) *There's Something about Mary: Essays on Phenomenal Consciousness and Frank Jackson's Knowledge Argument*. Cambridge, MA: MIT Press: 1–36.

ADDITIONAL DISCUSSIONS

Alter, Torin. 2023. *The Matter of Consciousness: From the Knowledge Argument to Russellian Monism*. Oxford: Oxford University Press.
Chalmers, David J. 2004. "Phenomenal Concepts and the Knowledge Argument." In P. Ludlow, D. Stoljar, and Y. Nagasawa (eds.) *There's Something about Mary: Essays on Phenomenal Consciousness and Frank Jackson's Knowledge Argument*. Cambridge, MA: MIT Press: 269–98.
Coleman, Sam. 2009. "Why the Ability Hypothesis is Best Forgotten." *Journal of Consciousness Studies* 16: 74–97.
Conee, Earl. 1994. "Phenomenal Knowledge." *Australasian Journal of Philosophy* 72: 136–50.
Dennett, Daniel C. 1991. "'Epiphenomenal' Qualia?" In *Consciousness Explained*. Boston: Little, Brown: 398–406.
Dennett, Daniel C. 2007. "What RoboMary Knows." In T. Alter and S. Walter (eds.) *Phenomenal Concepts and Phenomenal Knowledge: New Essays on Consciousness and Physicalism*. New York: Oxford University Press: 15–31.
Gertler, Brie. 1999. "A Defense of the Knowledge Argument." *Philosophical Studies* 93: 317–36.
Horgan, Terrance. 1984. "Jackson on Physical Information and Qualia." *Philosophical Quarterly* 34: 147–52.

Howell, R. J. 2013. *Consciousness and the Limits of Objectivity: The Case for Subjective Physicalism*. Oxford: Oxford University Press.

Jackson, F. 1995. "Postscript." In P. K. Moser and J. D. Trout (eds.) *Contemporary Materialism: A Reader*. New York: Routledge: 184–89.

Jackson, Frank. 1986. "What Mary Didn't Know." *Journal of Philosophy* 83: 291–5.

Jackson, Frank. 2003. "Mind and Illusion." In A. O'Hear (ed.) *Minds and Persons*. New York: Cambridge University Press: 251–71.

Lewis, David K. 1988. "What Experience Teaches." In *Proceedings of the Russellian Society*. Sydney: University of Sydney. Reprinted in W. Lycan (ed.) *Mind and Cognition: A Reader*. Cambridge, MA: Blackwell, 1990: 499–518.

Loar, Brian. 1997. "Phenomenal States." In N. Block, O. Flanagan, and G. Güzeldere (eds.) *The Nature of Consciousness: Philosophical Debates*. Cambridge, MA: MIT Press: 597–616.

Montero, Barbara G. 2007. "Physicalism Could Be True Even If Mary Learns Something New." *Philosophical Quarterly* 57: 176–89.

Nemirow, Lawrence. 1990. "Physicalism and the Cognitive Role of Acquaintance." In W. Lycan (ed.) *Mind and Cognition: A Reader*. Cambridge: Blackwell: 490–99.

Nida-Rümelin, Martine. 1995. "What Mary Couldn't Know: Belief about Phenomenal States." In T. Metzinger (ed.) *Conscious Experience*. Paderborn: Schöningh/Imprint Academic: 219–42.

Stoljar, Daniel. 2005. "Physicalism and Phenomenal Concepts." *Mind and Language* 20: 469–94.

OTHER REFERENCES

Balog, Katalin. 1999. "Conceivability, Possibility, and the Mind-Body Problem." *Philosophical Review* 108: 497–528.

Chalmers, David J. 1996. *The Conscious Mind: In Search of a Fundamental Theory*. New York: Oxford University Press.

Chalmers, David J. 2010. *The Character of Consciousness*. New York: Oxford University Press.

Howell, Robert J. 2019. "The Knowledge Argument and the Self." In S. Coleman (ed.) *The Knowledge Argument*. Cambridge: Cambridge University Press: 254–68.

Prinz, Jesse J. 2012. *The Conscious Brain: How Attention Engenders Experience*. New York: Oxford University Press.

ZOMBIES

BACKGROUND

According to physicalism, consciousness is in reality nothing more than a physical phenomenon. This view has strong implications. In particular, it is widely taken to imply that consciousness *supervenes* on physical phenomena: any world that is exactly like the actual world in all physical respects (and contains nothing else) must be exactly like the actual world with respect to consciousness. That physicalist supervenience claim runs into a challenge from *zombies*: hypothetical creatures that are exactly like conscious human beings in all physical (and functional) respects, but that lack consciousness entirely. The zombie challenge was presented by Robert Kirk (see Kirk and Squires 1974, pp. 135–52) and popularized by David J. Chalmers (1996).

THE CASE

Here is how to imagine your zombie twin. Don't imagine a zombie from the movies, who is "undead" and likes to snack on human brains. Instead, imagine someone who is physically indistinguishable from you. Cell for cell, molecule for molecule, quark for quark, they are your counterpart. They also behave exactly as you do. At this moment, their eyes are positioned just as yours are, as you read these words. More

DOI: 10.4324/9781003179191-9

generally, you and this creature are physically and functionally indistinguishable. There is only one difference: you have conscious experiences, and they do not. They could be described as "seeing" words right now, in the sense that their brains register information. But there is nothing it's like for them to see those words. There's nothing it's like for them, period—ever. They are a *zombie*: a physical/functional duplicate of a human being who lacks consciousness entirely. Not that anyone could tell. If your zombie twin were asked what they are seeing, they will answer exactly as you would. And they will insist that they are *not* a zombie, just as you would. But while you are right, they are wrong.

Your zombie twin probably does not exist. But their existence does not seem impossible. Indeed, it seems possible for there to be an entire zombie world: a world that lacks consciousness but is identical to the actual world in all physical and functional respects. And that possibility is hard to reconcile with physicalism. By definition, a zombie world has every physical and functional feature that the actual world has. If such a world is possible, then how could consciousness be just a physical phenomenon? In the actual world, consciousness exists. So, if consciousness were physical, then duplicating the actual world's physical and functional features should guarantee the existence of consciousness.

For comparison, consider rocks. Could there be a world that duplicates the actual world in all physical and functional respects but that does not contain rocks—a rock-zombie world? This seems doubtful, precisely because rocks are physical phenomena. There is nothing more to a rock than what would be captured in a complete physical and functional description of it. But while a rock-zombie world seems impossible, a consciousness-zombie world seems possible—contrary to what physicalism seems to imply.

The zombie argument has three main premises, which can be stated roughly as follows:

1. A zombie world is ideally conceivable (that is, conceivable on ideal reflection).
2. If a zombie world is ideally conceivable, then it is metaphysically possible (that is, possible in the broadest sense, rather than, say, relative to natural laws).
3. If a zombie world is metaphysically possible, then physicalism is false.

Conclusion: physicalism is false.

The features of consciousness that distinguish you and your zombie twin are sometimes called "phenomenal properties" or "qualia". Zombies lack qualia. For that reason, zombie cases are sometimes described as "absent qualia" cases (see Chapter 16).

DISCUSSION

Some respond to the zombie argument by rejecting physicalism and exploring non-physicalist alternatives, such as dualism (Chalmers 1996; see Chapter 4). Others respond by rejecting one or more of the zombie argument's three main premises. Though all three premises have been challenged, most accept the third and reject either the first or the second (though for a challenge to the third, see Montero 2013, and for a reply see Alter 2023). The discussion tends to get pretty technical. But the basic ideas are fairly intuitive.

To reject the first premise is to deny that a zombie world is ideally conceivable. Sometimes something seems conceivable at first, but on reflection we realize we are just confused. Recall an example from Chapter 3. In objecting to Descartes' conceivability argument, Arnauld (1641) suggests that someone might be able to conceive of a right triangle that doesn't conform to the Pythagorean theorem: the sum of the squares of its sides is slightly greater than its hypotenuse squared. But such a triangle isn't *ideally* conceivable. Enough reflection would reveal that it makes no sense. (To put the point in the language that we used in Chapter 3, their idea of the right triangle is not clear and distinct; they are not using concepts that are sufficiently comprehensive.) Some argue that the same is true of the zombie scenario: enough reflection would reveal that the zombie scenario is incoherent (see Chapter 32).

On one version of that objection, the reason zombies seem conceivable is that we don't yet know enough about what a zombie world would be like (Stoljar 2006). Such a world would be exactly like the actual world in all physical respects. But how can we claim to know what that entails? The physical sciences aren't completed. There is much about the physical world we don't know. Perhaps future discoveries in physics will reveal some inconsistency in the idea of a physical/functional duplicate of the actual world without consciousness—discoveries that would prove that any such physical/functional duplicate would *have* to contain consciousness. If we can't see that inconsistency today, that might be because current physics is incomplete. In response, proponents of the zombie argument argue that any future discovery in physics could only reveal information of the same kind that current physics reveals—namely, information about causal, spacetime structure. In their view, no revelation of that sort would undermine, or even weaken, the intuition that a zombie world is conceivable (see Chapter 4; Chalmers 2003, Alter 2023).

Another physicalist response to the zombie argument is to deny its second premise: the claim that the ideal conceivability of a zombie world entails that it is metaphysically possible. Here, one might invoke an analogy to hydrogen-free water. Many philosophers regard such a thing as metaphysically impossible, on the grounds that water *is* H_2O. But suppose you don't know anything about the chemical composition of water. You might nevertheless well understand the *concept* of water. Plausibly, many people had that concept well before the chemical composition of water was discovered. So, suppose you are in that sort of position: you know what water is in an everyday sense, but you don't know that it's really H_2O. In that case, even if you know I'm drinking water, you could conceive of my glass containing no hydrogen—and you could do so without making any mistake in reasoning. There's nothing about the *concept* of water that prevents you from conceiving of hydrogen-free water. For you, such a thing is *conceptually* possible. But for all that, it might be *metaphysically* impossible. Likewise, one might reason, perhaps a zombie world is impossible despite being conceivable.

However, the analogy between conceiving of zombies and conceiving of hydrogen-free water has been questioned. Hydrogen-free water is ideally conceivable only if we fail to consider some of the world's physical features, including water's chemical composition. By contrast, the zombie-world scenario duplicates *all* of the actual world's physical features. So, without saying more, physicalists can't explain the ideal conceivability of a zombie world in the way they can explain the ideal conceivability of hydrogen-free water. But these philosophers have a lot more to say. Recall the phenomenal concept strategy from Chapter 4. Phenomenal concept strategists attribute the ideal conceivability of zombie world not to distinctive features of consciousness itself but rather to distinctive features of how we *think* about consciousness—that is, to phenomenal concepts (Loar 1997, Balog 1999, Hill and McLaughlin 1999, Papineau 2002). Maybe it's just built into phenomenal concepts that consciousness is independent of physical and functional features. If so, we should blame the ideal conceivability of a zombie world not on the nature of phenomenal *consciousness* but instead on the nature of phenomenal *concepts*.

If the phenomenal concept strategy succeeds, then we can have our cake and eat it too: we can accept the intuition that a zombie world is ideally conceivable, but deny that this ideal conceivability entails that such a world is metaphysically possible. On this strategy, dualism is built into our concepts; but that is perfectly consistent with a physicalist view about what our concepts pick out. Non-physicalists counter that this strategy doesn't succeed. It merely relocates the problem the zombie case brings out. If phenomenal concepts are really so distinctive—if their features can explain the ideal conceivability of a zombie world—then those concepts will themselves be non-physical, and so the anti-physicalist argument can be reinstated (Chalmers 2007; for further discussion, see Balog 2012, Alter 2023).

RECOMMENDED READING

CANONICAL PRESENTATIONS

Chalmers, David J. 1996. *The Conscious Mind: In Search of a Fundamental Theory.* New York: Oxford University Press.

Kirk, Robert and Squires, J. E. R. 1974. "Zombies v. Materialists." *Proceedings of the Aristotelian Society Supplementary Volumes* 48: 135–63.

OVERVIEWS

Chalmers, David J. 2003. "Consciousness and Its Place in Nature." In S. Stich and T. Warfield (eds.) *The Blackwell Guide to Philosophy of Mind.* Malden, MA: Blackwell: 102–42. Reprinted in D. J. Chalmers (ed.) *Philosophy of Mind: Classical and Contemporary Readings*, second edition. New York: Oxford University Press, 2021: 260–82.

Kirk, R. 2021. "Zombies." *The Stanford Encyclopedia of Philosophy* (Spring 2021 Edition), Edward N. Zalta (ed.), URL = <https://plato.stanford.edu/archives/spr2021/entries/zombies/>.

ADDITIONAL DISCUSSIONS

Alter, Torin. 2023. *The Matter of Consciousness: From the Knowledge Argument to Russellian Monism.* Oxford: Oxford University Press.

Balog, Katalin. 2012. "A Defense of the Phenomenal Concept Strategy." *Philosophy and Phenomenological Research* 84: 1–23.

Balog, Katalin. 1999. "Conceivability, Possibility, and the Mind-Body Problem." *Philosophical Review* 108: 497–528.

Chalmers, David J. 2007. "Phenomenal Concepts and the Explanatory Gap." In T. Alter and S. Walter (eds.) *Phenomenal Knowledge and Phenomenal Concepts: New Essays on Consciousness and Physicalism.* New York: Oxford University Press: 167–94.

Hill, Christopher S., and McLaughlin, Brian P. 1999. "There are Fewer Things in Reality than are Dreamt of in Chalmers's Philosophy." *Philosophy and Phenomenological Research* 59: 445–54.

Howell, Robert J. 2013. *Consciousness and the Limits of Objectivity: The Case for Subjective Physicalism.* Oxford: Oxford University Press.

Loar, Brian. 1997. "Phenomenal States." In N. Block, O. Flanagan, and G. Güzeldere (eds.) *The Nature of Consciousness: Philosophical Debates.* Cambridge, MA: MIT Press: 597–616.

Montero, Barbara G. 2013. "Must Physicalism Imply Supervenience of the Mental on the Physical?" *Journal of Philosophy* 110: 93–110.

Papineau, David, 2002. *Thinking about Consciousness.* New York: Oxford University Press.

Stoljar, Daniel. 2005. "Physicalism and Phenomenal Concepts." *Mind and Language* 20: 469–94.

Stoljar, Daniel. 2006. *Ignorance and Imagination: The Epistemic Origin of the Problem of Consciousness.* New York: Oxford University Press.

OTHER REFERENCES

Arnauld, Antoine. 1641. "Fourth Set of Objections." In J. Cottingham, R. Stoothoff, D. Murdoch, and A. Kenny (eds.) *The Philosophical Writings of Descartes, vol. II.* Cambridge: Cambridge University Press, 1985: 138–53.

Campbell, Keith. 1970. *Body and Mind.* London: Doubleday.

Dennett, Daniel C. 1991. *Consciousness Explained.* Boston: Little, Brown.

Gendler, Tamar, and Hawthorne, John (eds.). 2002. *Conceivability and Possibility.* New York: Oxford University Press.

Nagel, Thomas. 1998. "Conceiving the Impossible and the Mind-Body Problem." *Philosophy* 73 (285): 337–52.

Pereboom, Derk. 2011. *Consciousness and the Prospects of Physicalism.* New York: Oxford University Press.

YOGIS

BACKGROUND

According to the zombie argument against physicalism, the conceivability of zombies entails that they are metaphysically possible, which in turn entails that consciousness is not physical (see Chapter 7). Katalin Balog (1999) responds that the zombie argument cannot be correct. She argues that zombie philosophers could use similar reasoning to show that they themselves have non-physical mental states—and yet, by hypothesis, they do not. She builds her case by developing a thought experiment involving creatures she calls "yogis."

THE CASE

The zombie argument against physicalism is based on a thought experiment. We are asked to conceive of a world that is physically and functionally the same as the actual world, except no one is conscious. In a zombie world, there is a molecule-for-molecule duplicate of you who is "seeing" worlds indistinguishable from the worlds you're presently seeing—except they have no inner, subjective life at all. If such a world is conceivable, that is partly because we can refer to our experiences directly, rather than *via* physical or functional descriptions.

DOI: 10.4324/9781003179191-10

For example, we can refer to pain not just as a state that has certain physical causes and physical effects—events that have zombie counterparts. We can refer to pain more directly, as a state that feels a certain way—that is, a state with a certain distinctive phenomenal quality. Phenomenal qualities are what the zombie world is supposed to lack.

Katalin Balog rejects the zombie argument. To show why we should too, she asks us to imagine a world with people that are much like us, except that some of them are *yogis*. Just as philosophical zombies are different from the zombies of horror films, philosophical yogis are different from the yogis who practice certain forms of eastern religions. Balog's yogis have a special concept-forming ability. They can detect some of their own brain states in a direct way, without the mediation of any physical or functional description. Indeed, they do not know how they do this. In detecting these brain states, they do not conceive of them *as* brain states, or as physical or functional states of any kind. Their direct detection of these brain states enables them to refer to them. Indeed, they refer to them in something like the way we refer to states of consciousness. But there is a difference: their reference is not mediated by phenomenal qualities.

Call one of the yogi's brain states "A" and suppose they use the term "flurg" to refer directly to A. Now imagine a yogi philosopher considering the nature of flurgs. Are flurgs physical? They might well conclude that flurgs are not physical, reasoning as follows. It is ideally conceivable that there should be a world that is physically and functionally just like our world but in which no flurgs occur. Therefore, such a world is possible, and so flurgs are non-physical. That yogi philosopher's argument seems to parallel the zombie argument in all relevant respects. And yet their conclusion is clearly false. We *stipulated* that flurgs are brain states, which are physical. Thus, any physical duplicate of the yogi world is guaranteed to contain flurgs. The world the yogi philosopher conceives is impossible. Something is amiss.

Balog takes the case of yogis to reveal an error in the zombie argument. The reason yogi philosophers can conceive of a flurg-free world that is physically and functionally just like theirs can't be that such a world is possible, because it isn't possible. The reason is rather that their flurg concept refers directly, without the mediation of physical or functional concepts. Likewise, according to Balog, the reason we can conceive of a zombie world is not that such a world is possible, but rather because our phenomenal concepts refer directly, without the mediation of physical or functional concepts. Thus, the physicalist can respond to the zombie argument by rejecting the premise that a zombie world is possible if conceivable (that's premise (2) of the zombie argument, as presented in Chapter 7).

DISCUSSION

Balog's argument could be seen as an instance of the phenomenal concept strategy for rejecting the zombie argument (and related arguments, such as the knowledge argument). This strategy accepts the conceivability of zombies, but explains it in terms of special features of phenomenal concepts rather than special features of the phenomenal properties those concepts pick out (Stoljar 2005). Balog's argument also has much in common with a related strategy, on which phenomenal concepts are construed as conditional concepts: they refer to physical states if the world is entirely physical, and to non-physical states if the world is not entirely physical (Hawthorne 2002, Stalnaker 2002, Braddon-Mitchell 2003; but see Alter 2007.). Like the phenomenal concept strategy, the conditional analysis strategy defends physicalism by appealing to claims about phenomenal concepts. But, unlike the phenomenal concept strategy, the conditional analysis is used to challenge the premise that zombies are conceivable rather than the premise that zombies are possible if conceivable.

Zombie-argument proponents, such as David J. Chalmers (2007, 2010), respond to Balog's argument by rejecting her analogy between zombies and yogis. Chalmers suggests that the yogis' flurg concept differs significantly from phenomenal concepts (or at least from the sorts of phenomenal concepts that are most relevant to the zombie argument). The yogis' flurg concept is a kind of *demonstrative* concept: its content could be roughly expressed as "*this* inner state, whatever that turns out to be." By contrast, phenomenal concepts do not seem to be demonstrative concepts. For example, the pain concept picks out a state with a certain distinctive phenomenal quality. That state might or might not be physical; but, either way, it must have that distinctive phenomenal quality if it is to be the reference of the pain concept.

That difference between the yogis' concepts and our phenomenal concepts is significant. Suppose the yogis are supplied with the complete physical truth about their world. That includes the information that flurgs are brain states. Perhaps they could wonder if that information pertains specifically to *their* flurgs. But they need not wonder about that for very long; suppose they are also supplied with information enabling them to locate themselves in their world. They would then be positioned to know that *their* flurgs are brain states, and therefore to exclude the possibility that flurgs are non-physical. By contrast, supplying a person with the complete physical truth plus information about their place in the actual world would *not* position them to know whether pains are brain states. The nature of pains and other states of consciousness would remain open (see Chapter 4). If so, then the analogy between the yogi case and the zombie case is less compelling than Balog suggests.

RECOMMENDED READING

CANONICAL PRESENTATION

Balog, Katalin. 1999. "Conceivability, Possibility, and the Mind-Body Problem." *Philosophical Review* 108: 497–528.

OVERVIEWS

Chalmers, David J. 2003. "Consciousness and Its Place in Nature." In S. Stich and T. Warfield (eds.) *The Blackwell Guide to Philosophy of Mind*. Malden, MA: Blackwell: 102–42. Reprinted in D. J. Chalmers (ed.) *Philosophy of Mind: Classical and Contemporary Readings*, second edition. New York: Oxford University Press, 2021: 260–82.

Kirk, Robert. 2021. "Zombies." *The Stanford Encyclopedia of Philosophy* (Spring 2021 Edition), Edward N. Zalta (ed.), URL = <https://plato.stanford.edu/archives/spr2021/entries/zombies/>.

ADDITIONAL DISCUSSIONS

Balog, Katalin. 2012. "A Defense of the Phenomenal Concept Strategy." *Philosophy and Phenomenological Research* 84: 1–23.

Chalmers, David J. 2007. "Phenomenal Concepts and the Explanatory Gap." In T. Alter and S. Walter (eds.) *Phenomenal Knowledge and Phenomenal Concepts: New Essays on Consciousness and Physicalism*. New York: Oxford University Press: 167–94.

Chalmers, David J. 2010. *The Character of Consciousness*. New York: Oxford University Press. (See especially Chapter 9.)

Frankish, Keith. 2007. "The Anti-Zombie Argument." *Philosophical Quarterly* 57: 650–66.

Papineau, David. 2002. *Thinking about Consciousness*. New York: Oxford University Press.

Stoljar, Daniel. 2005. "Physicalism and Phenomenal Concepts." *Mind and Language* 20: 469–94.

OTHER REFERENCES

Alter, Torin. 2007. "On the Conditional Analysis of Phenomenal Concepts." *Philosophical Studies* 134: 235–53.

Block, Ned. 2006. "Max Black's Objection to Mind-Body Identity." In R. Zimmerman (ed.) *Oxford Studies in Metaphysics*, Volume 2. New York: Oxford University Press: 3–78.

Braddon-Mitchell, David. 2003. "Qualia and Analytical Conditionals." *Journal of Philosophy* 100: 111–35.

Hawthorne, John. 2002. "Advice for Physicalists." *Philosophical Studies* 109: 17–52.

Stalnaker, Robert. 2002. "What Is It Like to Be a Zombie?" In T. Gendler and J. Hawthorne (eds.) *Conceivability and Possibility*. New York: Oxford University Press: 385–400.

THE COFFEE TASTERS

BACKGROUND

The thought experiment we will consider in this chapter was put forth by Daniel C. Dennett in a paper called "Quining Qualia." The term "quining" is an homage to 20th-century philosopher Willard Van Orman Quine (1908–2000). Starting in 1969 and continuing through the 1970s and 1980s, Dennett published several editions of *The Philosophical Lexicon*, a humorous compilation of neologisms based on philosophers' names. "Quining" (used as a verb) was the very first term he coined, and he defined it as follows: "to deny resolutely the existence or importance of something real or significant." Indeed, the activity of quining was central to Quine's philosophy. In putting forth his naturalist view, one according to which he privileged the methods and techniques of science above all else, Quine frequently cast doubt on the usefulness of some of our most central philosophical notions—notions like meaning, thought, belief, experience, and necessity. In "Quining Qualia," Dennett offers a number of thought experiments—or what he refers to as "intuition pumps"—with the aim of casting similar doubt on the usefulness of the notion of qualia. Especially central to his case is the example of the coffee tasters, which we will focus on here.

Qualia (also known as phenomenal properties) are properties of experiences (see Chapters 4 and 5). For example, these are the properties in virtue of which there is something it is like to feel a sharp stitch of pain in your side or to smell the sweet and fragrant scent of a blooming lily. Dennett works with a notion of qualia that he takes to be firmly embedded in philosophical treatments of the mind: (1) qualia are ineffable, i.e., they cannot be fully or adequately described; (2) qualia are intrinsic properties, i.e., they cannot be analyzed merely in terms of their relations to other things; (3) qualia are directly or immediately apprehensible in consciousness, i.e., one can introspect them; and (4) qualia are private, i.e., no one other than the individual who is having them can directly or immediately apprehend them.

THE CASE

Imagine two individuals we'll call "Mr. Chase" and "Ms. Sanborn" who have worked for the last decade as coffee tasters in the quality control division of a coffee company. When Chase and Sanborn first started at the company, it seemed like a dream job. What could be better than spending a lot of time tasting the coffee that they both love? Recently, however, they are no longer quite as fond of their jobs, as each finds that they no longer like the taste of the company's distinctive coffee blend. They're each puzzled by this, since the recipe of the coffee has not changed at all over the years, and chemical analyses of current coffee samples show consistency with the chemical analyses of coffee samples from when they started at the company. Moreover, all the other members of the coffee tasting team affirm that the coffee tastes exactly the same as it always has, and that it's just as good as ever.

Imagine that one afternoon over tea Chase and Sanborn get to talking about their dissatisfaction. As they talk, they realize that, although they share their dislike for the company's coffee, they'd offer different diagnoses of what the problem is. Chase is convinced that his preferences have shifted over time. The coffee still tastes exactly the same to him, he reports, but he no longer likes that taste. In contrast, Sanborn denies that her preferences have shifted. Instead, she is convinced that her gustatorial system must have changed in some way, so that the way it processes the same coffee is now different. To cast it as Dennett does, we might explain their respective situations by saying that Chase thinks that his *tastes* have changed, while Sanborn thinks that her *tasters* (her tastebuds) have changed.

But now consider the following question: How does each know that they're right about what's happened? Perhaps Chase is really in the situation that Sanborn is in, or vice versa. Or perhaps they are each in a situation that's midway between the two, with some change of tastes and some change of tasters. How could they ever sort it out?

There doesn't appear to be any way they could do so from the inside, by reflecting on their experiences. But perhaps they could get clarity some other way. We might do some tests on Sanborn's gustatory system to see whether it is functioning normally. Suppose the tests come back with the result that the system is functioning just the same as it always did. If we take the test to be definitive, and thereby deny that the coffee is tasting any different to Sanborn from how it tasted in the past, then we would be overriding Sanborn' own subjective assessment of her qualia. After all, Sanborn insists that the coffee tastes different to her now. If we accept that she could be wrong about that, then it looks like she is no longer directly apprehending those qualia; if she were, says Dennett, then she would know what they are like.

On the other hand, to check things with Chase, suppose that we subject him to a bunch of tests where he is asked to re-identify samples of coffee, tea, and other beverages. If he does poorly at these tests, we might doubt his claim that the company's coffee still tastes the same to him. Insofar as we'd be willing to override an individual's own subjective assessments of their qualia, it again looks like we're denying that qualitative experience is directly or immediately apprehensible to consciousness.

Either way, it looks like we're departing from our initial notion of qualia. As Dennett says (1988, p. 60), if we accept that individuals have to do tests or consult experts in order to confirm what qualia they're having, then we've "surely" moved "far away from our original idea of qualia as properties with which we have a particularly intimate acquaintance."

Now let's take this one step further. Suppose we try to explain why Chase's qualia might be different from how they were before. A natural explanation would be to say that his shifting preferences have affected the way the coffee tastes to him—that is, that it's precisely because his preferences have changed that the taste has changed. Wine, for example, is often said to be an acquired taste. But what happens when you acquire that taste? One natural way to describe things would be to say that, as you come to appreciate certain aspects of the wine's flavor, your qualitative experience changes. Your preferences and reactions affect the qualia of your experience. If we accept this explanation, however, then we admit that qualia have a relational profile, and we would thus have to deny that they are intrinsic. This presents yet a further departure from the traditional conception of qualia.

DISCUSSION

Dennett takes the coffee tasters thought experiment to reveal a deep incoherence in the traditional conception of qualia. We can't really know what qualia we're having, and we can't really separate qualia from our reactions to them. In his view, the very notion of qualia is so thoroughly confused that it should be retired from philosophical discussion.

In rejecting the traditional notion of qualia, Dennett endorses a philosophical view known as *eliminativism* (or sometimes *eliminative materialism*). According to eliminativists, our ordinary and intuitive understanding of the mind is deeply wrong and misguided. To defend this point, eliminativists often draw a comparison to our ordinary and intuitive understanding of physics. There are deep mistakes interwoven throughout our intuitive conception of physics (often called *folk physics*)—for example, the idea that a heavier ball falls faster than a lighter one. Likewise, eliminativists say, there are also deep mistakes interwoven throughout our intuitive conception of the mind (often called *folk psychology*). In rejecting and replacing folk theories, we discard the mistaken posits of the theory. Thus, given that many of our mental state categories are posits of folk psychology, it shouldn't be surprising that they too need to be discarded as we come to develop a more sophisticated and scientific theory of mind.

Early eliminativists tended to focus on mental states like beliefs and desires (see, e.g., Churchland 1981). More recently, many philosophers of an eliminativist bent have turned their attention to consciousness and have developed a view that's come to be known as *illusionism* (Frankish 2016, Kammerer 2021). According to illusionism, qualia do not really exist; we are merely under the illusion that they exist.

Reflection on cases like Chase and Sanborn help bring attention to the nature of this illusion.

Though illusionism has some persistent supporters, it remains a minority view; and most philosophers remain unpersuaded that the Chase and Sanborn case presents a deep puzzle. Criticisms of this thought experiment often point to the role that memory seems to be playing in Dennett's discussion. For example, Ned Block (1995) suggests that Chase and Sanborn's mistakes are all traceable to problems with their memories of qualia. But when defenders of the traditional conception of qualia suggest that qualia are meant to be directly apprehensible, that is meant to apply to current qualitative experience. The fact that we might incorrectly remember the precise qualitative nature of past qualitative experiences does not show that the notion of qualia is confused.

A related criticism of Dennett's discussion suggests that he has interpreted the notion of direct and immediate apprehensibility too strongly. As Dennett interprets it, individuals are required to be completely infallible about their own qualitative experience. But we might accept that people can make various mistakes about their qualitative experiences while still holding onto the traditional conception of qualia. For example, suppose you are walking alone late at night and someone comes up behind you, presses something into your back, and says, "Don't move. I have a knife and I'm not afraid to use it." You take yourself to be experiencing a sharp pain. As the moments go by, however, you realize that the sensation you thought was painful is really just cold. It turns out that there was no knife, but just a frozen popsicle. It can still be the case that you were directly and immediately apprehending the sensation all along, even if your initial assessment of what you were experiencing was mistaken. More generally, not everyone who believes in qualia would accept Dennett's assumptions about such properties (see Chapters 19, 20, 38, 45).

RECOMMENDED READING

CANONICAL PRESENTATIONS

Dennett, Daniel C. 1988. "Quining Qualia." In Anthony J. Marcel and E. Bisiach (eds.) *Consciousness in Contemporary Science*. Oxford: Oxford University Press: 42–77.

Hofstadter, Douglas, and Dennett, Daniel C. 1981. *The Mind's I: Fantasies and Reflections on Self and Soul*. New York: Basic Books. (See pp. 427–29.)

OVERVIEWS

Mandik, Pete. 2018. "Cognitive Approaches to Phenomenal Consciousness." In Dale Jacquette (ed.) *Bloomsbury Companion to the Philosophy of Consciousness*. New York: Bloomsbury Academic: 347–70. (See Section 3, especially 3.3.)

ADDITIONAL DISCUSSIONS

Block, Ned. 1995. "Consciousness." In Samuel Guttenplan (ed.) *A Companion to Philosophy of Mind*. Oxford: Blackwell.

Churchland, Paul M. 1981. "Eliminative Materialism and the Propositional Attitudes." *Journal of Philosophy* 78: 67–90.

Dennett, Daniel C. 1991. *Consciousness Explained*. Boston: Little, Brown.

Dennett, Daniel C., and Kinsbourne, Marcel. 1992. "Time and the Observer: The Where and When of Consciousness in the Brain." *Behavioral and Brain Sciences* 15 (2): 183–201.

Frankish, Keith. 2016. "Illusionism as a Theory of Consciousness." *Journal of Consciousness Studies* 23 (11–12): 11–39.

Kammerer, François. 2021. "The Illusion of Conscious Experience." *Synthese* 198: 845–66.

Nida-Rümelin, Martine. 2016. "The Illusion of Illusionism." *Journal of Consciousness Studies* 23 (11-12): 160–71.

THE HORNSWOGGLE PROBLEM

BACKGROUND

In Chapter 4, we encountered the hard problem of consciousness, so named by David Chalmers (1995). There are many unsolved problems associated with consciousness—such as explaining why humans dream or determining exactly how anesthesia works. But as hard as these problems might be, they seem comparatively easy when compared with the problem of explaining why a given neural process has or gives rise to the particular experiential quality that it does. Why do I have an experience of searing pain, as opposed to an experience of a light tickle, or as opposed to no experience at all, when a particular group of neurons fire? Answering this kind of question has been singled out many philosophers as being uniquely hard, perhaps even unsolvable. Patricia Churchland disagrees. In her view, insofar as this assessment seems plausible, it's only because we've been *hornswoggled*. To be hornswoggled is to be deceived or cheated—as Churchland puts it, it's "to be fooled by something because you've been insufficiently sceptical. To be hornswoggled is to be sold a bill of goods, that once you've bought, turn out to be worthless" (2022, p. 81). In defending the charge of hornswoggling, she offers numerous examples drawn from the history of science designed to show that much of the contemporary philosophical discussion of consciousness is based on a misconception of scientific progress and how it can be achieved. We'll focus on one of her examples drawn from the history of astrophysics.

THE CASE

Consider a typical team of astronomers in the late 18th century. One thing they're studying is planetary orbits. Planets orbiting the sun do so in an elliptical fashion. But these orbits are not perfectly elliptical in nature. The point of the orbit where a planet is closest to the sun—called the *perihelion*—does not always occur at exactly the same place. This rotational change in the orbit is called a *precession*. The orbital precessions of the planets could be predicted and explained within the context of Newtonian theories, with one exception: Mercury. Though Newton's theories predict that Mercury's orbit will have a precession of 5557 seconds of arc per century, in fact the precession of Mercury's orbit is 5600 seconds of arc per century.

This discrepancy of 43 seconds poses a puzzle to the 18th-century astronomers, but they're not overly concerned by it. Perhaps it can be explained by interference from other planets, or perhaps it can be explained by the existence of space dust. Sure, no evidence of space dust has been found, but it's probably just a matter of time. From the perspective of the astronomy team, this is a problem that should be relatively easy to solve given enough time and study. But consider another problem that interests the team—namely, figuring out the composition of stars. As much as they would like to tackle this problem, they simply don't see how one could ever attain the kind of sample that one would need to do the analysis. It's not just a matter of needing more time and study. As a result, they're inclined to view the problem as extremely hard; so hard in fact, that it might well be impossible to solve.

In fact, both the "easy" problem of Mercury's precession and the "hard" problem of stellar composition have now long been solved. Moreover, the astronomers were wrong in their judgments about the comparative difficulty of the two problems. The development of spectroscopic analysis (a procedure that measures the radiation emitted by stars) made it a relatively straightforward matter to determine that stars are composed primarily of hydrogen and helium. This result was surprising, since these are the two lightest elements, and planets like Earth are composed of heavier elements such as iron, nickel, silicon, and aluminum; so the discovery was initially greeted with skepticism. But, as surprising as the result was, solving the problem itself proved to be much less difficult than had been thought. In contrast, solving the problem of Mercury's precession turned out to be considerably harder than had been thought. Solving it was not just a matter of discovering the source of interference, but required a conceptual revolution—namely, Einstein's development of relativity theory. The 43-second discrepancy could only be adequately explained within the context of the General Theory of Relativity. Crucial to the explanation was Einstein's insight that spacetime is curved; and it's the curvature of spacetime that affects the orbit of Mercury.

From these examples, Churchland concludes that we should be skeptical of philosophers' judgments about which problems concerning consciousness are particularly hard. Even more so, we should be skeptical of claims that certain problems about consciousness might be unsolvable. The history of science is "chock-full of phenomena deemed too mysterious ever to be understood by mere mortals, but which eventually did yield to explanation" (Churchland 2013, p. 57). As she suggests, in advance of the relevant scientific discovery, it can be very difficult to assess which problems are harder than others, which will be solved sooner, and which will be more tractable. Such judgments will too often have the effect of hornswoggling us. Summarizing the philosophical lesson she wants to draw, Churchland notes that, "when not much is known about a topic, don't take terribly seriously someone else's heartfelt conviction about what problems are scientifically tractable. Learn the science, do the science, and see what happens" (1996, p. 408).

DISCUSSION

A related response to the hard problem can be seen in Daniel C. Dennett's (1996) work (see Chapter 9). Though Dennett does not talk of hornswoggling, he too seems to think that the hard problem of consciousness seems hard to us only because we are being deceived or misled in some way. Moreover, like Churchland, Dennett calls upon scientific analogies in an attempt to show where things have gone wrong. One such analogy involves vitalism (an analogy also used by Churchland). When faced with the mystery of what life was and how to explain it, the vitalists too might be described as seeing a hard problem. In their view, life was something that needed to be explained over and above our explanations of various biological functions. As a result, they ended up postulating a new substance, *elan vital*, to explicate life. But the vitalists were wrong that there's any such thing as elan vital. It was only due to ignorance and misconception that they were led to think otherwise. In fact, science can give us a complete explanation of what distinguishes living from non-living things. Why should things be any different with respect to consciousness?

In a taxonomical discussion of possible responses to the hard problem, Chalmers (2003) distinguishes between various types of materialist approaches (see Chapter 4). The philosophers he classifies as *type-A materialists* typically claim that we will eventually be able to explain all the functions of consciousness and, in doing so, we will come to realize that this is all there is to be explained. The philosophers that he classifies as *type-B materialists* accept that there is an epistemic gap—that there really is a hard problem of consciousness; but they deny that the epistemic gap entails that there is an ontological gap, such that consciousness is not a physical phenomenon (see Chapter 7). The philosophers that Chalmers classifies as *type-C materialists* typically claim that the hard problem seems so hard only due to our current ignorance. Given the state of our current scientific understanding of the world, we cannot see how to solve the problem; but that does not mean that it is, in principle, unsolvable.

Churchland's overall position has elements in common with both type-A and type-C materialism, but her discussion of the hornswoggle problem seems to fit best within the type-C rubric. That said, Chalmers (2003) argues that type-C materialism is itself an unstable position, and ultimately collapses into one of the other types of materialism that he differentiates. On this way of looking at things, we could see Churchland as a type-C materialist whose view collapses into type-A materialism. In short, such a view suggests that the way the problem will ultimately be solved will be to explain the functions of consciousness, with the explanation likely being something that is hard to predict or anticipate given our current state of understanding. In virtue of our current ignorance of what a possible explanation could look like, we are hornswoggled into thinking that no such explanation is possible.

If this interpretation of Churchland is correct, then her argument can be addressed in similar fashion as other type-A materialist responses (see Chapter 11). For example, one might try to undercut the various scientist analogies that she draws in an effort to show that there is something different about the problem of consciousness. The scientific analogies involve cases where it was clear that what we were trying to explain involved functions. For example, in the case of life, it's hard to see how there is anything to be explained over and above the functions involved—how, for example, a living mammal manages to circulate its blood. But this fact differentiates the case of life (and the other scientific cases) from the case of consciousness. With respect to consciousness, the problem is not that we don't see how the functions could be explained, but rather that there seems to be something beyond functions for which we need to account (see Chapter 4).

RECOMMENDED READING

CANONICAL PRESENTATIONS

Churchland, Patricia S. 1996. "The Hornswoggle Problem." *Journal of Consciousness Studies* 3 (5–6): 402–8.

Churchland, Patricia S. 1994. "Can Neurobiology Teach Us Anything about Consciousness?" *Proceedings and Addresses of the American Philosophical Association* 67 (4): 23–40.

OVERVIEWS

Alter, Torin, and Howell, Robert. J. 2009. "The Hard Problem of Consciousness." *Scholarpedia* 4 (6): 4948. http://www.scholarpedia.org/article/Hard_problem_of_consciousness.

Weisberg, Joshua. n.d. "The Hard Problem of Consciousness." *Internet Encyclopedia of Philosophy*. https://iep.utm.edu/hard-problem-of-conciousness/.

ADDITIONAL DISCUSSIONS

Carruthers, Glenn, and Schier, Elizabeth. 2017. "Why Are We Still Being Hornswoggled? Dissolving the Hard Problem of Consciousness." *Topoi* 36: 67–79.

Chalmers, David J. 1995. "Facing Up to the Hard Problem of Consciousness." *Journal of Consciousness Studies* 2: 200–219.

Chalmers, David J. 2003. "Consciousness and Its Place in Nature." In S. Stich and T. Warfield (eds.) *The Blackwell Guide to Philosophy of Mind*. Malden, MA: Blackwell: 102–42.

Churchland, Patricia S. 2022. "The Hornswoggle Problem." In Jack Symes (ed.) *Philosophers on Consciousness: Talking about the Mind*. London: Bloomsbury Academic.

Churchland, Patricia S. 2013. *Touching a Nerve: Our Brains, Our Selves*. New York: Norton.

Dennett, Daniel C. 1996. "Facing Backward on the Problem of Consciousness." *Journal of Consciousness Studies* 3: 4–6.

THE SLUGS AND THE TILES

BACKGROUND

According to the knowledge and conceivability arguments, there is an epistemic gap (a gap in knowledge) between the physical and the phenomenal; and the epistemic gap entails a metaphysical gap (a gap in the world) that physicalists cannot abide. In the case of the knowledge argument, the epistemic gap is expressed in terms of the case of Mary in the black-and-white room (see Chapter 6). Here, the claim is that there are phenomenal truths about color experiences that Mary cannot deduce from the complete physical truth. In the case of the conceivability argument, the epistemic gap is often expressed in terms of the conceivability of a zombie world—that is, a consciousness-free world that is a physical/functional duplicate of the actual world. And in both the knowledge argument and the conceivability argument, the metaphysical gap often takes the form of a claim about possibility, such as the claim that there are truths about consciousness that might not obtain even if all the actual physical and functional truths were held fixed. Daniel Stoljar (2006) contends that the reasoning in both arguments is based on ignorance about either the nature of consciousness or the nature of the physical world, or both. He supports that contention with his case of the slugs and the tiles.

DOI: 10.4324/9781003179191-13

THE CASE

Imagine a community of intelligent slugs. They live on a mosaic containing circles, rectangles, figure eights, and various other shapes, all of which are constructed from two basic sorts of tiles: triangular tiles and pie-piece shaped tiles (sectors of circles). The slugs' perceptual access to the mosaic is limited. They have one shape-detecting system for triangles and another for circles, but that is all. They don't have a perceptual system enabling them to detect sector-shaped tiles.

Some slug philosophers believe that the circular tiles are composed entirely of non-circular tiles and, more specifically, of triangular tiles. Other slug philosophers reject that view on the basis of arguments analogous to the knowledge and conceivability arguments, and they treat facts about the circular tiles as basic. They conjure Slug Mary, who knows all non-circular truths about the mosaic, but who is not permitted to exercise her circle detector. They contend that she would be in no position to know whether the mosaic contains circles. Then they continue to reason in a way that parallels the knowledge argument, concluding that the circular tiles are *basic* tiles: they are not composed of non-circular tiles. In other words, they give their own version of the knowledge argument. They also give their own version of the zombie argument. They claim it is conceivable that there be a mosaic that is the same in all non-circular respects as the actual mosaic and yet lack circular tiles entirely. They infer that such a mosaic is possible, and conclude again that the circles tiles are basic.

The slug versions of the knowledge and conceivability arguments are unsound. Their conclusions are false. According to Stoljar, the reason they seem convincing to some slug philosophers is that those philosophers don't know some basic facts about the mosaic on which they live. Their ignorance derives from the limitation in their perceptual system that prevents them from being able to perceive pie-shaped tiles. Perhaps they'll eventually overcome that limitation. Or perhaps they won't. In any case, the story is suggestive. Some human philosophers find the knowledge and conceivability arguments convincing. But perhaps those arguments are unsound too, just like the slug versions are. Maybe they seem convincing only because we humans are ignorant of some basic (or non-basic) physical facts—physical facts that, together with known physical facts, undermine a premise of the knowledge and conceivability arguments. For example, maybe there are unknown physical facts that would, if known, reveal why any world that's physically and functionally indistinguishable from the actual world *must* contain consciousness—and thus why zombie worlds are inconceivable. Perhaps we'll eventually learn those physical facts, or perhaps we won't. In any case, how can proponents of the knowledge and conceivability arguments be confident that they're not making the same sort of error that their slug counterparts are making?

DISCUSSION

Stoljar's slug-and-tiles case is a variation of a similar thought experiment that Frank Jackson devised for a different purpose. Jackson imagined intelligent sea slugs that "have only a very restricted conception of the world by comparison with ours, the explanation for this being the nature of their immediate environment" (1982, pp. 135–6). His moral concerned humility: some "tough-minded slugs" incorrectly thought their science, or mere extensions thereof, could explain all of nature. The discussion of Jackson's slugs appears at the end of the 1982 article where he first presents the knowledge argument. By contrast, Stoljar (2006) takes his own slug example to *undermine* Jackson's knowledge argument. Stoljar's moral is that the knowledge and conceivability arguments owe their apparent force to ignorance—ignorance of physical facts that are, at least currently, unknown (see Chapter 10; for similar responses, see Nagel 1974, McGinn 1989, van Gulick 1993, Polger 2004, Churchland 1996).

Stoljar argues in detail that our situation parallels that of the slugs and the tiles. He invokes historical precedents: situations where arguments similar to the knowledge and conceivability arguments turned out to derive from ignorance. For example, in 1925 C. D. Broad presented an argument similar to the knowledge argument to show that there are irreducible truths about chemical bonding—an argument that can no longer be sustained in light of the quantum-mechanical theory of chemical bonding (which was not widely known in 1925).

In response, proponents of the knowledge and conceivability arguments sometimes point to disanalogies between those arguments and the historical precedents Stoljar cites (Alter 2023). Broad's argument concerns whether certain truths about chemical bonding can be deduced from truths about more fundamental physical properties. Plausibly, all truths concerned—including both the chemical truths and the more fundamental physical truths—are *structural*: they are all truths about spatiotemporal causal structure. They are the sorts of truth that can be fully expressed in an abstract, mathematical language. By contrast, the knowledge argument concerns whether certain phenomenal truths (truths about consciousness) can be deduced from structural physical truths. And it is far from obvious that those phenomenal truths are structural (Alter 2023). The relevant phenomenal truths are truths such as the truth Mary would express when she first sees red and says, "So that's what it's like to see red!" It's hard to see how that truth is about spatiotemporal causal structure.

Proponents of the knowledge and conceivability arguments have also scrutinized Stoljar's description of the slugs' reasoning (Gertler 2009, Alter 2023). As Stoljar describes that reasoning, their conclusion is that the circular tiles aren't composed of *any* non-circular tiles. That false conclusion is clearly not justified. But why would the slugs draw that conclusion? Based on what they know, the only reasonable conclusion they could draw would be that circular tiles aren't composed of triangular tiles. And that conclusion is true. So, perhaps their arguments aren't fallacious after all. The analogous conclusion in the human case would be that consciousness isn't composed of a specific sort of physical phenomenon, namely, structural phenomena—physical phenomena that can be fully explained in black-and-white media of the sort that Mary has access to in her black-and-white room. That conclusion does not show that consciousness is not composed of *non-structural* physical phenomena. On the other hand, it is not clear how physical phenomena could be non-structural.

RECOMMENDED READING

CANONICAL PRESENTATION

Stoljar, Daniel. 2006. *Ignorance and Imagination: The Epistemic Origin of the Problem of Consciousness*. New York: Oxford University Press.

OVERVIEWS

Chalmers, David J. 2003. "Consciousness and Its Place in Nature." In S. Stich and T. Warfield (eds.) *The Blackwell Guide to Philosophy of Mind*. Malden, MA:

Blackwell: 102_42. Reprinted in D. J. Chalmers (ed.) *Philosophy of Mind: Classical and Contemporary Readings*, second edition. New York: Oxford University Press, 2021: 260–82.

Van Gulick, Robert. "Consciousness." 2021. *The Stanford Encyclopedia of Philosophy* (Winter 2021 Edition), Edward N. Zalta (ed.), URL = <https://plato.stanford.edu/archives/win2021/entries/consciousness/>.

ADDITIONAL DISCUSSIONS

Alter, Torin. 2023. *The Matter of Consciousness: From the Knowledge Argument to Russellian Monism*. Oxford: Oxford University Press.

Bennett, Karen. 2009. "What You Don't Know Can Hurt You." *Philosophy and Phenomenological Research* 79 (3): 766–74.

Churchland, Patricia S. 1996. "The Hornswoggle Problem." *Journal of Consciousness Studies* 3: 402–8.

Gertler, Brie. 2009. "The Role of Ignorance in the Problem of Consciousness: Critical Review of Daniel Stoljar, *Ignorance and Imagination*." *Noûs* 43 (2): 378–93.

Jackson, Frank. 1982. "Epiphenomenal Qualia." *Philosophical Quarterly* 32: 127–36.

McGinn, Colin. 1989. "Can We Solve the Mind-Body Problem?" *Mind* 98: 349–66.

Nagel, Thomas. 1974. "What Is It Like to Be a Bat?" *Philosophical Review* 83: 435–50.

Polger, Thomas W. 2004. *Natural Minds*. Cambridge, MA: MIT Press.

Stoljar, Daniel. 2009. "Response to Alter and Bennett." *Philosophy and Phenomenological Research* 76: 775–84.

Van Gulick, Robert. 1993. "Understanding the Phenomenal Mind: Are We All Just Armadillos?" In M. Davies and G. Humphreys (eds.) *Consciousness: Philosophical and Psychological Aspects*. Oxford: Blackwell: 137–54.

PART II

PHYSICALIST THEORIES AND THE METAPHYSICS OF MIND
Introduction

Physical events sometimes cause mental events. For example, light reflecting the page you're reading affects your eyes and brain, thereby causing you to think certain thoughts. Also, mental events sometimes cause physical events. For example, your intention to turn the page causes your fingers to move and bring about that page-turning. At least, many philosophers believe in such two-way mental–physical causal interaction. This leads to a problem for dualist views such as the one offered by Descartes. If dualism is true, then mental–physical causal action is hard, if not impossible, to explain. How could an event occurring in a non-spatial, mental realm cause, or be caused by, an event occurring in a wholly distinct, spatially extended, physical realm?

Princess Elisabeth of Bohemia, who was a student of Descartes, presented that argument in letters to him. Although she failed to convince him, versions of her argument eventually won endorsement by many philosophers of mind. Today, Cartesian dualism is widely rejected, and physicalism is the most popular view on the mind–body problem— both due to causal arguments along the lines of Princess Elisabeth's and to advances in science that suggest we can give a complete causal explanation of bodily events in physical terms. But how exactly does the causal argument for physicalism go? And can all physicalist theories avoid the sort of problem Elisabeth raised for Cartesian dualism? This section begins by addressing those questions in Chapters 12 and 13.

As interest in physicalism grew, so did the question of what form a physicalist theory should take. In the 20th century, some physicalists endorsed *behaviorism*—the theory that identifies mental phenomena with behavioral phenomena. For example, the mental state of pain was identified with the disposition to wince, frown, etc. when one's body is damaged. But problems for behaviorism quickly arose. For example, Hilary Putnam offers a thought experiment involving an imagined species of super-spartans to show that a mental state such as pain can occur independently of any specific pattern of behavior. We discuss that thought experiment in Chapter 14.

As a result of considerations such as the ones developed by Putnam, a widespread consensus has emerged among contemporary philosophers that behaviorism erred in failing to account for the both the inner states that underlie behavior and relations among such inner states. This has led many to embrace *functionalism*, a view on which the mental is characterized not only in terms of behavioral phenomena but also in terms of such inner states and relations. That view and some thought experiments that raise objections to it are discussed in Chapters 15 and 16. These thought experiments suggest that functionalism is unable to account for phenomenally conscious experience (i.e., for qualia). Chapters 17 and 18 turn to a closely related set of ideas concerning artificial intelligence, though here the focus is primarily on how our mental states can have representational content rather than on how our mental states can have qualitative character. Chapter 17 centers on the so-called Turing test for intelligence, and Chapter 18 centers on a well-known criticism of the claim that running a computer program is sufficient for mentality.

As we saw in Part I, a main challenge for physicalist theories is whether they can explain phenomenal consciousness—that is, consciousness in the "what it's like" sense (see Chapters 4 and 5). Some argue that the problem is misconceived. In their view, phenomenal consciousness should be understood as a sort of representational/intentional property—that is, a property of representing the world in a certain way. For example, on this view, the phenomenal property associated with seeing a red circle just is the property of visually representing the presence of something that is red and circular. Some go further and argue that representational properties can be characterized in physicalism-friendly terms. Thought experiments used to support and challenges those ideas are discussed in Chapters 19 and 20.

The debate between physicalists and their opponents assumes we have a reasonably clear understanding of what it means for something to be (or not to be) physical. But the notion of physicality is vexed. This was not always so. Descartes defined the notion in terms of spatial extension. But most regard that definition as antiquated. Modern physics posits phenomena that are not extended in Descartes' sense (gravity might be an example). Today, physicalists often characterize the physical by deferring to science. Physical phenomena, they say, are the fundamental phenomena described by theories in physics. But which theories? Current physical theories are incomplete, and future (or idealized) physical theories are unknown. That problem is discussed in Chapter 21. And what if there are no *fundamental* physical phenomena? A thought experiment illustrating that problem is discussed in Chapter 22.

THE EXCLUSION PROBLEM

BACKGROUND

As soon as Descartes kicked off the modern discussion of the mind–body problem by arguing for substance dualism, he faced a crucial objection from his correspondent, Princess Elisabeth of Bohemia. Princess Elisabeth asks how an immaterial substance, like a soul, that lacks any extension in space can causally interact with a spatially extended material substance like the body. Physical events sometimes cause mental events. For example, when my hand touches a flame, I feel pain as a result. Likewise, mental events sometimes cause physical events. When my hand touches the flame, my pain causes me to jerk my hand back; and my pain—along with my beliefs about how to ameliorate it—causes me to hold my hand under a cold tap. Mental–physical causal interaction seems commonplace. But, as Princess Elisabeth points out, our conception of one thing causing another is closely tied to the way bodies are related in space. A pool cue moves the ball by being in contact with it. Explaining the ball's movement across the table, as it collides with other balls and caroms off the rails, is always a matter of explaining spatial contact between extended things. How, then, can something that is not extended in space explain the movements of things in space?

DOI: 10.4324/9781003179191-15

This is the traditional problem of mental causation for dualism. Although Descartes' attempts to answer this challenge are often thought to be inadequate, Princess Elisabeth's challenge seems to presuppose a mechanistic account of causation that is often rejected, even by physicalists. It's open to a dualist to insist that causation between mental and physical phenomena is a brute fact, underwritten by no further mechanism. While that proposal might not be completely satisfying, perhaps that's the cost of recognizing the world isn't made of one type of thing. The exclusion problem developed by Jaegwon Kim is a contemporary version of the mental-causation problem that doesn't yield so easily to this solution.

THE CASE

While you're cooking dinner, your hand comes into contact with the flame. You pull your hand away. How is your reaction to be explained? On the one hand, it seems like we can give a complete explanation in physical terms—we can explain why a given set of neurons fire and why the firing of those neurons leads to the contraction of muscles, etc. On the other hand, it seems that *pain* is involved in causing your hand to move. That's not a problem if you think pains are identical to physical states such as the firing of neurons. But many philosophers think pain and other mental states aren't identical to physical states of any kind. Most of these philosophers are not substance dualists, like Descartes, but are property dualists. They believe that even if all things are physical, some things have non-physical properties. These philosophers face a problem: given that everything physical can be fully explained in physical terms, what causal role is left for these distinct mental phenomena to play? They would seem to be excluded from the action by the physical events. The mental can be subtracted from the universe and nothing about physical events would change. The only hope seems to be for the mental phenomena to overdetermine the physical events—your moving your hand from the burner is fully caused by the physical events, but is also caused, somewhat redundantly, by your pain. But that your hand movement should be caused twice over in that way seems implausible. Since it seems implausible that mental events are either causally irrelevant to the physical or causally redundant, the exclusion problem puts serious pressure on the claim that mental and physical properties are distinct (Kim 1989, 1998).

Unlike the problem Princess Elisabeth raised for Descartes, the exclusion problem doesn't rule out mental causation based on the natures of the properties involved—that non-spatial mental things can't interact with physical things in space. Instead, the exclusion argument turns on an empirical premise often referred to as *the completeness of physics*: every physical event can be fully explained in physical terms. This leaves the mental with nothing to do.

One of the upshots is that the exclusion problem arises not only for the dualist—who thinks the mental is something over and above the physical—but for the *non-reductive physicalist* as well. Non-reductive physicalists accept that mental properties are nothing over and above the physical, in the sense that such properties are metaphysically necessitated by physical properties; but they deny that the mental properties are identical to those physical properties. For example, the non-reductive physicalist might hold that, while beliefs and all other mental states are nothing over and above brain states, being a belief cannot be identified with any particular physical property. According to non-reductive forms of functionalism, for example, what makes a belief a belief is the role it plays in a cognitive system—it stores information for use by the system, etc. That role might happen to be played by brain states; but things made of different stuff (robots perhaps) can have beliefs too because other materials (silicon chips and circuits, perhaps) play the belief role. So, even though in humans belief roles are played by physical states and processes, being a belief is not identical with some type of physical state or process. The non-reductive physicalist faces the exclusion problem no less than the dualist: as long as mental properties are distinct from a set of properties that can do all the causal work, they would seem to be epiphenomenal with respect to the physical world, lacking physical efficacy of their own.

DISCUSSION

Although the exclusion problem applies to both dualism and non-reductive physicalism, these different camps tend to offer different responses to the problem. The non-reductive physicalist, but not the dualist, can take advantage of the fact that mental properties bear very close relations to physical properties. Mental properties are, for example, *realized* or *constituted* by physical properties. To return to the functionalist example we considered earlier, brain states that play the belief role are said to be the physical "realizers" for the belief, or might be said to "constitute" the belief. So, for the non-reductive physicalist, although being a pain is distinct from a particular physical kind—such the firing of a particular group of neurons—it doesn't exist independently of the physical. As a rough analogy, being a queen in chess isn't identical with a physical type either: I can have a plastic queen shaped like Marge Simpson and you can have a marble queen shaped like Daenerys Targaryen; but what makes these things queens in chess aren't those physical characteristics. Nevertheless, a movement of those pieces isn't independent of the physical movement of the shaped plastic or marble. Moving the queen still requires movement of the material that makes her up, and if that material is moved, the queen moves. If the relation between mental states and physical states is like this, the mental is involved in the causal story even though it doesn't insert a novel causal power into the world. This might reduce the force of the exclusion problem for the non-reductive physicalist.

To be successful, the non-reductive physicalist's response will need to satisfy two opposing desiderata: it needs to give the mental some "autonomy," thus preserving the distinctness of the mental and physical events (and causal relations) while denying the causal power will compete with the causal powers on the physical level. Though this is tricky, there are plenty of plausible attempts to thread this needle. Take an example: "Jimmy grabs his umbrella because he believes it is raining." This seems to give us a case of mental causation—Jimmy's beliefs and desires cause him to grab his umbrella. The mental part is autonomous because, although beliefs and desires must all be physically realized, the explanation doesn't depend on the idiosyncrasies of Jimmy's particular physical make-up—the explanation would be just as true if slightly different neurons were involved or if Jimmy were a robot. What matters is that Jimmy had those beliefs, not that those particular physical processes were involved. Nevertheless, there is no novel causation here, in that the mental causation is underwritten, every step along the way, by physical processes. Or, to put it another way, the mental causation doesn't compete, in this instance, with the physical causation because of the intimate relationship between the mental properties and the physical properties. (There are many variations and twists on this story, but for important versions of the story and some important moves along the way see Fodor 1974, Yablo 1992, Baker 1993, Antony 1991, Pereboom 2002, Bennett 2003, Wilson 1999 and 2002, and Shoemaker 2001.)

In responding to the exclusion problem, the dualist needs to take a different tack from that of the non-reductive physicalist. For, while the non-reductive physicalist can appeal to the intimate relation of realization or constitution between the mental and the physical to downplay the novelty (or the competition) of the causal contribution of the mental, the dualist has no such recourse. Take the property dualist as an example—though similar problems face substance dualists. If pains are wholly metaphysically distinct from the physical, being neither constituted nor necessitated by the physical, then it seems that any causal contribution they make must be novel. This novel contribution would then seem to compete with the physical. The property dualist thus faces a choice about which of two bullets to bite. One option would be to see the mental cause as making something happen that the physical did not make happen. In this case, however, they have to deny the completeness of physics. The other option would be to see the mental cause as being redundant, overdetermining an effect already determined by the physical.

Some property dualists have taken the first option (Kane 1996, Stapp 2005): they deny the completeness of the physical and insist that some physical events need non-physical explanations. Notice that this is more than saying that some physical events lack physical explanations. At least on some interpretations of quantum mechanics, nothing fully explains the decay of a radium atom, for example. Still, that's a far cry from saying that something mental does determine it. The problem is that such quantum indeterminacy is everywhere (assuming it is anywhere) and not just in the vicinity of human minds. If this is where mental causation gets its grip, we should expect to see different quantum behavior in places where there are minds. But there's not much evidence for this.

Other dualists have taken the second option (Mills 1996, Lowe 2003): they claim that mental properties do, as a matter of fact, overdetermine their effects; while the physical cause is there, so too is an additional mental cause. This would be a curious state of affairs, but it seems possible. Even though it gives us an inelegant world, and one where it doesn't seem mentality is causally needed, perhaps there is room here to save our intuitions about mental causation.

In recent years, a number of philosophers who reject the traditional physicalist picture of mental phenomena have sought to avoid the exclusion argument by turning away from traditional property dualism to something like Russellian monism (see Chapter 4.) On that view, mental properties—or proto-mental properties that are not themselves mental but contain the seeds of mentality—actually ground all of the physical properties in the world. In contrast to the traditional picture, on which mental properties do not emerge until you get to the level of brains, Russellian monists see the world as having a mental or proto-mental base which ultimately explains the physical phenomena. Though this requires the denial of completeness, the Russellian monist will argue that they can do so in an empirically unobjectionable way. For a critical discussion of the Russellian strategy as a solution to the exclusion problem see Howell (2015), and for a response see Alter and Coleman (2021).

RECOMMENDED READING

CANONICAL PRESENTATIONS

Kim, Jaegwon. 1989. "Mechanism, Purpose, and Explanatory Exclusion." *Philosophical Perspectives* 3: 77–108.
Kim, Jaegwon. 1998. *Mind in a Physical World*, Cambridge, MA: MIT Press.

OVERVIEWS

Bennett, K. 2007. "Mental Causation." *Philosophy Compass* 2: 316–37.
Moore, Dwayne. 2018. "Mind and the Causal Exclusion Problem." *Internet Encyclopedia of Philosophy*. https://iep.utm.edu/mind-and-the-causal-exclusion-problem/.
Robb, David, and Heil, John. 2018. "Mental Causation." *The Stanford Encyclopedia of Philosophy* (Spring 2021 Edition), Edward N. Zalta (ed.), URL = <https://plato.stanford.edu/archives/spr2021/entries/mental-causation/>.
Yoo, Julie. 2007. "Mental Causation." *Internet Encyclopedia of Philosophy*. https://iep.utm.edu/mental-c/.

ADDITIONAL DISCUSSIONS

Alter, Torin, and Coleman, Sam. 2021. "Russellian Monism and Mental Causation." *Noûs* 55 (2): 409–25.

Antony, L. M. 1991. "The Causal Relevance of the Mental: More on the Mattering of Minds." *Mind & Language* 6: 295–327.

Baker, L. R. 1993. "Metaphysics and Mental Causation." In J. Heil and A. Mele (eds.) *Mental Causation*. Oxford: Clarendon: 75–95.

Bennett, K. 2003. "Why the Exclusion Problem Seems Intractable, and How, Just Maybe, to Tract It." *Noûs* 37: 471–97.

Fodor, J. A. 1974. "Special Sciences (Or: The Disunity of Science as a Working Hypothesis)." *Synthese* 28 (2): 97–115.

Heil, J., and Mele, A. (eds.). 1993. *Mental Causation*. Oxford: Clarendon.

Howell, R. 2015. "The Russellian Monist's Problems with Mental Causation." *Philosophical Quarterly* 65 (258): 22–39.

Kane, Robert. 1996. *The Significance of Free Will*. New York: Oxford University Press.

List, Christian, and Stoljar, Daniel. 2017. "Does the Exclusion Argument Put Any Pressure on Dualism?" *Australasian Journal of Philosophy* 95 (1): 96–108.

Lowe, E. J. 2003. "Physical Causal Closure and the Invisibility of Mental Causation." In S. Walter and H.-D. Heckmann (eds.) *Physicalism and Mental Causation: The Metaphysics of Mind and Action*. Exeter: Imprint Academic: 137–54.

Mills, Eugene O. 1996. "Interactionism and Overdetermination." *American Philosophical Quarterly* 33 (1): 105–15.

Pereboom, D. 2002. "Robust Nonreductive Materialism." *Journal of Philosophy* 99: 499–531.

Shoemaker, S. 2001. "Realization and Mental Causation." In C. Gillett and B. Loewer (eds.) *Physicalism and Its Discontents*. Cambridge: Cambridge University Press: 74–98.

Stapp, H. 2005. "Quantum Interactive Dualism: An Alternative to Materialism." *Journal of Consciousness Studies* 12: 43–58.

Wilson, Jessica. 1999. "How Superduper Does a Physicalist Supervenience Need to Be?" *Philosophical Quarterly* 49: 33–52.

Wilson, Jessica M. 2002. "Causal Powers, Forces, and Superdupervenience." *Grazer Philosophische Studien* 63 (1): 53–77.

Yablo, S. 1992. "Mental Causation." *Philosophical Review* 101: 245–80.

THE PUZZLE OF THE SPECIAL SCIENCES

BACKGROUND

Many, if not most, philosophers are physicalists. Those philosophers usually believe that a complete physics would be a fully general science, leaving nothing out. Nevertheless, many also believe that sciences with more limited domains—the so called "special sciences" like psychology and biology—are essential to getting a full picture of the world. The special sciences discover things physics does not. And they help us see nature's joints, so to speak, even if those joints aren't the fundamental ones. This view about the relationship between the sciences is often reflected in beliefs about the nature of the mind.

THE CASE

Two popular beliefs seem to be in tension: (1) physics is complete in the sense that everything that happens is covered by physical law, and if you fix everything described by physics, you fix the nature of the world as a whole; and (2) sciences such as psychology and biology discover important truths about the world that physics does not capture. Can these views be reconciled?

One reaction is concessive: the "special sciences" are just different ways of talking about the same events, perhaps at different levels of descriptions—zoomed out or zoomed in—or restricted to different contexts; but physics ultimately doesn't leave anything out. The value of the special sciences is epistemological, in the sense that they help us comprehend events that would be hard to understand in the language of physics. But for many, such as Jerry Fodor in "Special Sciences" (1974), this concessive reaction is incorrect. According to Fodor, it underestimates the sense in which sciences such as psychology really do discover new laws—interesting, predictively important, and counterfactually robust generalizations—that are not present in the laws of physics. Just as important, the special sciences discover unified types of phenomena that relate to each other in a lawlike manner.

Though Fodor's main concern is psychology, a consideration of economics makes things particularly plain. Consider the law that, other things being equal, prices are higher if there is more money in the economy. If this is true, it's not because of the physical stuff money is made of. Bits of currency can be made of paper, coins, or entries in electronic ledgers, all of which have dramatically different physical properties. The law of economics holds despite the diversity of these physical properties. While no law of physics is ever broken in economic transactions, the laws of economics are independent of physical laws. Someone who could see only physical properties and interactions probably wouldn't even know there was an economy, much less understand why prices were suddenly high!

The same thing is true of the laws of psychology. Beliefs and desires can be made of different physical things. In extreme cases, perhaps between androids and humans, some beliefs could be carbon based and others silicon based. But even among animals there is certainly no guarantee—or need for a guarantee—that the same neural or subatomic activity is going on in two creatures with the same beliefs. Nevertheless, it is all-things-considered true that if an organism believes it is in danger and desires to get out of danger, it will try to do so. Someone studying only physics would predict all of the movements of the subatomic activity that underlies the organism's behavior—its attempt to get out of danger. But they would miss what causes that behavior, and would probably fail to understand that there was *behavior*—as opposed to mere physical motions—in the first place.

Although psychology neither talks about anything non-physical nor contravenes the laws of physics, it is an autonomous science all the same. Some (such as Fodor himself, and many of the non-reductive materialists mentioned in the previous chapter) draw a moral for the philosophy of mind: mental states are physical states, but they are not identical to those states (and cannot be reduced to them) because they are governed by distinct laws.

DISCUSSION

Probably the most influential counterpoint to Fodor's picture of the special sciences comes from Jaegwon Kim (1992). Kim finds something suspicious about Fodor's story in "Special Sciences." The story, in Kim's view, depends on claiming that there is a law in the special sciences but no corresponding law in the physical sciences. Kim questions this assumption: Why not take the special-sciences law to be a law in physical science? Staying with the economics analogy, Fodor's answer might seem obvious: units of currency are not physical kinds like quarks, charge, mass, etc. But that seemingly obvious answer itself raises questions. Granted, any particular instance of currency is realized by something physical (paper, copper, electrons, etc.), but the kind itself is not physical. One might wonder, though, why there can't be a *disjunctive kind:* "P1 or P2 or P3 or P4"—where P1 is the physical basis of paper money, P2 of copper money, P3 of digital currency, and so on? Though it's a disjunctive kind, it involves only physical terms. So, why isn't it a physical kind that can be included in physical laws? Fodor's answer is that there cannot be disjunctive kinds. But why not?

Kim offers an example to help us see what might be problematic about disjunctive kinds. Jade, it turns out, is not a single mineral. Instances of jade are either instances of the mineral nephrite or the mineral jadeite. It is, in fact, a disjunctive kind. Can we treat that as just a kind like any other? The problem is that there is no guarantee of any causal similarity between jadeite and nephrite. They could be—and in fact are—very different physically. This means that, as a kind, jade cannot be used to confirm interesting generalizations. Suppose one found 1000 pieces of jade and discovered they were all green. Suppose further that all the pieces of jade one found were jadeite. Kim claims this would not support the generalization that all jade was green. You would have found some confirmation that all jadeite is green; but, because of the disunified nature of jade as a kind, you can't conclude anything about other instances of jade from your evidence—they might be nephrite and you don't know anything about nephrite! In particular, you don't know that all—or indeed any—nephrite is green. What makes something apt for inclusion in scientific laws—i.e., what makes it a natural kind—is that it has enough unity as a kind for observations about one instance to bear on observations on all instances of the kind. So, the reason we should reject disjunctive kinds like jade is that they lack such unity.

At this point, Kim seems only to have given Fodor a premise for his own argument—since disjunctions can't be kinds and can't enter into laws, there can be no disjunctive physical law corresponding to the special science laws. But, says Kim, there is a problem. Jade is disjunctive whether you call it "jade" or whether you call it "jadeite or nephrite." So why aren't economic kinds disjunctive, whether you call them "dollar" or "P1 or P2"? The language you use doesn't matter. What matters is whether they have a unified enough nature to enter into laws. Now, though, there seems to be a dilemma. Either the special science kinds such as "money" or "belief" are unified enough to be in laws or not. If they are, then there is no problem with there being a kind including them. But Fodor's own argument insists that they aren't unified enough to be a kind. The various physical instances of currency are too motley, too disparate to have much in common at all. If that's the case, though, they seem more like jade—they have too little in common to support lawful generalizations or to support scientific inferences. If this is true, we shouldn't count these disjunctive kinds as scientific kinds at all, whether in special sciences or physical sciences. In essence, Kim's point can be put as follows: if special science kinds are too causally heterogeneous to support scientific generalizations, then they cannot support special-science generalizations. Since the motley causal nature of the special science kinds are an essential part of the argument for the autonomy of the special sciences, the autonomy of those sciences comes at the cost of their not being scientific after all.

How does this bear on psychology and mental kinds? One way to think of it is to ask whether beliefs are like jade. The argument was supposed to be that beliefs are independent (non-physical) kinds because there can be, for example, human beliefs and robot beliefs with very little in common physically. But, if that is the case, we seem to be in a very jade-like situation with beliefs. Beliefs come in two varieties—carbon based and silicon based. We've made a lot of observations about beliefs in psychology—but they've all been about carbon-based beliefs. How much confidence should this give us that these generalizations hold about beliefs in general? The jade example suggests not much. The worry, in essence, is that the more the mental kinds are independent, the less they are reliable as scientific kinds.

RECOMMENDED READINGS

CANONICAL PRESENTATIONS

Fodor, Jerry A. 1974. "Special Sciences." *Synthese* 28 (2): 97–115.
Kim, Jaegwon. 1992. "Multiple Realization and the Metaphysics of Reduction." *Philosophy and Phenomenological Research* 52 (1): 1–26.

OVERVIEWS

Robb, David, Heil, John, and Gibb, Sophie. 2023. "Mental Causation." *The Stanford Encyclopedia of Philosophy* (Spring 2023 Edition), Edward N. Zalta and Uri Nodelman (eds.), URL = <https://plato.stanford.edu/archives/spr2023/entries/mental-causation/>.

ADDITIONAL DISCUSSIONS

Antony, Louise. 2003. "Who's Afraid of Disjunctive Properties?" *Philosophical Issues* 13 (1): 1–21.
Clapp, Leonard J. 2001. "Disjunctive Properties: Multiple Realizations." *Journal of Philosophy* 98 (3): 111–36.
Fodor, Jerry A. 1997. "Special Sciences: Still Autonomous after All These Years." *Philosophical Perspectives* 11: 149–63.
Gillett, Carl. 2003. "The Metaphysics of Realization, Multiple Realizability, and the Special Sciences." *Journal of Philosophy* 100 (11): 591–603.
Kim, Jaegwon. 2005. "Laws, Causation, and Explanation in the Special Sciences." *History and Philosophy of the Life Sciences* 27 (3–4): 325–38.
Loewer, Barry. 2009. "Why Is There Anything Except Physics?" *Synthese* 170 (2): 217–33.
Millikan, Ruth Garrett. 1999. "Historical Kinds and the 'Special Sciences'." *Philosophical Studies* 95 (1–2): 45–65.
Sober, Elliott. 1999. "The Multiple Realizability Argument against Reductionism." *Philosophy of Science* 66 (4): 542–64.

THE SUPER-SPARTANS

BACKGROUND

From the early 1930s until about 1960, behaviorism was the reigning methodological approach in research psychology. The approach was to study mental phenomena by examining their observable causes and observable effects: environmental stimuli and behavioral responses. Consideration of any inner mechanisms underlying behavioral dispositions fell outside the scope of the behaviorist paradigm. During that same period, a corresponding view was widely discussed in philosophy (Carnap 1932, Hempel 1935, Ryle 1949). *Philosophical* behaviorism does not concern methodology. Instead, its central thesis is that mental states consist in behavioral dispositions. The relevant behavioral dispositions might be highly complex, but the implication is that the mental is nothing over and above the dispositional. Prior to Putnam's (1963) super-spartans argument, the debate about philosophical behaviorism focused largely on whether the meaning of statements containing mentalistic terms—such as "belief" and "pain"—can be adequately characterized in terms of statements describing behavioral dispositions (Chisholm 1957, Geach 1957). Putnam regarded such issues, which are linguistic and conceptual, as peripheral to behaviorism's central thesis, which is about mental states themselves: about pain rather than the concept of pain, for example. Often when people feel pain they exhibit characteristic pain behavior, such as wincing, screaming, gritting their teeth, etc. Sometimes people feel pain but suppress such behavior. But even then they are *disposed* to exhibit such behavior, at least normally. That much is not controversial; but, according to philosophical behaviorism, to experience pain *is* to have the associated sorts of dispositional states. According to Putnam, that thesis is false. He devises a series of thought experiments designed to demonstrate its falsity.

THE CASE

Imagine a community of *super-spartans* in which the adults can suppress all involuntary pain behavior. They feel pain; but when they do, they don't wince, scream, etc. Then, after millions of years, the super-spartans begin to have children who are born with the capacity to suppress pain behavior and the spartan belief that one should always do so. In those imagined communities, pain is less closely related to the behavioral *responses* that we associate with pain. Now imagine creatures that feel pain but whose pain is not *caused* in the way ours typically is—for example, when our bodies are damaged. Instead, they feel pain only when a certain sort of magnetic field is present—a field that does not damage their bodies. Such creatures might also be super-spartans, in which case their pain experiences are accompanied by neither the causes nor the effects that normally accompany human pain.

Perhaps those super-spartans nonetheless report having pain when they have it. That is potentially significant because some behaviorists accord a central role to verbal expressions of mental states. That inspired Putnam's final variation on his thought experiment: the *super-super-spartans* (he also calls them "X-worlders"), who do not even report having pain when they have pain. Individual members of that community might have their own private way of thinking about pain, and they might well dislike pain just as we do. But, publicly, they are silent about it. The super-super-spartans feel pain but have *none* of the dispositions we normally associate with pain.

Putnam concludes that behaviorism is false. His argument could be summarized as follows. If behaviorism is true, then experiencing pain consists in having the dispositional states normally associated with pain (wincing, etc.). If experiencing pain consists in having those dispositional states, then it's impossible that any creatures experience pain unless their pain is accompanied by those dispositional states. The super-super-spartans case demonstrates that such creatures are possible. Therefore, behaviorism is false.

DISCUSSION

Putnam's super-spartans case premiered in his 1963 article "Brains and Behavior." By that time, methodological behaviorism was being supplanted by cognitivist approaches in psychology, which focuses as much on inner, mental representational states as on their behavioral causes and effects. Philosophical behaviorism's popularity was also waning. Nevertheless, Putnam anticipated potential behaviorist responses to his argument. One response was that the claim that super-super-spartans feel pain is unverifiable, and therefore meaningless. That response assumes a verificationist theory of meaning, on which a statement is meaningful only to the extent that it can be empirically verified or empirically falsified. Like behaviorism, that theory had fallen out of favor by 1963. (If verificationism sounds plausible, then consider that the verificationist principle is itself unverifiable!) But Putnam argued that it would be possible to empirically verify that the super-super-spartans feel pain, for example, by detecting relevant brain activity.

In fact, the main behaviorist response was to not to defend their theory, at least not as a general theory of mind (with exceptions; see, for example, Gibbs 1969). Some proposed that behaviorism applies to cognitive states, such as belief and desire, but not to sensations such as pain (Smart 1959); and some rejected even that weakened variety of the theory. Even so, many embraced successor theories, including functionalism (see Chapters 15, 16, and 18). These philosophers often attributed the implausibility of behaviorism to its narrow focus on the external causes (stimuli) and external effects (behavioral responses) of mental states. A better theory, they thought, would include a place for inner states and relationships among such inner states. Mental states should be understood as states that play certain functional roles, where the components of functional roles include not only external stimuli and behavioral responses but also relations among mental states (Lewis 1966, Putnam 1967, Armstrong 1968).

Although the possibility of super-super-spartan pain is incompatible with behaviorism, functionalism might be able to accommodate it. After all, as Putnam describes the super-super-spartans, their pain is related to their beliefs, desires, etc. in much the same way as ours is. Even so, important critiques of functionalism and related views could be seen as variations on a Putnamian theme. For example, consider Galen Strawson's (1994) *weather watchers*: sentient, intelligent creatures that are rooted in the ground and profoundly interested in the local weather. They have sensations, emotions, thoughts, etc. But their physiology prevents them from behaving. Strawson claims such imaginary creatures are possible, and that this possibility refutes *neobehaviorism*: the view that the nature of almost all, if not all, mental states is constitutively linked to behavior. Mainstream functionalism could be classified as neobehaviorist since, on mainstream functionalism, behavioral dispositions figure into the very nature of mental states. Strawson's case would seem to mirror Putnam's cases, in which some creatures have mental states of the same sort we humans have but lack relevant (or all) behavioral components. Although neobehaviorism, in the form of functionalism, remains a contender view today, Putnam-style cases, such as Strawson's, are widely considered important problems for the view.

RECOMMENDED READING

CANONICAL PRESENTATION

Putnam, Hilary. 1963. "Brains and Behavior." In R. Butler (ed.) *Analytical Philosophy: Second Series*. London: Blackwell: 1–19.

OVERVIEWS

Graham, George. 2019. "Behaviorism." *The Stanford Encyclopedia of Philosophy* (Spring 2019 Edition), Edward N. Zalta (ed.), URL = <https://plato.stanford.edu/archives/spr2019/entries/behaviorism/>.

Levin, Janet. 2021. "Functionalism." *The Stanford Encyclopedia of Philosophy* (Winter 2021 Edition), Edward N. Zalta (ed.), URL = <https://plato.stanford.edu/archives/win2021/entries/functionalism/>.

ADDITIONAL DISCUSSIONS

Block, Ned. 1981. "Psychologism and Behaviorism." *Philosophical Review* 90: 5–43.

Carnap, Rudolf. 1932. "Psychologie in Physikalischer Sprach." *Erkenntnis* 3: 162–76. Translated as "Psychology in Physical Language" in A. J. Ayer (ed.) *Logical Positivism*. New York: Free Press, 1959.

Hempel, Carl G. 1935. "Analyse Logique de la Psychologie." *Revue de Synthèse* 9–10: 27–42. Translated as "The Logical Analysis of Psychology" in N. Block (ed.) *Readings in Philosophy of Psychology, volume 1*. Harvard, CT: Harvard University Press, 1980: 14–23.

Malcolm, Norman. 1968. "The Conceivability of Mechanism." *Philosophical Review*, 77: 45–72.

Ryle, Gilbert. 1949. *The Concept of Mind*. London: Hutchinson.

Strawson, Galen. 1994. *Mental Reality*. Cambridge, MA: MIT Press.

OTHER REFERENCES

Armstrong, David. 1968. *A Materialist Theory of Mind*. London: Routledge & Kegan Paul.

Chisholm, Roderick M. 1957. *Perceiving*. Ithaca, NY: Cornell University Press.

Geach, Peter. 1957 *Mental Acts*. London: Routledge & Kegan Paul.

Gibbs, B. 1969. "Putnam on Brains and Behavior." *Analysis* 30: 53–5.

Lewis, David K. 1966. "An Argument for the Identity Theory." *Journal of Philosophy* 63: 17–25.

Putnam, Hilary. 1967. "The Nature of Mental States." Originally entitled "Psychological Predicates." In W. H. Capitan and D. D. Merrill (eds.) *Art, Mind, and Religion: Proceedings of the 1965 Oberlin Colloquium in Philosophy*. Pittsburgh: University of Pittsburgh Press: 37–48.

Smart, J. J. C. 1959. "Sensations and Brain Processes." *Philosophical Review* 68: 141–56.

MAD PAIN AND MARTIAN PAIN

BACKGROUND

Two popular versions of physicalism are known as *the identity theory* and *functionalism*. According to the identity theory, mental phenomena are identical to physical phenomena. For example, pain is identical to certain brain processes, such as c-fiber stimulation, in much the same way that lightning is identical to electrical discharge and water is identical to H_2O. (C-fiber stimulation is no longer considered an empirically plausible candidate for the relevant brain process; but here it will serve as a placeholder for one that is.) According to functionalism, mental states are explained in functional terms—that is, in terms of (i) environmental stimuli, (ii) behavioral responses, and (iii) relations among mental states. For example, very roughly, pain is that mental state that typically: (i) is caused by damage to the body; (ii) causes wincing and saying things like "ouch"; and (iii) combines with the desire to avoid the state and the belief that aspirin will help do that to cause one to take aspirin. In short, pain is explained in terms of its characteristic causal role. David K. Lewis raises a challenge for these theories, based on the possibility of what he calls *mad pain* and *Martian pain*.

THE CASES

Mad pain is pain that doesn't play pain's characteristic causal role. For example, imagine Maddy. She feels pain not when her body is cut, burned, etc., but instead when she does moderate exercise or has an empty stomach. And, though to us pain is distracting, to her it is not. Instead, her pain makes her think about mathematics.

Unlike mad pain, *Martian pain* plays pain's characteristic causal role. But Martian pain differs from our pain in its physical realization. For example, imagine Marty. He feels pain but has no neurons. Instead, he has a hydraulic mind, consisting of many inflatable cavities. The inflation of a cavity opens some valves and closes others. When you pinch his skin, certain cavities in his feet inflate. He experiences that process as pain. This motivates him to avoid getting pinched, just as our pain motivates us to avoid getting pinched.

According to Lewis (1980), any credible theory of mind should account for the possibility of mad pain and the possibility of Martian pain. And it is not clear how the identity theory or functionalism can account for both possibilities. The identity theory easily accounts for the possibility of mad pain. Maddy feels pain when her c-fibers are stimulated, just like the rest of us—even though her c-fiber stimulation is causally connected to other parts of her neural system in atypical ways. But the identity theory seems to exclude the possibility of Martian pain. Marty feels pain but lacks c-fibers. On the identity theory, he can no more experience pain than lightning can occur without electricity or water can exist without hydrogen.

Functionalism has the reverse problem. Marty experiences pain because he has states that play that role. That those role-playing states are hydraulic rather than neural is irrelevant. But now the possibility of mad pain would seem to be excluded: none of Maddy's states play pain's characteristic causal role.

So, how can a physicalist theory account for *both* the possibility of mad pain (such as Maddy's pain) and the possibility of Martian pain (such as Marty's pain)?

DISCUSSION

Lewis (1966) proposes a solution cast in terms of a physicalist theory known as *analytic functionalism* (see also Armstrong 1968). This theory has two main components. One concerns the *concept* of pain. That concept is characterized in terms of pain's typical causal role. (That is why the theory is called *analytic* functionalism: it is partly based on an *analysis* of mental concepts, such as the concept of pain—or, as it is sometimes put, an analysis of the *meaning* of mental terms, such as "pain.") The other main component concerns *pain itself*. Pain itself is identified with whatever state plays pain's typical causal role. For example, if in typical humans c-fiber stimulation plays the pain role, then human pain is identical to c-fiber stimulation. And, if in typical Martians a certain hydraulic state plays that role, then Martian pain is identical to that hydraulic state. And the same goes for all other mental states. For example, the concept of belief is characterized in terms of the typical causal role belief plays; and belief itself is identified with whatever state typically plays that role.

On analytic functionalism, the explanation of how Martian pain is possible is straightforward. What it means to feel pain, on this view, is to have a state (any state) that plays pain's characteristic causal role. That causal role is explained in a way that makes no essential reference to human (or non-human) physiology. Marty's pain is possible because he has states that play that role. Analytic functionalism also delivers an explanation of the possibility of mad pain. The theory identifies pain itself with the state that *typically* plays pain's characteristic causal role, relative to some population. Maddy is human, and in humans c-fiber stimulation typically plays that role. Maddy feels pain because she has that neural state, even though in her that neural state does not play its typical causal role. Further, as Lewis explains, analytic functionalism can explain not only mad pain and Martian pain but also *mad Martian pain*. Mad Martian pain is the Martian version of mad pain, and can be explained in the same way. The mad Martian is a member of the Martian species despite their madness. They feel pain because they have the state that *typically* plays the relevant causal role in Martians, even though in them that state does not play that role.

Key to Lewis's solution is species (or population) relativity. The states that play the relevant causal role can differ from one species (or population) to the next, as the cases of human pain and Martian pain illustrate. Significantly, although Maddy feels pain, she does so partly in virtue of her membership in the human species. But that aspect of Lewis's solution can seem implausible. Whether an individual human feels pain would seem to be entirely a matter of what is happening in that individual, regardless of how they might relate to others.

Lewis recognizes the difficulty. Indeed, he illustrates it by considering a phenomenon that initially seems no less possible than pain experienced by Maddy or Marty: pain experienced by a creature who is mad (like Maddy), physiologically alien (like Marty), and unique (like neither Maddy nor Marty). Analytic functionalism can't explain how mad, alien, unique pain is possible. Because this creature is mad, the state realizing their pain doesn't play the relevant causal role. Because they are alien, they do not have c-fiber stimulation—the state that plays that role in humans. And, because they are unique, their state doesn't realize pain in other members of their species: their species has no other members! Lewis concludes that such a case is impossible, despite initial appearances to the contrary. That intuitive cost, he suggests, is outweighed by other benefits of his theory. Even so, the case helps bring out the oddity of the view that whether an individual creature feels pain depends on their relationship to other members of their species.

Martian pain illustrates a doctrine known as the *multiple realizability* of the mental (Putnam 1967, Bickle 2020). A given mental kind, such as pain, can be realized in (or constituted by) many distinct kinds: brain states in humans, other biological states in non-human animals, perhaps hydraulic states in Martians, silicon or electronic states in some digital computers, and maybe even non-physical states in ghosts. Many, including Lewis, take accounting for multiple realizability as an important goal for a theory of mind (Putnam 1967, Kripke 1972). But some philosophers are more skeptical (Polger and Shapiro 2016). Mad pain has received less attention, though some—including some analytic functionalists—have expressed skepticism about that too (Shoemaker 1981).

RECOMMENDED READING

CANONICAL PRESENTATION

Lewis, David K. 1980. "Mad Pain and Martian Pain." In N. Block (ed.) *Readings in Philosophy of Psychology*, vol. 1. Cambridge, MA: Harvard University Press: 216–22.

OVERVIEWS

Levin, Janet. "Functionalism." 2021. *The Stanford Encyclopedia of Philosophy* (Winter 2021 Edition), Edward N. Zalta (ed.), URL = <https://plato.stanford.edu/archives/win2021/entries/functionalism/>.

Smart, J. J. C. 2017. "The Mind/Brain Identity Theory." *The Stanford Encyclopedia of Philosophy* (Spring 2017 Edition), Edward N. Zalta (ed.), URL = <https://plato.stanford.edu/archives/spr2017/entries/mind-identity/>.

ADDITIONAL DISCUSSIONS

Armstrong, David. 1968. *A Materialist Theory of Mind*. London: Routledge & Kegan Paul.

Block, N. 1978. "Troubles with Functionalism." *Minnesota Studies in the Philosophy of Science* 9: 261–325.

Kripke, Saul. 1972. "Naming and Necessity." In D. Davidson and G. Harman (eds.) *Semantics of Natural Language*. Dordrecht: Reidel: 253–355.

Lewis, David K. 1966. "An Argument for the Identity Theory." *Journal of Philosophy* 63: 17–25.

Lewis, David K. 1983. "Postscript to 'Mad Pain and Martian Pain'." In *Philosophical Papers*, vol. 1. New York: Oxford University Press: 130–32.

Putnam, Hilary. 1967. "The Nature of Mental States." Originally entitled "Psychological Predicates." In W. H. Capitan and D. D. Merrill (eds.) *Art, Mind, and Religion: Proceedings of the 1965 Oberlin Colloquium in Philosophy*. Pittsburgh: University of Pittsburgh Press: 37–48.

Schwitzgabel, Eric. 2012. "Mad Belief?" *Neuroethics* 5 (1): 13–17.

Shoemaker, Sydney. 1981. "Some Varieties of Functionalism." *Philosophical Topics* 12: 93–119.

OTHER REFERENCES

Aydede, Murat. 2019. "Pain." *The Stanford Encyclopedia of Philosophy* (Spring 2019 Edition), Edward N. Zalta (ed.), URL = <https://plato.stanford.edu/archives/spr2019/entries/pain/>.

Bickle, John. 2020. "Multiple Realizability." *The Stanford Encyclopedia of Philosophy* (Summer 2020 Edition), Edward N. Zalta (ed.), URL = <https://plato.stanford.edu/archives/sum2020/entries/multiple-realizability/>.

Kim, Jaegwon. 1998. *Mind in a Physical World*. Cambridge, MA: Bradford.

Pereboom, Derk, and Kornblith, Hilary. 1991. "The Metaphysics of Irreducibility." *Philosophical Studies* 63: 125–45.

Polger, Thomas W., and Shapiro, Lawrence A. 2016. *The Multiple Realization Book*. New York: Oxford University Press.

16

THE BLOCKHEAD

BACKGROUND

The thought experiment to be considered in this chapter has a lot in common with the zombie thought experiment that we considered in Chapter 7. In contrast to the zombie argument, however, the Blockhead thought experiment has a narrower target. Instead of focusing broadly on physicalism, it is directed specifically at functionalism. According to functionalism, mental states are to be identified with functional states. Functional states can be defined in terms of three things—input, output, and relations to other states. So, for example, the functional state of foot pain can be defined in terms of the inputs that bring it about (stepping on a stray Lego brick or a nail, etc.), the outputs that it produces (crying out, clutching one's foot, etc.), and the relations in which it stands to other states (anger at whoever left the Lego or the nail on the floor, desire to avoid such objects in the future, etc.) This definition does not require any physical specification. On the functionalist view, we might think of a brain analogously to a complex computer, where what matters for mentality is the software, not the hardware.

The functionalist analysis of mentality entails that if two systems are in the same functional state, they are in the same mental state. But many philosophers have thought that it's conceptually possible for there to be two systems in the same functional state that are different with respect to qualia—that is, the experiential, "what it's like" features of consciousness, such as the distinctive way it feels to see red or feel pain (see Chapters 4 and 5). Since qualia seem essential to making a mental state the state that it is, this possibility poses a serious threat to functionalism. The Blockhead thought experiment aims to show that a system could be in the very same functional state as a human being who is experiencing a qualitative state even though the system lacks qualia altogether.

THE CASE

Imagine a giant robot called *the Blockhead*. It has a body that, outwardly, looks very much like a human body. On the inside, however, it is very different. In its head is a hollow cavity containing a bank of lights, an array of buttons, a bulletin board covered with a very large number of note cards, and a correspondingly large number of miniature individuals. The Blockhead's sensory organs are all connected to the bank of lights, with different sensory inputs causing different lights to blink on or off. The buttons are connected to the Blockhead's motor system, with different buttons causing different motor activities to occur. The note cards on the bulletin board each indicate the current state of the system. All of this works to mirror the complex computer program in which your mentality consists. In you, this program is implemented by biological neurons; in the Blockhead, it is implemented by the mini-individuals, each of whom plays the role of a single neuron. More specifically, each mini-individual is assigned a very simple task. Take one particular mini-individual that we'll call "G-72." All that G-72 has to do is wait for the note card to display G and for input light I-53 to come on. When that happens, G-72 presses output button O-97 and changes the card on the bulletin board to M. G-73 has a similar task: When the note card displays G and input light I-54 comes on, press output button O-98 and change the card to N. And so on for all the other mini-individuals. The mini-individuals are very good at their operations, and, as a result, the overall system is functionally equivalent to you. Perhaps it would be hard to keep the mini-individuals working for very long; but suppose that we can keep the whole thing going for an hour.

Now imagine that during that hour there's a moment that you step on a piece of Lego and feel a sharp stab of pain in your right foot. The Blockhead is functionally equivalent to you for this hour, so at the very same moment that you are feeling the pain, it is in the same functional state as you. Just as you cry out and grab your foot, so too does the Blockhead cry out and grab its foot. But is the Blockhead feeling a sharp stab of pain? Is it experiencing any qualitative state at all? Insofar as we're inclined to answer no, it looks like functionalism cannot be an adequate theory of mind.

DISCUSSION

The Blockhead thought experiment takes its name from Ned Block, the philosopher who first proposed it in 1978. But it has often been referred to by other names as well. As Block first describes the case, the mini-individuals are referred to as "homunculi," and so the thought experiment is thus often referred to as the *homunculi-headed robot*. Though it's now believed that the human brain contains approximately 86 billion neurons, at the time Block was writing the estimate was considerably lower, about a billion neurons. So Block thought that about 1 billion homunculi would be needed. Since that roughly matched the population of China at the time, he supposes that we might recruit the entire population of China to serve as the homunculi. The thought experiment is thus also sometimes referred to as the *China Nation case*.

The thought experiment serves as the linchpin of what Block refers to as *the absent qualia argument*. The reasoning proceeds roughly as follows: You and the Blockhead are in the same functional state. But you have qualia and the Blockhead does not. So the Blockhead is not in the same mental state that you are in. Since, according to functionalism, two systems are in the same mental state if and only they are in the same functional state, and since you and Blockhead are in the same functional state without being in the same mental state, functionalism must be false.

The argument has the same overall structure as the disembodied pain thought experiment that we considered in Chapter 3 and the zombie thought experiment that we considered in Chapter 7. Having imagined the Blockhead scenario, we use that to establish a claim about what is or is not possible, and then draw a conclusion about the falsity of a particular theory of mind. Since the debate here is basically the same as the debate discussed in Chapter 7, we won't rehearse the worries that relate to this kind of argumentative structure. Instead, we will focus on worries that are specific to this thought experiment.

One such worry that Block explores is that the Blockhead system would operate too slowly. Even if the mini-individuals are very fast at carrying out their very simple tasks, they would still operate much more slowly than the firing of a neuron. In Block's view, however, timescale shouldn't matter. Were your own mental operations to be slowed down, even considerably so, he claims that they would still count as the same mental operations.

Another possible objection owes to the work of Sydney Shoemaker (1975, 1981), who worries about how cases of absent qualia would be detectable. In particular, he argues that the Blockhead thought experiment suggests that each of us would be unable to tell if we are ourselves were lacking qualia. All we have in our own case is behavioral and introspective evidence. And, as Shoemaker puts it, if that's not adequate evidence, then nothing could be. But the Blockhead must have that same evidence about itself; if it had different evidence, then some kind of functional difference would be manifested—you and the Blockhead would not be functionally equivalent. Thus, unless we are prepared to admit that we might be wrong about whether we have qualitative states, we should accept that the Blockhead too has qualitative states.

A third possible objection owes to the work of Hilary Putnam (1967; see also Tononi 2012). Consider a swarm of bees. Though each individual bee in the swarm might be conscious, Putnam notes that we tend not to think of the swarm as a whole as conscious. According to Putnam, we're intuitively committed to an anti-nesting principle: No conscious being can be broken down into decomposable parts that are themselves conscious. Because this principle is violated in the Blockhead case—since each mini-individual is itself conscious—the case is not really conceivable. In response, Block has suggested that the anti-nesting principle has unintuitive consequences. Suppose that scientists were to develop tiny chips that could serve as replacements or enhancements for neurons, and suppose that the tiny chips themselves had low levels of consciousness. If we commit to the anti-nesting principle, then we would have to accept that a person who opts to have one of these tiny chips inserted into their brain is rendered unconscious as a result. Because the person now has a part that is conscious, they cannot themselves be conscious. That seems implausible.

That said, it's worth noting that accepting that minds can nest leads to results that strike many as implausible. Eric Schwitzgebel (2015) has leveraged the claim that minds can nest to conclude that the entirety of the United States might reasonably be thought of as conscious (or at least, that this is what a materialist should think). To make his argument, he relies on two different thought experiments. The first involves a supersquid whose neural system is spatially distributed throughout its body, including among its limbs. Moreover, the supersquid can detach its limbs from its body. This suggests that consciousness need not be spatially continuous; spatially discrete components can be integrated into a single conscious being. The second thought experiment involves a species of creatures Schwitzgebel calls the Antarean antheads. The Antareans, which look like woolly mammoths but manifest human-like intelligence, have a sophisticated society. Their society has a political structure, an educational system, social institutions like marriage, and thriving commerce. Interestingly, however, their brains contain not neurons but instead millions and millions of conscious antlike insects. The ant colony within an Antarean's head is wholly responsible for its behavior—just as the mini-individuals of the Blockhead are wholly responsible for its behavior. This suggests that consciousness can nest. What does that show about the United States? On Schwitzgebel's view, the United States has all the types of properties that a materialist takes to be generally characteristic of conscious beings: it has sufficiently sophisticated information processing and sufficiently sophisticated behavioral responses. Thus, the only thing that would be keeping us from considering it to be conscious would be a prejudice against spatially distributed group entities. According to Schwitzgebel, if we accept that "weirdly formed aliens" like the supersquid and Antarean anthead are conscious, then we should accept that there can be consciousness in spatially distributed group entities like the United States.

RECOMMENDED READING

CANONICAL PRESENTATION

Block, Ned. 1978. "Troubles with Functionalism." *Minnesota Studies in the Philosophy of Science* 9: 261–325.

OVERVIEW

Levin, Janet. 2018. "Functionalism." *The Stanford Encyclopedia of Philosophy* (Winter 2021 Edition), Edward N. Zalta (ed.), URL = <https://plato.stanford.edu/archives/win2021/entries/functionalism/> (See Section 5.5, "Functionalism and the Problem of Qualia.")

ADDITIONAL DISCUSSIONS

Block, Ned. 1980. "Are Absent Qualia Impossible?" *Philosophical Review* 89 (2): 257–74.

Fodor, Jerry A. 1981. "The Mind-Body Problem." Scientific American 244: 114–25.

Huebner, Bryce, Bruno, Michael, and Sarkissian, Hagop. 2010. "What Does the Nation of China Think about Phenomenal States?" *Review of Philosophy and Psychology* 1: 225–43.

Lycan, William. 1995. *Consciousness*. Cambridge, MA: MIT Press. (See Chapter 5, "Homunctionalism and Qualia.")

Schwitzgebel, Eric. 2015. "If Materialism Is True, the United States is Probably Conscious." *Philosophical Studies* 172: 1697–721.

Shoemaker, Sydney. 1975. "Functionalism and Qualia." *Philosophical Studies* 27 (5): 291–315.

Shoemaker, Sydney. 1981. "Absent Qualia are Impossible: A Reply to Block." *Philosophical Review* 90 (4): 581–99.

Tye, Michael. 2019. "Homunculi Heads and Silicon Chips: The Importance of History to Phenomenology." In Adam Pautz and Daniel Stoljar (eds.) *Blockheads! Essays on Ned Block's Philosophy of Mind and Consciousness*. Cambridge, MA: MIT Press: 545–69.

OTHER REFERENCES

Putnam, Hilary. 1967. "Psychological Predicates". In W. H. Capitan and D. D. Merrill (eds.) *Art, Mind, and Religion: Proceedings of the 1965 Oberlin Colloquium in Philosophy*. Pittsburgh: University of Pittsburgh Press: 37–48.

Tononi, Giulio. 2012. "The Integrated Information Theory of Consciousness: An Updated Account." *Archives Italiennes de Biologie* 150: 290–326.

THE IMITATION GAME

BACKGROUND

In the first half of the 20th century, advances in mathematics and computer science led to the development of what's become known as the Church–Turing thesis. Roughly put, this thesis holds that digital computers have the capacity to compute every possible rule-governed input–output function. This entails that digital computers can achieve whatever humans can achieve by way of formal reasoning. Given this result, the question naturally arises of whether we should treat the computers as engaging in reasoning themselves. Are they merely simulating the processes of thinking, or are they actually thinking? And how could we ever make this determination? The imitation game discussed in this chapter was proposed as a way to help us explore and answer this question.

THE CASE

Suppose you were given the following task: Communicate via separate text message exchanges with two unknown subjects, one of whom is a computer and one of whom is a human being, and determine which is which. You can take the conversation in whatever direction you want and pose whatever questions you want—whether they be about the weather, mathematics, football, poetry, politics, celebrity gossip, or something else entirely. Any topic is fair game. Carry out the conversation for enough time to get a good sense of each of the two subjects—perhaps an hour. Now suppose that, at the end of the allotted time, you're unable to make the determination that you've been charged to make. You really can't tell which subject is the computer and which subject is the human being. You take a guess that subject Alpha is the human being. But you're wrong; subject Alpha is the computer. We know that humans think. Given that subject Alpha has fooled you, a neutral interrogator, into identifying it as the human, should we conclude that it thinks?

This basic set-up describes the imitation game, also known as the Turing Test, proposed by Alan Turing in the early 1950s. Though we've updated the description slightly—Turing put it in terms of communication by teletype and not by text messaging—the key elements of the thought experiment remain the same. In Turing's view, the question "Can a machine think?" is too loaded for us to answer directly. Humans have too much bias against the machine. We are biased by the way it looks, by the mechanical sound of any "voice" we would give it, and also by our basic knowledge that it is a non-biological entity lacking an organic brain. Turing thus suggests that we would do better to approach the question indirectly. As he argues, if a computer can successfully imitate a human being—if it can produce the kind of performance in the imitation game that fools a neutral investigator—then we would have no grounds to deny thought to the computer. In his view, a computer that could pass the imitation game should be counted as thinking.

DISCUSSION

When Turing first proposed this test, he predicted that computers would be able to pass it within 50 years. That has not come to pass. Granted, computing systems have achieved remarkable feats, especially those that have been designed to focus on a specific task. Such systems are often referred to as Narrow (or Weak) Artificial Intelligence (AI), and they are contrasted with Artificial General Intelligence (AGI)—that is, systems that would be able to solve tasks and problems across a wide range of domains. Narrow AI systems have beaten human experts in contests involving chess, Go, and Jeopardy! They have composed music and written poetry that are in many ways indistinguishable from the kinds of music and poetry that humans produce, and they have created art that has sold for record-breaking prices at auction. But, despite an annual competition (sponsored by Hugh Loebner) that ran for 30 years and promised a prize of $100,000 to the first computing system that could successfully fool a panel of judges into thinking it was a human, no computer has yet managed to pass the Turing Test—at least as at the time of writing; though, given the fast pace of current technological development, some iteration of the language model-based chatbot ChatGPT might well do so in the near future, perhaps even before this book is published!

Some critics of the Turing Test accuse it of having a humancentric bias. Why should the imitation of human thought be considered an appropriate standard for thought in general? In response, however, we can point to the fact that Turing was not trying to define thinking; nor was he saying that passing the Turing Test was necessary for a machine to count as thinking. Rather, he was simply offering a sufficient condition for the attribution of thought to a machine.

But, even though we can dismiss this criticism, a related criticism proposed by Robert French (1990) has more bite. Suppose we were trying to figure out whether some machine we were building should count as flying. Of course, not everything that travels through air counts as flying—consider soap bubbles. So, it might prove difficult to come up with a precise definition of flying. To avoid the problem, we decide to use the Seagull Test: If our machine can fool someone looking at a radar screen into thinking that they are seeing a seagull in flight, then the machine counts as flying. Passing the Seagull Test is thus sufficient for an entity to count as flying. The Seagull Test does well with respect to bullets and bubbles, both of which will be easily distinguished from seagulls on radar. But it does less well with helicopters, airplanes, bats, and hummingbirds. Since all of these things will also be easily distinguished from seagulls on radar, the Seagull Test will not be able to deliver the result that they count as flying. The standard it sets is far too high. Yes, something that is indistinguishable from a seagull on radar should count as flying; but there are far too many things that should count as flying that won't be indistinguishable from seagulls, and so, for practical purposes, the Seagull Test is useless. French wants to say something similar about the Turing Test. Yes, something that is indistinguishable from a human in conversation should count as thinking; but there are far too many things that should count as thinking that won't be indistinguishable from humans, and so, for practical purposes, the Turing Test is useless.

In line with this criticism, some philosophers have suggested that we should jettison the Turing Test because it fails to set an appropriate goal for the field of artificial intelligence (Hayes and Ford 1995). According to this line of criticism, focus on passing the Turing Test forces researchers to work towards an unreasonable and perhaps unreachable goal. Moreover, it requires researchers to spend too much time worrying about issues irrelevant to intelligence—for example, mimicking the speed of typical human response or mimicking the kind of common errors that humans might make. In short, working to develop machines that pass the Turing Test might not be the best way to achieve machine intelligence.

A different kind of criticism of the Turing Test worries that it sets too low a standard for the attribution of intelligence. This kind of criticism has been offered by John Searle (1980), who claims that we can see the central problem with the Turing Test by way of a first-person thought experiment. If we imagine a scenario in which we ourselves are furnished with a sufficiently powerful rulebook, we can see that we could produce answers to questions without actually having any genuine understanding of what we were doing. We could do this without knowing what either the questions or the answers mean. Since all a computer does is work with that kind of rulebook, we should thus conclude that the computer doesn't have any genuine understanding either. We will discuss this thought experiment, commonly known as the *Chinese Room*, in the next chapter. Other philosophers have raised related worries, focusing not just on understanding but on consciousness. A machine that passes the Turing Test might just be a very good actor—so good that it can fool us into thinking that it is consciously thinking even though it lacks consciousness altogether.

In response to this kind of worry, Susan Schneider (2019) has suggested that we should move beyond our sole focus on the Turing Test and use alternative tests in addition (or instead) when trying to determine whether machines can think (see also Harnad 1991). Even if a machine cannot pass for human, it might nonetheless have behavioral manifestations of consciousness, and we might have other good reasons to think that is genuinely conscious. Schneider's AI Consciousness Test (ACT) aims to determine whether the machine has developed views of its own about consciousness, and whether it is reflective about and sensitive to the qualitative aspects of experience. If so, that would give us reason to think that it is genuinely conscious and not just faking it. She also describes another test called *the chip test*. In contrast to ACT, the chip test focuses not on machine behavior but on machine composition. Suppose that there are technological devices that, when integrated into a human brain, seem to support the presence of consciousness. Schneider suggests that if there are machines that utilize this same technology, then we should take seriously the possibility that they are conscious.

Finally, it's worth noting that when Turing proposed his imitation game, he based it on a different kind of imitation game—one involving a man, a woman, and an interviewer of either sex. In this game, the man is trying to convince the interviewer that he is the woman. Whether and how this gendered imitation game influences the way we should think about Turing's imitation game has been the subject of some discussion, with some arguing that it has no relevance for how the test should be understood (e.g., Piccinini 2000) and others arguing the reverse (Genova 1994, Kind 2022).

RECOMMENDED READING

CANONICAL PRESENTATION

Turing, Alan M. 1950. "Computing Machinery and Intelligence." *Mind* 59: 433–60.

OVERVIEWS

Copeland, B. Jack. 2000. "The Turing Test." *Minds and Machines* 10: 519–39.

French, Robert M. 2009. "The Turing Test." In Timothy Bayne, Axel Cleeremans, and Patrick Wilken (eds.) *The Oxford Companion to Consciousness*. Oxford: Oxford University Press: 641–3.

Oppy, Graham, and Dowe, David. 2016. "The Turing Test." *The Stanford Encyclopedia of Philosophy* (Spring 2016 Edition), Edward N. Zalta (ed.), URL = <https://plato.stanford.edu/archives/spr2016/entries/turing-test/>.

ADDITIONAL DISCUSSIONS

French, Robert M. 1990. "Subcognition and the Limits of the Turing Test." *Mind* 99: 53–65.

Genova, Judith. 1994. "Turing's Sexual Guessing Game." *Social Epistemology* 8: 313–26.

Harnad, Steven. 1991. "Other Bodies, Other Minds: A Machine Incarnation of an Old Philosophical Problem." *Minds and Machines* 1: 43–54.

Hayes, Patrick, and Ford, Kenneth. 1995. "Turing Test Considered Harmful." *Proceedings of the Fourteenth International Joint Conference on Artificial Intelligence.* San Mateo, CA: Morgan Kaufmann: 972–7.

Kind, Amy. 2022. "Computing Machinery and Sexual Difference: The Sexed Presuppositions Underlying the Turing Test." In Keya Maitra and Jennifer McWeeny (eds.) *Feminist Philosophy of Mind.* Oxford: Oxford University Press: 54–69.

Moor, James H. 1976. "An Analysis of the Turing Test." *Philosophical Studies* 30 (4): 249–57.

Piccinini, Gualtiero. 2000. "Turing's Rules for the Imitation Game." *Minds and Machines* 10: 573–85.

Schneider, Susan. 2019. *Artificial You: AI and the Future of Your Mind.* Princeton: Princeton University Press.

Searle, John R. 1980. "Minds, Brains, and Programs." *Behavioral and Brain Sciences* 3 (3): 417–57.

Traiger, Saul. 2000. "Making the Right Identification in the Turing Test." *Minds and Machines* 10: 561–72.

THE CHINESE ROOM

BACKGROUND

In 1956, a workshop held at Dartmouth College in New Hampshire gave rise to the research program known as Artificial Intelligence (AI). Research in AI has two main strands. One strand focuses on systems that engage in symbol manipulation, while the other focuses on connectionist networks. For the purpose of this chapter, we will focus on the first of these strands. Some AI researchers working with systems engaged in symbol manipulation are concerned only with developing systems that produce certain intelligent behaviors. Although such systems may simulate intelligence, it is not claimed that they are actually intelligent. There are other researchers, however, who aim to develop systems that not only simulate intelligence but also exhibit actual intelligence. In developing the thought experiment discussed in this chapter, Searle (1980) refers to the former as "weak" AI and the latter as "strong" AI. Though Searle was not the first philosopher to mount an attack on AI (see especially Dreyfus 1972), his thought experiment has proved especially influential.

THE CASE

Imagine that you are alone in a room that contains a rulebook and a bunch of pieces of paper with characters that you cannot parse. They mean nothing to you. Indeed, you do not even know whether they are characters in a language; to you, they are just meaningless shapes. The rulebook contains a very long list of rules that all have the same form: "If ____, then do _____." In each rule, the blanks are filled in with some of the same characters written on the pieces of paper. Soon someone outside the room slips a piece of paper in via a slot in the door. The paper is inscribed with some of these same characters. Consulting the rulebook, you find that the rule numbered 572 has the relevant characters in the first blank. You then find the piece of paper inscribed with the characters from the second blank in rule 572 and slip it out through the slot in the door. Almost immediately, another piece of paper comes through. The characters written on this paper correspond to the characters in the first blank for the rule numbered 394. Once you find the piece of paper inscribed with the characters from the second blank for rule 394, you slip it out through the slot. And on and on this goes. After you've been in the room a while, you find yourself becoming more and skilled in using the rulebook. You still have no idea what any of the characters mean, or what the point of this whole enterprise is, but you get extremely fast at your task. You can almost instantly locate the relevant rule and pass out the relevant piece of paper.

But now suppose that it turns out that the characters inscribed on the pieces of paper and in the rulebook are all actually characters in Mandarin. (If you are a Mandarin-speaker, or can recognize Mandarin characters, then substitute a different language with characters that you wouldn't recognize—perhaps Arabic or Greek or Sanskrit.) From the perspective of the person outside the room who has been slipping in the pieces of paper, it seems that they have been having a conversation with someone who is fluent in Mandarin—a conversation that has ranged across a great variety of subjects.

This scenario presents a thought experiment proposed by John Searle and commonly referred to as the *Chinese Room*. According to Searle, while in the room you are equivalent to a computer running a program—and, indeed, the best possible program for understanding Mandarin there could be. Your program is so good that you have fooled someone into thinking you speak Mandarin. You have passed the Turing Test for Mandarin (see Chapter 17). But you don't speak Mandarin. You don't understand what the characters mean, and you can't come to understand them in virtue of the program that you are running. In Searle's view, this shows that no computer can come to achieve understanding in virtue of running a symbolic program consisting of syntactically specified rules. As he often puts the point, syntax is not sufficient for semantics. His argument runs roughly as follows:

1. If strong AI is true, then the person in the Chinese Room understands Mandarin.
2. The person in the Chinese Room doesn't understand Mandarin.
3. Thus, strong AI is false.

The Chinese Room example also seems to pose a problem to functionalism—a theory of mind that treats mental states as functional states. While we have already seen other problems for functionalism that arise from its inability to handle the phenomenal character of our mental states (see Chapters 15 and 16), this example suggests that functionalism cannot adequately handle the intentional content of our mental states—that is, the aspect of our mental states in virtue of which they are about or directed at objects or states of affairs. One slogan commonly associated with functionalism is that the mind is to the brain as a computer software is to its hardware. In the Chinese Room, however, you are running the right software for understanding Mandarin, but yet you are not in the state of understanding Mandarin. Though Mandarin speakers use these characters to refer to objects or states of affair, to you they are every bit as meaningless after you've mastered the rulebook as when you first entered the room. Thus, if this example succeeds, it seems that functionalism must be false.

DISCUSSION

One common response to the Chinese Room is to argue that Searle was looking for understanding in the wrong place. When strong AI claims that computers can achieve understanding, they attribute the understanding to the entire computing system. But the person inside the room is only one part of the system—there is also the rulebook. Though you may not understand Mandarin as a result of being in the Chinese Room, that does not mean that the whole system lacks such understanding (see Copeland 1993). In terms of the argument outlined above, premise 1 is rejected. To try to rebut this objection, which

Searle refers to as the *Systems Reply*, he suggests that the individual in the room could memorize the entire rulebook. The individual now constitutes the entire system, but it doesn't seem that memorization of the rulebook would be sufficient for them to understand Mandarin.

Another common response (also directed against premise 1), often called the *Robot Reply*, contends that the lack of understanding results from the fact that the system lacks any sensory organs and cannot interact with the world (see Fodor 1980, Harnad 1991). These deficiencies prevent it from being able to connect the symbols that it is manipulating to the objects and states of affair that those symbols are meant to represent. To try to rebut this objection, Searle suggests another modification to the original thought experiment. Suppose we put the entire room inside the head of a giant robot. This robot has cameras and other sensors that take input from the world, and now some of the characters that are slipped into the room come via the cameras and sensors. According to Searle, the fact that these symbols are coming from a different source doesn't have any effect on your understanding. You are still just doing what you have always been doing—namely, manipulating symbols without understanding what they symbolize. Searle also suggests that, in granting that something like sensory perception is needed for understanding, the Robot Reply tacitly concedes his conclusion: no computer can come to achieve understanding *merely* in virtue of running a symbolic program consisting of syntactically specified rules.

A different kind of response targets the structure of Searle's example. Paul and Patricia Churchland (1990) propose a parallel argument—what they call the *Luminous Room*. You inside the room are given a magnet, and told to wave it as fast as you can. No matter how much you wave it, however, you don't produce any visible light. It thus looks like we could conclude that electromagnetic forces are not sufficient to produce light. But of course, electromagnetic forces *are* sufficient to produce light, as was shown by James Clerk Maxwell in the 19th century. So, something must be wrong with the structure of this reasoning and, correspondingly, with the structure of the Chinese Room example. As the Churchlands diagnose it, the problem is that waving a magnet around will not generate enough force to produce light that is detectable to the human eye. But there is luminance there. Likewise, the fact that the person in the Chinese Room cannot detect understanding does not mean that there isn't understanding there. It just might be at too low a level to be detectable.

In criticizing the Chinese Room, the Churchlands also suggest that Searle's Chinese Room, with only a single individual and rulebook, is based on a problematic model of what kind of computation is done by the brain. Brain processes operate via parallel processing. In the Churchlands' view, connectionist networks are a much more promising computational model than the kind of symbol processing on which Searle focuses.

Responding to this kind of case, Searle suggests that we could consider a whole Chinese gym with numerous individuals working together instead of just the original case of a single individual inside a single room. Still, he says, there won't be understanding. Note, however, that in moving from a single individual to a group of individuals, some of the force of the original thought experiment is blunted. In the initial version of the case, an individual can imagine being in the Chinese Room and assessing from a first-person perspective that they would lack understanding. If many individuals are involved, the relevant assessment can no longer be made from this perspective.

RECOMMENDED READING

CANONICAL PRESENTATIONS

Searle, John R. 1980. "Minds, Brains, and Programs." *Behavioral and Brain Sciences* 3 (3): 417–57.

Searle, John R. 1990. "Is the Brain's Mind a Computer Program?" *Scientific American* 262 (1): 26–31.

OVERVIEW

Crane, Tim. 1996. *The Mechanical Mind: A Philosophical Introduction to Minds, Machines and Mental Representation*. London: Penguin. (See especially Chapter 7.)

ADDITIONAL DISCUSSIONS

Boden, Margaret. 2004. "Escaping from the Chinese Room." In John Heil (ed.) *Philosophy of Mind: A Guide and Anthology*. Oxford: Oxford University Press: 253–66.

Churchland, Paul, and Churchland, Patricia. 1990. "Could a Machine Think?" *Scientific American* 262 (1): 32–37.

Copeland, Jack. 1993. "The Curious Case of the Chinese Room." In Jack Copeland (ed.) *Artificial Intelligence: A Philosophical Introduction*. Oxford: Blackwell: 121–39.

Dennett, Daniel. 1980. "The Milk of Human Intentionality." *Behavioral and Brain Sciences* 3 (3): 428–30.

Dreyfus, Hubert. 1972. *What Computers Can't Do*. New York: Harper & Row.

Fodor, Jerry. 1980. "Searle on What Only Brains Can Do." *Behavioral and Brain Sciences* 3 (3): 431–2.

Harnad, Steven. 1991. "Other Bodies, Other Minds: A Machine Incarnation of an Old Philosophical Problem." *Minds and Machines* 1: 43–54.

Preston, John. 2002. *Views into the Chinese Room: New Essays on Searle and Artificial Intelligence*. Oxford: Oxford University Press.

19

ELOISE AND THE TREE

BACKGROUND

Many of our mental states have intentional content. Intentionality in the relevant sense doesn't have to do with having an intention or doing something intentionally, but rather with representational content. The notion is often characterized in terms of "aboutness" or "directedness." For example, my belief that Mike Trout plays for the Los Angeles Angels is *about* a particular person, Mike Trout, and a certain state of affairs—his playing for that particular baseball team. My belief represents, or is directed at, those things. It's not just beliefs that have intentionality. My desire to see tonight's Angels game and my hope that Trout wins the Most Valuable Player (MVP) award also have aboutness. Do all of our mental states have intentional content? Representationalists answer this question in the affirmative, and they typically attempt to explain phenomenal consciousness in terms of intentionality. In an attempt to support their view, they often argue that when we attempt to attend to the phenomenal character of a given phenomenally conscious mental state, we have nothing to attend to except what the mental state represents. In this chapter we'll consider a thought experiment put forth in an effort to support this claim about attention and its relationship to representationalism.

DOI: 10.4324/9781003179191-22

THE CASE

Consider Eloise, who is in her front yard looking at an oak tree. As she looks at the canopy of leaves overhead, she is having a visual experience with a greenish character; and, as she touches the bark, she is having a tactile experience with a rough, bumpy character. But now suppose that she tries to attend to her experience, its greenishness say. What happens? Though she is aiming to focus her attention inward, she can't find any intrinsic features there on which to focus, and her attention slips through to the greenishness of the tree. An attempt to attend inward ends up being an act of outward attention. The color Eloise experiences is experienced as a feature of the tree.

There's nothing special about Eloise and her visual experience, as you can see if you try this attentional task yourself. If there's no tree nearby, you can just focus on the experience you're having right now while reading. As you read these words, you're having an experience of black text against a white background (or, if you're looking at a screen in dark mode, you're having an experience of white text against a black background). Try to turn inwards away from the black text itself and focus on the blackness of your experience. What happens when you do? Does your attention slip through to the blackness of the text before you? Can you keep it from doing so and focus on the blackness of your experience itself, rather than the blackness of the text?

DISCUSSION

The example of Eloise comes from Gilbert Harman (1990), but other representationalists use similar examples to make the same point (see, e.g., Tye 1995, p. 30). This point about attention seems to have been first noticed by G. E. Moore, who claimed that, when we're having a blue experience and we "try to introspect the sensation of blue, all we can see is the blue: the other element is as if it were diaphanous" (1903, p. 25). In line with this notion of diaphanousness, contemporary philosophers talk of the *transparency* of experience, and they tend to take examples like Eloise to establish what's often referred to as the *transparency thesis*. According to this thesis, experience is transparent in the way that a pane of glass is transparent. Just as we see right through a pane of glass to whatever is on the other side of it, we "see" right through our experience to whatever it is representing.

Though transparency has been most commonly discussed with respect to visual experience, many philosophers take it to be true for perceptual experiences generally (Tye 1995). For example, Clare Batty (2010) has argued that olfactory experience is transparent. On her view, when we're having an olfactory experience, the properties we're smelling are presented to us as out in the world or as around us. Granted, we might not always know what object in particular has produced the relevant odor. But, she argues, when we try to attend to an olfactory experience, we "smell" through that experience directly to the world, even if not to particular external objects in the world.

In addition to extending transparency to non-visual perceptual experiences, Michael Tye has extended it even more broadly to all kinds of phenomenal experience whatsoever. Consider bodily sensations and emotions. On Tye's view, when you have a toothache, if you try to attend to the pain your attention slips right through to the painful tooth itself. Likewise, when you're scared of a giant rattlesnake coiled on the trail ahead of you, if you try to attend to your fear your attention slips right through to what you're scared of; in this case, that's the rattlesnake itself.

How does the transparency thesis support representationalism? We might best see the representationalist as offering an argument that takes the form of an inference to the best explanation. Qualia are meant to be intrinsic features of experience. But if there really were such intrinsic features, features that were over and above functional and representational properties, then we should be able to attend to them. According to the representationalists, the fact that we can't attend to any intrinsic properties of experience is best explained by the hypothesis that there are no intrinsic properties of experience. The phenomenal properties of an experience that have been presumed to be intrinsic properties are really just representational properties.

In responding to this thought experiment, some philosophers deny that representationalists have described the Eloise case properly. In their view, we can introspectively attend to more than the representationalists think we can (e.g., Block 1996, Robinson 1998). To help defend this claim, they often point to kinds of experiences where there doesn't really seem to be anything represented by the experience. For example, consider phosphene experiences—the kind of visual experience you have when you push (lightly!) on your eyeball. When you're having a phosphene experience of a moving, colored expanse, the sensation doesn't really seem to be suggesting that there are actually moving, colored expanses out there in the world somewhere; and so it seems implausible to say that, in attending to our phosphene experiences, our attention to slips through to the world. Rather, we seem to be attending to the experiences themselves. Relatedly, consider afterimages. If you stare at a picture of a green dot for about half a minute and then you shift your attention to a blank piece of white paper, you will visually experience a red dot on the paper similar in size and location to the green dot you had been staring at. Given that we don't take there to be any red dot actually on the paper, it seems implausible to suppose that we attend to our afterimage experience by attending to the red dot.

Another example often mentioned involves blurry experiences (see Pace 2007). Suppose you're not wearing your glasses and you're trying to read a text that just came through on your phone. You can see that it says "Home by 6 pm," but it looks blurry to you. When you put your glasses on, the phenomenal character of your experience changes from blurry to clear (or, at least, clearer). But what's represented by the experience needn't seem to change. The same words, "Home by 6 pm," were represented both before and after you put your glasses on. Before you put your glasses on, you could attend to the blurriness of your experience without taking it to be a blurriness out there in the world.

A different way of responding to the transparency thesis notes that it appears to be importantly ambiguous. As Amy Kind (2003) has argued, we can distinguish two different interpretations of what it means to say that experience is transparent. When experience is *strongly transparent*, it is impossible to attend to the experience itself independent of what the experience represents. In contrast, when experience is *weakly transparent*, it is merely difficult to attend to the experience itself independent of what the experience represents. But the fact that this task is difficult does not mean that it is impossible. With appropriate introspective effort, we can pull it off. For the transparency thesis to support representationalism, it must be interpreted in terms of strong transparency. Because Kind thinks that the strong transparency thesis is false—that experience is only weakly transparent—she concludes that the transparency-based case for representationalism fails.

Worries have also been raised about whether the transparency thesis is meant to be a negative thesis, a positive thesis, or both (see, e.g., Stoljar 2004). Understood as a negative thesis, the claim that experience is transparent would be a claim about what we can't directly attend to. Understood as a positive claim, it would be making a claim about what we can directly attend to. It looks like the negative claim is required for the representationalist case to go through. Simply claiming that we directly attend to what's represented does not establish that there is nothing else to attend to. Arguably, the more plausible interpretation of transparency is the positive one. It seems clear that we can directly attend to the tree when attending to our experience of the tree. But if that's all that transparency amounts to, then it would not provide the support for representationalism that it is often thought to provide (see Molyneux 2009).

RECOMMENDED READING

CANONICAL PRESENTATIONS

Harman, Gilbert. 1990. "The Intrinsic Quality of Experience." *Philosophical Perspectives* 4: 31–52

Moore, G. E. 1903. "The Refutation of Idealism." *Mind* 12 (48): 433–53.

Tye, Michael. 1995. *Ten Problems of Consciousness*. Cambridge, MA: MIT Press.
Overview

Kind, Amy. 2010. "Transparency and Representationalist Theories of Consciousness." *Philosophy Compass* 5: 902–13.

ADDITIONAL DISCUSSIONS

Batty, Clare. 2010. "Scents and Sensibilia." *American Philosophical Quarterly* 47 (2): 103–18.

Block, Ned. 1990. "Inverted Earth." *Philosophical Perspectives* 4: 53–79.

Block, Ned. 1996. "Mental Paint and Mental Latex." *Philosophical Issues* 7: 19–49.

Byrne, Alex. 2001. "Intentionalism Defended." *Philosophical Review* 110: 199–240.

Dretske, Fred. 1995. *Naturalizing the Mind*. Cambridge, MA: MIT Press.

Kind, Amy. 2003. "What's So Transparent about Transparency?" *Philosophical Studies* 115: 225–44.

Molyneux, Bernard. 2009. "Why Experience Told Me Nothing about Transparency." *Noûs* 43 (1): 116–36.

Pace, Michael. 2007. "Blurred Vision and the Transparency of Experience." *Pacific Philosophical Quarterly* 88: 328–54.

Robinson, William S. 1998. "Intrinsic Qualities of Experience: Surviving Harman's Critique." *Erkenntnis* 47: 285–309.

Shoemaker, Sydney. 1990. "Qualities and Qualia: What's in the Mind?" *Philosophy and Phenomenological Research* 50: 109–31.

Stoljar, Daniel. 2004. "The Argument from Diaphanousness." In M. Ezcurdia, R. Stainton, and C. Viger (eds.) *New Essays in the Philosophy of Language and Mind*. Calgary: University of Calgary Press: 341–90.

Tye, Michael. 2000. *Consciousness, Color, and Content*. Cambridge, MA: MIT Press.

INVERTED QUALIA

BACKGROUND

Qualia are phenomenal properties: experiential, "what it's like" features of consciousness, such as the distinctive way it feels to see red or feel pain. In inverted qualia cases, we consider the possibility of people whose color qualia are reversed. For example, when an invert sees red blood, her color experience feels to her like the color experience most of us have when we see green grass; and when she sees green grass, her color experience feels to her like the color experience most of us have when we see red blood.

Such cases are discussed in philosophy today largely because they are thought to threaten important theories in the philosophy of mind. One such theory is functionalism, on which qualia are characterized in terms of functional properties: external stimuli, behavioral responses, and relations among mental states (see Chapter 16). Another is representationalism, on which qualia are identified with representational properties, which are themselves characterized in causal, historical, or functional terms (see Chapter 19). A third is physicalism, on which everything, including color experience, is physical (see Chapters 4 and 12).

THE CASE

Imagine two people we will call *Invert* and *Non-vert*. Non-vert is a typical color-sighted person. When she sees oxygenated blood, fire engines, and stop signs, she has a visual experience with a distinctive phenomenal quality (or quale) that might be called *phenomenal redness*. When she sees grass, cucumbers, and unripe bananas, she has a visual experience with a different phenomenal quality, which might be called *phenomenal greenness*. Invert is atypical. When she sees oxygenated blood, fire engines, and stop signs, her visual experience is not phenomenally red but rather phenomenally green. When she sees grass, cucumbers, and unripe bananas, her visual experience is not phenomenally green but rather phenomenally red.

This inverted qualia case is interpersonal. There are also intrapersonal cases. Imagine that someone who has never been inverted becomes inverted overnight (Wittgenstein 1968, Shoemaker 1982, Block 1990). Perhaps this happens because inverting lenses were surreptitiously placed on his eyes while he slept. At first, he might well say things like, "To me, grass looks red and blood looks green!" But we can suppose he learns to adapt to use color words, calling grass "green" and blood "red." Once he is fully adapted, he is functionally undetectable from people whose color vision is not inverted, except that he remembers how he experienced the world prior to his inversion. But that exception can be removed. We can simply suppose that he develops amnesia about that earlier period.

Inverted qualia cases have been discussed at least since John Locke imagined one in 1689. The inversion issue could be raised for any sense modality, at least in principle. For example, one might wonder whether inverted gustatory qualia are possible. But inverted visual qualia are the most commonly discussed kind.

Inverted qualia cases raise epistemological questions. For example, how do you know your own qualia are not inverted? Such cases have also been used to challenge functionalism, physicalism, and representationalism. To see why such cases threaten functionalism, let us add an additional claim to the above description of Invert: suppose Invert is not functionally atypical. That does not seem especially difficult to imagine. Suppose her red/green experiences have always been inverted. If so, then she might well behave similarly to people whose color experiences are not inverted. Indeed, it seems she might be similar to those people *in all relevant functional respects*. The anomaly might never be detected, either by her or by others. For example, because we learn words for colors by example, Invert describes blood as being red and grass as being green, just as Non-vert does. But if Invert is not functionally atypical, then it is hard to see how color qualia could be just functional properties. Your "red" experiences are phenomenally different from those of others; the qualia differ. And yet, functionally, your "red" experiences are the same as those of others, or so we are imagining.

Inverted qualia cases have also been used to challenge physicalism. This time, suppose Invert is not *physically* atypical. For example, suppose that, in humans, phenomenally red experience is correlated 1-to-1 with a certain brain state B1, and phenomenally green experience is correlated 1-to-1 with a different brain state B2. Now imagine that, just like Non-vert, when Invert sees blood, her brain goes into B1. Imagine also that, just like Non-vert, when Invert sees grass, her brain goes into state B2. That seems possible, despite the fact that Invert's qualia are inverted. But then color qualia can vary independently of the physical properties with which they are supposed to be identical. So, it is hard to see how color qualia could be physical properties.

Parallel reasoning has also been used to challenge representationalism. On representationalism, phenomenal properties are identified with (or at least supervene on) representational properties—properties of representing the world (Harman 1990, Chalmers 2004). Further, on significant versions of this view, representational properties are themselves characterized in functional, causal, and historical terms (Dretske 1995, Lycan 1996, Tye 2000). For example, on this view, phenomenal redness is the property of representing redness. Also on this view, what it is to represent redness is fully determined by such things as the fact that certain sorts of visual experiences (described in objective, scientific terms) are typically caused by interacting with red objects. In other words, there is "causal co-variation" between phenomenally red experiences and interaction with red objects. However, it seems possible that Invert is just like Non-vert with respect to all relevant representational properties, including such things as causal history. If such a thing is possible, then it is hard to see how color qualia could be such representational properties.

DISCUSSION

Inverted qualia cases raise a number of contested issues. One is whether such cases can actually happen. Martine Nida-Rümelin (1996) argues that there is scientific evidence that they do happen, though the cases she has in mind are ones in which the inverts are both functionally and physically atypical. There are three types of retinal photoreceptor that play a central role in human color vision, known as B-cones, G-cones, and R-cones. Usually, they contain chemically distinct photopigments. Due to genetics, it's likely that sometimes (though rarely) G-cones contain the photopigment that R-cones usually contain, and vice versa. According to Nida-Rümelin, this can result in red/green qualia inversion. Moreover, she suggests that the resulting inverts might be behaviorally indistinguishable from non-inverts.

Others argue that the scientific evidence points in the opposite direction—that is, that such behaviorally indistinguishable inverts are empirically impossible (e.g., Hardin 1988, Hilbert and Kalderon 2000). For example, for behaviorally indistinguishable inverts to exist, experiences of red and green would have to be symmetrical, and that is not so. For example, C. L. Hardin (1988) argues that, for humans, red is "warm" whereas green is "cool." Perhaps that particular asymmetry could also be inverted (Block 1990), but some argue that others cannot (Hilbert and Kalderon 2000). Some of the debate concerns not just red/green inversion, but inversion of the entire color spectrum; traditionally, inverted qualia cases are called "inverted spectrum" cases. But red/green qualia inversion suffices for the central philosophical arguments, such as the argument against functionalism.

To succeed, the inverted qualia argument against functionalism requires more than *behavioral* indistinguishability. Invert would have to be *functionally* indistinguishable from non-inverts. Her phenomenally red experiences would have to relate to her other mental states in the way phenomenally green experiences do in non-inverts, and vice versa. That is even harder to vindicate empirically. However, at least as stated above, the argument against functionalism requires only that functionally indistinguishable inverted qualia are possible, in the broadest (metaphysical) sense (Shoemaker 1982, Block 1990, Chalmers 1996). Indeed, the inverts need not even be human. And many find the possibility of inverted qualia plausible (but see, for example, Speaks 2011).

Some functionalists respond by denying that inverted qualia are possible (Harman 1982, Lycan 1987). But not all do. Sidney Shoemaker (1975, 1982) argues instead that the possibility of inverted qualia can be reconciled with functionalism, if functionalism is combined with the physicalist view that functional properties are realized in us by brain states. In his view, while the general property of having a conscious experience is a functional property, any specific phenomenal property we have, such as phenomenal redness, is a neurophysiological property. But that strategy faces a problem. As we have seen, the possibility of inverted qualia threatens not just functionalism but physicalism as well (Chalmers 1996).

Another noteworthy inversion case is known as *Inverted Earth* (Harman 1982, Block 1990). Inverted Earth differs from Earth in only two ways. First, everything there has the complementary color of its Earthly counterpart. The sky is yellow, ripe bananas are blue, grass is red, fire hydrants are green, etc. Second, the language is inverted. The English-speaking inhabitants describe the sky's color as "blue," the color of ripe bananas as "yellow," etc. Now imagine that evil scientists knock you unconscious, insert color-inverted lenses on your eyes, and transport you to Inverted Earth, where you are substituted for your counterpart.

Inverted Earth seems to pose a problem for representationalism, on which qualia are identified with representational properties. When you first wake up on Inverted Earth, everything looks normal to you; the lenses reverse the inverted colors. In terms of qualia, there is no inversion. But what happens regarding what your experiences represent? Suppose you describe the red grass you see as "green." At first, your description would be incorrect. That's because your use of "green" is grounded in events that took place on Earth, such as your perceiving green things and interacting with others. But, according to Ned Block (1990), this will gradually change. For example, after enough time has passed, the typical cause of your phenomenally green experiences will be interaction with red things. And Block takes this to show that qualia can't be identified with representational properties, at least as representational properties are typically characterized. He also takes Inverted Earth to vindicate qualia realism, on which there are *intrinsic* mental features of our experience: features that are not grounded in relations—environmental relations, functional relations, or any other relations. In Block's view, if there were no such intrinsic features, then your qualia would gradually change as their representational features do. But your qualia don't gradually change in that way.

Block's argument depends on controversial premises. For example, some challenge the premise that the phenomenal (qualitative) character of your mental states remains constant as their representational character shifts (Lycan 1996, Tye 2000). And some detach representationalism from the causal co-variation account of representational properties. For example, on one view, the phenomenal character of color experiences is intrinsically representational; what it represents depends only partially on the environment (Chalmers 2004). But it is interesting to note that the Inverted Earth case involves an inversion that is the converse of the more traditional inverted qualia cases. Instead of inverting the qualia and keeping the representational (or functional or physical) properties constant, in this case it is the representational properties that are inverted while the qualia are kept constant.

RECOMMENDED READING

CANONICAL PRESENTATION

Locke, John. 1689/1975. *An Essay Concerning Human Understanding*, edited by P. H. Nidditch. Oxford: Oxford University Press, 1975.

OVERVIEW

Byrne, Alex. 2020. "Inverted Qualia." *The Stanford Encyclopedia of Philosophy* (Fall 2020 Edition). Edward N. Zalta (ed.), URL = <https://plato.stanford.edu/archives/fall2020/entries/qualia-inverted/>.

ADDITIONAL DISCUSSIONS

Block, Ned. 1990. "Inverted Earth." *Philosophical Perspectives* 4: 53–79.
Chalmers, David J. 1996. *The Conscious Mind: In Search of a Fundamental Theory*. New York: Oxford University Press.
Hardin, C. L. 1988. *Color for Philosophers: Unweaving the Rainbow*. Indianapolis: Hackett.
Harman, Gilbert. 1982. "Conceptual Role Semantics." *Notre Dame Journal of Formal Logic*, 23: 242–56.
Harman, Gilbert. 1990. "The Intrinsic Quality of Experience." *Philosophical Perspectives* 4: 31–52.

Lycan, Willian G. 1987. *Consciousness*. Cambridge, MA: MIT Press.

Nida-Rümelin, Martine. 1996. "Pseudonormal Vision: An Actual Case of Qualia Inversion?" *Philosophical Studies* 82: 145–57.

Shoemaker, Sydney. 1975. "Functionalism and Qualia." *Philosophical Studies* 27 (5): 291–315.

Shoemaker, Sydney. 1982. "The Inverted Spectrum." *Journal of Philosophy* 74: 357–81.

Speaks, Jeffrey. 2011. "Spectrum Inversion without a Difference in Representation is Impossible." *Philosophical Studies* 156: 339–61.

Wittgenstein, Ludwig. 1968. "Notes for Lectures on 'Private Experience' and 'Sense-Data'." *Philosophical Review* 77: 275–320.

OTHER REFERENCES

Chalmers, David J. 2004. "The Representational Character of Experience." In B. Leiter (ed.) *The Future for Philosophy*. Oxford: Clarendon: 153–81.

Dretske, Fred. 1995. *Naturalizing the Mind*. Cambridge, MA: MIT Press.

Hilbert, David R., and Kalderon, Mark E. 2000. "Color and the Inverted Spectrum." In S. Davis (ed.) *Color Perception: Philosophical, Psychological, Artistic, and Computational Perspectives*. Oxford: Oxford University Press: 187–214.

Kripke, Saul. 1972. "Naming and Necessity." In D. Davidson and G. Harman (eds.) *Semantics of Natural Language*. Dordrecht: Reidel: 253–55.

Lycan, William G. 1996. *Consciousness and Experience*. Cambridge, MA: MIT Press.

Tye, Michael. 2000. *Consciousness, Color, and Content*. Cambridge, MA: MIT Press.

HEMPEL'S DILEMMA

BACKGROUND

According to physicalism, everything is physical. But what does it mean for something to be physical? According to Descartes, to be physical is to be extended in three spatial dimensions. But that 17th-century definition is out of line with current science. Contemporary philosophers often characterize the physical by deferring to physics: physical phenomena are those that are described by physical theory. But such deference leads to a problem known as Hempel's dilemma.

THE CASE

Physicalists claim that the mind is a physical phenomenon. Dualists reject that claim, holding that the mind is non-physical or that there are non-physical mental properties. The disagreement seems substantial, but it is not entirely clear what the disagreement amounts to. What does it mean to say (or deny) that something is *physical*?

Descartes had a clear answer: to say that something is physical is to say that it is extended in space. But that answer is outdated. For example, modern physics posits phenomena that are not extended in the sense Descartes meant, such as gravitational force. How should we, in the 21st century, understand what it means to be physical?

A natural strategy for answering that question is to defer to science. Physical phenomena are those physical theory posits—or those plus the entities that such phenomena constitute (Loewer 2001). For example, if physical theory posits quarks and leptons, then quarks and leptons qualify as physical—and so does anything that is constituted by quarks and leptons, such as rocks, tables, and planets. Non-physical phenomena are defined correspondingly as phenomena that are neither posited by physical theory nor constituted by such posits.

The deferential strategy is popular, but it leads to a problem. *Which* physical theory is relevant? Presumably not *current* physical theory. Current physical theory is incomplete and probably inaccurate in some ways. How about *completed* (or *ideal*) physical theory? Completed physical theory is, by definition, complete and accurate, and so the concerns about current physical theory do not arise. But there is another concern. We don't know the content of completed physical theory, at least not yet. So, we don't know what phenomena ideal physics will posit. What if that science ends up positing fundamental mental features? For all we know, it might (Chalmers and McQueen 2022). And if it does, then even fundamental, irreducible mentality, of the sort dualists claim exists, would qualify as physical. And that's problematic. It would undermine the contrast between physicalism and dualism. This problem was raised by Carl Hempel (1966) and has been developed more recently by Barbara Gail Montero (1999).

DISCUSSION

Some take Hempel's dilemma to imply that the physicalism/dualism contrast, along with the surrounding debate, should be discarded (Crane and Mellor 1990). But most respond in a less extreme fashion.

Some accept the first horn of the dilemma, arguing that we should define the physical by reference to current physical theory despite its shortcomings. Andrew Melnyk (1997) takes this line, noting that a scientist might favor a scientific hypothesis without believing it is true—and, indeed, without believing that it is even more likely to be true than false. They might favor that hypothesis because it is better than all contemporary and historical rival hypotheses. Similarly, Melnyk suggests, for the purposes of defining the physical, what matters is only that current physical theory is better than all contemporary and historical rival theories.

But, as Montero (1999) observes, recognizing that a theory is superior to historical and contemporary rival theories need not commit one to accepting the theory. For example, one might be a libertarian about free will, and yet take Humean compatibilism to be superior to all historical and contemporary rival theories (perhaps one regards all such theories as failures but takes Hume's theory to be the most elegant). Yet physicalism is typically understood to involve a commitment to its main thesis, that everything is physical, being *true*. A further problem with Melnyk's approach is that limiting the competition to historical and contemporary rivals seems hard to justify, given that some future physical theories will be more accurate and more complete.

Some accept the second horn of the dilemma, arguing that we should define the physical by reference to future or ideal physical theory and that the problems this causes can be solved. Jessica M. Wilson (2005, 2006) does this. On her characterization, physical phenomena are phenomena posited by ideal physical theory. But those posited phenomena must satisfy a further constraint: none can be fundamentally mental. Wilson's approach is to embrace the second horn of Hempel's dilemma; but, thanks to her *No Fundamental Mentality* constraint, she can avoid the concern that ideal physics might posit the sort of mentality that dualists accept and physicalists reject.

Other philosophers avoid Hempel's dilemma by providing a substantive characterization of the physical rather than deferring to science. One response of this sort involves characterizing the physical as the class of entities that are, in relevant respects, similar to paradigmatically physical entities, such as rocks and trees (Snowdon 1989, Stoljar 2001). Such a characterization involves no reference to physical theory, and thus avoids both horns of Hempel's dilemma. But there are problems. One is that it is not entirely clear what is to count as a paradigmatically physical entity. Here it is worth noting that idealists, who maintain that everything is mental, would not agree that rocks and trees are physical if their being physical is meant to be inconsistent with their being composed of mental phenomena, such as ideas. Similarly, on this response, physicalism could be true even if rocks and trees turn out to involve some fundamental mental features, as panpsychists claim—and many take that result to be unacceptable. Further, it is not clear what the "relevant respects" are supposed to be (Montero 1999).

Another way to provide a substantive characterization of the physical is to update Descartes' conception. Thus, Robert J. Howell (2013) proposes that a physical property is one that can be fully characterized in terms of its implications for the distribution of things in space over time. According to Howell, even if gravitational force is not extended *per se*, it can be fully characterized in terms of its spatiotemporal implications.

Yet another approach to Hempel's dilemma is to identify features common to any physical theory, including ideal/completed physical theory. In particular, some argue that any physical theory will concern only spatiotemporal/causal structure and dynamics (Chalmers 2020). If so, then perhaps we can characterize the physical as the structural-and-dynamic, or perhaps as structural-and-dynamic phenomena and those composed of such phenomena. But the relevant notion of structure and dynamics needs to be spelled out adequately, and it is controversial whether doing so is possible (Stoljar 2015, Alter 2016).

On all of the foregoing responses the physical is characterized positively—that is, in terms of what it *is* to be physical. But some regard the search for an adequate *positive* characterization as misguided. They argue that we should instead characterize the physical negatively, in terms of what it is *not*: to be physical is to be not fundamentally mental (Spurrett and Papineau 1999, Levine 2001, Montero and Papineau 2005, Worley 2006, Fiorese 2016; cf. Montero 1999). Such a negative characterization involves no mention of physical theory, and so Hempel's dilemma is circumvented. Proponents of this approach, known as *via negativa physicalism*, also argue that such a negative characterization is adequate for the purposes of the mind–body problem.

However, it is unclear what falls under the description "not fundamentally mental." And that threatens to make claims central to the mind–body debate especially difficult to evaluate. For example, consider a premise of the zombie argument, that a zombie world—a minimal physical/functional duplicate of the actual world but without consciousness—is conceivable (see Chapter 7). That premise is controversial as it is. But it seems especially hard to assess if "physical" means "not fundamentally mental." There might be all manner of features that satisfy that description, perhaps including some that no one has even dreamt of; and perhaps some such features imply that the zombie-world scenario is incoherent.

Some combine the negative characterization of the physical with a positive one. For example, Wilson's account, discussed above, fits that description: the positive characterization is expressed by her characterization of the physical in terms of future/ideal physics; and the negative characterization is expressed by her No Fundamental Mentality constraint. This view might seem a reasonable comprise. Still, there remains a concern that, like *via negativa* physicalism, the proposed characterization of the physical is overly open-ended since, again, we do not know the content of ideal physical theory.

RECOMMENDED READING

CANONICAL PRESENTATIONS

Hempel, Carl. 1966. *Philosophy of Natural Science*. Englewood Cliffs, NJ: Prentice Hall.

Montero, Barbara G. 1999. "The Body Problem." *Noûs* 33: 183–200.

OVERVIEW

Stoljar, Daniel 2022. "Physicalism." *The Stanford Encyclopedia of Philosophy* (Summer 2022 Edition), Edward N. Zalta (ed.), URL = <https://plato.stanford.edu/archives/sum2022/entries/physicalism/>.

ADDITIONAL DISCUSSIONS

Crane, Timothy, and Mellor, Hugh. 1990. "There Is No Question of Physicalism." *Mind* 99: 185–206.

Fiorese, Raphaël. 2016. "Stoljar's Dilemma and Three Conceptions of the Physical: A Defence of the Via Negativa." *Erkenntnis* 81: 201–29.

Howell, Robert J. 2013. *Consciousness and the Limits of Objectivity: The Case for Subjective Physicalism*. Oxford: Oxford University Press.

Loewer, Barry M. 2001. "From Physics to Physicalism." In C. Gillett and B. Loewer (eds.) *Physicalism and Its Discontents*. Cambridge: Cambridge University Press: 37–56.

Melnyk, Andrew. 1997. "How to Keep the 'Physical' in Physicalism." *Journal of Philosophy* 94: 622–37.

Montero, Barbara G. 2001. "Post-Physicalism." *Journal of Consciousness Studies* 8: 61–80.

Montero, Barbara G., and Papineau, David. 2005. "A Defence of the *Via Negativa* Argument for Physicalism." *Analysis* 65: 233–7.

Snowdon, Paul. 1989. "On Formulating Materialism and Dualism." In J. Heil (ed.) *Cause, Mind, and Reality: Essays Honoring C.B. Martin*. Dordrecht: Kluwer Academic: 137–58.

Stoljar, Daniel. 2001. "Two Conceptions of the Physical." *Philosophy and Phenomenological Research* 62: 253–81.

Wilson, Jessica M. 2005. "Supervenience-Based Formulations of Physicalism." *Noûs* 39: 426–59.

Wilson, Jessica M. 2006. "On Characterizing the Physical." *Philosophical Studies* 131: 61–99.

Worley, Sara. 2006. "Physicalism and the Via Negativa." *Philosophical Studies* 131 (1): 101–26.

OTHER REFERENCES

Alter, Torin. 2016. "The Structure and Dynamics Argument against Materialism." *Noûs* 50: 794–815.

Chalmers, David J. 2020. "Spatiotemporal Functionalism v. the Conceivability of Zombies." *Noûs* 54 (2): 488–97.

Chalmers, David J., and McQueen, Kelvin J. 2022. "Consciousness and the Collapse of the Wave Function." In S. Gao (ed.) *Consciousness and Quantum Mechanics*. New York: Oxford University Press: 11–63.

Levine, Joseph. 2001. *Purple Haze: The Puzzle of Consciousness*. Oxford: Oxford University Press.

Spurrett, David, and Papineau, David. 1999. "A Note on the Completeness of 'Physics'." *Analysis* 59: 25–9.

Stoljar, Daniel. 2015. "Russellian Monism or Nagelian Monism?" In T. Alter and Y. Nagasawa (eds.) *Consciousness in the Physical World: Perspectives on Russellian Monism*. New York: Oxford University Press: 324–45.

BRAINS WITHIN BRAINS

BACKGROUND

According to physicalism, everything is physical. But what does it mean to be physical? Contemporary philosophers often characterize the physical by deferring to physics: physical phenomena are the entities described by fundamental physics, or those plus entities that are constructed from them (Loewer 2001; see Chapter 21). In other words, to be physical is to be, or to be made of, entities that exist at the fundamental level of physical reality. For example, if quarks and leptons are posited by fundamental physics, then they and the things they compose are physical. But what if there is no fundamental level? For example, what if quarks and leptons are composed of more basic entities? And what if those more basic entities are composed of still more basic entities, and so on forever (*ad infinitum*)? Physicalism shouldn't rule that possibility out. But how can that be avoided?

Barbara Gail Montero (2006) develops an elegant solution to the problem described above—of how to reconcile physicalism with the possibility that there are no fundamental physical phenomena. Her solution begins with a constraint on physicalism that Jessica Wilson (2006) calls the *No Fundamental Mentality constraint*: physicalism is true only if there is no fundamental mentality (see Chapter 21). That constraint is widely accepted. Montero proposes a sort of generalization of it, which could be called the *No Low-Level Mentality constraint*: physicalism is true only if there is neither fundamental mentality nor an infinite descent of mentality (Montero 2006; cf. Brown and Ladyman 2009, Schaffer 2017).

Initially, the No Low-Level Mentality constraint might seem to be just what is called for. Suppose everything physical is infinitely decomposable: quarks are composed of more elementary phenomena, which in turn are composed of yet more elementary phenomena, and so on forever. Physicalism could still be true if the chain of decomposition includes only physical phenomena. What would seem incompatible with physicalism would be if, below a certain point in that chain of decomposition, the more basic phenomena are mental. In that case, the world would be grounded in (that is, based on) mental phenomena. But that sort of scenario is exactly what the No Low-Level Mentality constraint specifies is incompatible with physical. Problem solved!

Or so it might seem. Christopher Devlin Brown describes what appears to be a counterexample to the No Low-Level Mentality requirement: a scenario in which physicalism could be true even though there is an infinite descent of mentality. To construct his counterexample, Brown appeals to a "compositional account of mentality" that, he suggests, all versions of physicalism entail. On this account, if a physical system has mental properties, then it has those properties solely in virtue of the arrangement of its constituent parts. For example, he writes:

> If a mental type is identical to a neural type, then just get the chemical and other constituents of nerves together in the right way, set them acting correctly and—voilà! There is a brain that has mental properties, no further specifications required.
>
> (Brown 2017, p. 1435)

THE CASE

Imagine a world that has only one thing, a brain called Alex. On the compositional account of mentality, Alex has mental properties: they have "parts that are dynamically arranged in such a way that they produce mentality for the thing they compose" (Brown 2017, p. 1435). The same point extends to Alex's parts. They too are brains, which Brown calls "Bretts." These smaller brains are mental beings for the same reason Alex is. Each Brett is composed of parts, Charlies, arranged in such a way as to produce Brett's mentality. And each Charlie is also an even smaller brain, composed of yet smaller brains, Devins, which are also mental beings—and so on infinitely. Brown (2017, p. 1435) calls that world the "all-mental and all-physical world—MPW for short."

Physicalism could be true of MPW. That world only contains brains: nothing but brains all the way down. But the brains all have mentality, so there is also mentality all the way down. Thus, physicalism could be true of MPW even though that world contains an infinite descent of mentality. Evidently, the No Low-Level Mentality constraint is incorrect. If so, we need a different solution—a different way to explain how physicalism could be true if it turns out that there is no fundamental physical level of reality.

DISCUSSION

One might be tempted to dismiss Brown's counterexample on the grounds that physicalism is a thesis about the actual world, not other conceivable worlds. But that would be too quick. For one thing, it is widely accepted that the content of the physicalist thesis is determined partly by its consequences for other conceivable (and possible) worlds. Moreover, as noted above, it has been argued that the actual world could turn out to be, in relevant respects, like MPW. That is, it might be that, not just in MPW but also in reality, everything is infinitely decomposable and there are no fundamental physical phenomena (Schaffer 2003). And that possibility should be compatible with physicalism. So, an explanation of that compatibility is needed if, as Brown contends, MPW shows that Montero's solution fails.

Two alternative solutions have been proposed. Both follow Montero's template: they explain how physicalism could be true in MPW by specifying necessary conditions on physicalism that MPW satisfies. But the specified conditions differ from Montero's. She identified *a pattern of infinite decomposition* that is (she thought) incompatible with physicalism. By contrast, the first alternative solution identifies *a type of mentality* that is incompatible with physical: the type that does not conform to Brown's compositional account of mentality—that is, mentality that something has but *not* solely in virtue of the arrangement of its constituent parts (Alter 2022). This suggests an Only Compositional Mentality constraint: physicalism is true only if all mentality is merely compositional (in the sense of the compositional account of mentality). The thesis helps support the claim that physicalism could be true of MPW: physicalism is compatible with the existence of compositional mentality, no matter how such mentality is distributed—even if such mentality is present at every level, as in MPW. However, there's a snag: despite what Brown suggests, it's not so clear that all versions of physicalism entail the compositional account of mentality.

The second alternative solution combines insights of the other two, identifying both a pattern of infinite decomposition that's incompatible with physicalism and a type of mentality that's incompatible with physicalism (Alter et al. 2022). The proposal is based on the following No Low-Level Mental Constitution constraint: physicalism is true only if there's neither (a) fundamental mentality nor (b) an infinite descent of mentally constituted (mentally composed) mentality—that is, an infinite descent of phenomena that are constituted by mental phenomena.

MPW could satisfy the condition that the No Low-Level Mental Constitution constraint specifies. MPW does contain an infinite descent of mentality, but it need not contain an infinite descent of *mentally constituted* mentality. To see this, imagine a drawing made up of little circles arranged in a big circle. The big circle is circular in virtue of the arrangement of the little figures. But the fact that the arranged figures are themselves circular is irrelevant to constituting the circularity of the big circle. The little figures might have been squares, and they nonetheless would have constituted a big circle because of how they were arranged. Likewise, although Alex's mentality exists in virtue of the arrangement of mental beings, the Bretts, the fact that the Bretts are mental beings is irrelevant to constituting Alex's mentality. That's why physicalism could be true of MPW.

Is the No Low-Level Mental Constitution constraint plausible? Arguably, it is. What physicalists cannot abide is the presence of mentally constituted mentality all the way down—an infinite descent of levels where mentally constituted mentality exists. From the physicalist's perspective, the latter is no more palatable than fundamental mentality is. However, the relevant notion of constitution is itself controversial (Bliss and Trogdon 2021), and some physicalists might hesitate to rely on it.

There is another factor to consider. As Brown (2017) points out, his MPW example also raises a problem for characterizing *panpsychism*—the view that mentality occurs everywhere, even at the microphysical level. In recent philosophy of mind, panpsychism has increasingly been taken seriously (Goff et al. 2022). The problem for panpsychism is the reverse of the problem MPW raises for characterizing physicalism. In MPW, mentality is everywhere. Yet MPW seems compatible with the denial of panpsychism. After all, MPW contains nothing but brains within brains—it's brains all the way down. And if one supposes that panpsychism must be true of MPW, one should bear in mind that panpsychism is widely taken to be incompatible with physicalism (Wilson 2006). If the two theories are indeed incompatible, then either: (i) panpsychism could be false of MPW, in which case an explanation of how that could be is called for; or (ii) physicalism could not be true of MPW, even though all that world contains are brains—that is, physical things.

RECOMMENDED READING

CANONICAL PRESENTATIONS

Brown, Christopher D. 2017. "Minds within Minds: An Infinite Descent of Mentality in a Physical World." *Erkenntnis* 82: 1339–50.

Montero, Barbara G. 2006. "Physicalism in an Infinitely Decomposable World." *Erkenntnis* 64: 177–91.

OVERVIEW

Stoljar, Daniel. 2022. "Physicalism." *The Stanford Encyclopedia of Philosophy* (Summer 2022 Edition), Edward N. Zalta (ed.), URL = <https://plato.stanford.edu/archives/sum2022/entries/physicalism/>.

ADDITIONAL DISCUSSIONS

Alter, Torin, Coleman, Sam, and Howell, Robert J. 2022. "Physicalism, Infinite Decomposition, and Constitution." *Erkenntnis*. doi:10.1007/s10670-022-00582-2.

Alter, Torin. 2022. "Physicalism without Fundamentality." *Erkenntnis* 87: 1975–86.

Brown, Robin, and Ladyman, James. 2009. "Physicalism, Supervenience and the Fundamental Level." *Philosophical Quarterly* 59 (234): 20–38.

Loewer, Barry M. 2001. "From Physics to Physicalism." In C. Gillett and B. Loewer (eds.) *Physicalism and Its Discontents*. Cambridge: Cambridge University Press: 37–56.

Schaffer, Jonathan. 2003. "Is There a Fundamental Level?" *Noûs* 37: 498–517.

Schaffer, Jonathan. 2017. "The Ground between the Gaps." *Philosophers' Imprint* 17 (11): 1–26.

Wilson, Jessica. 2006. "On Characterizing the Physical." *Philosophical Studies* 131: 61–99.

OTHER REFERENCES

Bliss, Ricki, and Trogdon, Kelly. 2021. "Metaphysical Grounding." *The Stanford Encyclopedia of Philosophy* (Winter 2021 Edition), Edward N. Zalta (ed.), URL = <https://plato.stanford.edu/archives/win2021/entries/grounding/>.

Goff, Philip, Seager, William, and Allen-Hermanson, Sean. 2022. "Panpsychism." *The Stanford Encyclopedia of Philosophy* (Summer 2022 Edition), Edward N. Zalta (ed.), URL =<https://plato.stanford.edu/archives/sum2022/entries/panpsychism/>.

PART III

CONTENT, INTENTIONALITY, AND REPRESENTATION
Introduction

It seems to be an essential feature of minds that they *think*, and it seems to be an essential feature of thinking that it is *about* something. Sarah can think her grandmother is stylish. She can hope that she inherits her grandmother's fancy shawls. She can remember the first time she beat her grandmother at gin rummy. All of these thoughts have what philosophers call *intentionality*: they are about something. By having these thoughts, Sarah *represents* the world as being a certain way. Sarah's thoughts are about inheriting shawls, beating her grandmother at rummy, and so on. The thought's *content* is what the thought represents as being the case. In many cases, the content of a thought is what philosophers call a *proposition*. Propositions are, roughly, the things designated by that-clauses. For example, Sarah believes that her grandmother was born in Peoria, Illinois. This thing Sarah believes—that her grandmother was born in Peoria—could be true or it could be false. This is a crucial feature of propositions—that they can be true or false. One can take many different stances or attitudes toward the same content or proposition. Sarah could doubt that her grandmother was born in Peoria, she could wonder whether her grandmother was born in Peoria, she could hope it, and so on. These are all *propositional attitudes*. They are attitudes that have propositions as their content.

One of the most significant problems in the philosophy of mind is explaining the intentionality of mental states. Providing such an explanation involves at least two important parts. We might call them *the general question* and *the particular question*. The general question is: What makes a mental state about anything at all? This problem is clearest, perhaps, for the naturalist who believes that the mind is physical. Your liver, though a sophisticated and complex system, doesn't seem to have intentional states. And non-organic matter—such as an outcropping of rock—also doesn't represent anything. What, then, makes the brain, or some states of the brain, be about the world? The particular question is: Why are thoughts about the specific things they are about? What makes a certain firing of neurons be about Sarah's grandmother and not the little old lady who lives next door? Even if one isn't a naturalist, and one believes the mind involves some non-physical stuff or set of properties, the problem would still arise as we still need an explanation for what makes that stuff be about anything, and we also need an explanation for what makes it be about the specific things it is about.

This section considers several puzzles concerning intentionality and content. Chapter 23 concerns the particular question, and stems from a puzzle developed by Quine: in any given situation, there are many candidates for what a thought might be about. Suppose one sees a rabbit hopping by and one thinks, "Ooh, a rabbit!" We naturally think that thought is about a rabbit. But what makes the thought about a rabbit as opposed to something like "connected rabbit parts" that are also right in front of you? Quine thinks there is no determinate fact of the matter. Chapter 24 might be seen as being more concerned with the general question—or, more specifically, a certain answer to the general question. It is tempting to think that what makes a thought about something has to do with the history of the individual who has that thought, or perhaps the evolutionary process that gave rise to such a thought type. Sarah's thought is about her grandmother and not the lady next door because Sarah has been in contact with her grandmother and not the lady next door. But what if there were a creature without such a history? The answer to the general aboutness question, which emphasizes historical connections, would seem to imply that this creature wouldn't have intentionality at all. This appears implausible to many. Chapter 24 concerns that problem.

It is tempting to think that, whatever makes a person's thoughts about something, it must be something about the particular person—the constitution of their brain, the way they feel, and so forth. But Chapter 25 presents an argument that challenges this assumption. At least some of our thoughts have the particular content they do partly because of our environment. When I think about water, I think about one thing: H_2O. But if I grew up in a world where almost everything was the same but the thing people called "water" and that ran in rivers and streams was not H_2O but XYZ, my thoughts about water would be about XYZ. Things outside of our brains and bodies can determine what content we are thinking. Philosophers often call this view about content *externalism*. Chapter 26 presents a thought experiment that supports a different sort of externalism. On this view, there can be *extended minds* in the sense that part of our mind—the states and activities that make up our minds—can be located outside of our bodies. On this view, for example, a state of my iPhone might constitute one of my beliefs. Take Sarah's belief that her grandmother is from Peoria. On the extended-mind view, Sarah might have that belief even if it does not reside anywhere in her head. If it is on her iPhone and plays the appropriate role in her cognitive system, it counts as her belief.

Some philosophers think externalist views of content have implications for traditional philosophical problems such as skepticism about the external world. Such skepticism often results from reflection on scenarios such as the "brain in a vat", discussed in Chapter 27. You think you have a body. But you might be just a brain in a vat being fed information by a complicated computer. Everything would seem the same to you. It looks like in such a case you'd be radically wrong about the world. For example, your belief that you have hands would be false. But externalism complicates matters. Even though in such a scenario it would seem to you just like it does now, would you be thinking the same thing? If your thoughts are partially determined by your environment, maybe you are in fact right about things in that world. After all, in that scenario you do have *virtual* hands.

One of the tricky issues raised by externalism is that, if our beliefs are determined by things outside of our heads, there is a sense in which we are likely to be insensitive to some of the features of our mental states. It might be that we could wind up rationally believing complete contradictions. Chapter 28 considers such a case, and discusses its implications for theories of content.

Content isn't the only puzzling thing about propositional attitudes. There is also the question of what makes them the attitudes they are. It seems there are at least two types of attitude that can be usefully distinguished. First, there are attitudes like predictions, suspicions, and beliefs that, in some sense, try to *get something right about the world*. Second, there are also attitudes such as desires, hopes, and wishes that potentially lead the agent to *change the world*. Chapter 29 attempts to get at this contrast by considering two sorts of list. On the one hand, there is a shopping list where the purpose of the list is to get the world—or rather the shopping basket—to reflect what is on the list. On the other hand, there is a receipt, which should be a list that matches what is in the basket.

RABBITS AND RABBIT STAGES

BACKGROUND

Sometimes what we say is ambiguous. When I tell you that I've gone to the bank, you might wonder whether I went to a financial institution or to a river. Also, some ordinary terms are vague, e.g., "tall" and "bald." Even so, often what we say would seem to have determinate meaning. For example, suppose I say of my friend Smith, "Smith is tall." Here "Smith" refers to my friend, even though there are many others who go by the name "Smith." Also, here "is tall" refers to the property of being tall, even if there is no precise minimal height required for being tall. Such claims might seem obviously true—perhaps too obvious to bother stating. Not according to Willard Van Orman Quine. According to Quine, such claims are actually *false*. In his view, understanding linguistic meaning requires analyzing language from an objective, scientific viewpoint. And that, he holds, involves setting aside our pre-theoretical intuitions about meaning and instead focusing only on objective facts. For example, in the case of translating unknown languages into one's own language, those objective facts include only dispositions to exhibit verbal behavior in response to external stimuli. As Quine (1987, p. 5) writes: "There is nothing in linguistic meaning ... beyond what is to be gleaned from overt behavior in observable circumstances." The results of Quine's influential analysis are startling. Contrary to what might have seemed obvious, what we say generally lacks determinate meaning. Whenever we use ordinary language meaningfully, there are multiple, mutually inconsistent things that our words could mean, and there is no fact of the matter about which of those things is correct. Quine uses the case we consider in this chapter to help motivate these startling results.

THE CASE

Imagine that you're an explorer in an unfamiliar place. You come across a tribe of people who speak a language that is wholly unknown to you. You try to write a translation manual that translates sentences of their language into English. They say "Gavagai!" when a rabbit scurries by. What does that translate into, in English? "There goes a rabbit!"? At first, that seems reasonable. After all, that's what you'd probably say if you retained your mastery of English but found yourself in the position of the person saying "Gavagai!"

But then you realize that there are other possibilities—for example, "There goes an undetached part of a rabbit!" and "There goes a temporal stage in a rabbit's life history!" And you remind yourself that you're concerned with what the people of the tribe mean, not with what you yourself might have said. Still, you think, it was an actual rabbit that scurried by, not merely an undetached rabbit part or a rabbit stage. But then you remember two other things. First, the translation manual should concern "Gavagai!" as that sentence is used generally, not just on this one occasion. For that reason, you shouldn't assume that the fact that there was actually a rabbit present plays an essential role in determining the sentence's meaning. The same sentence might be prompted by, for example, seeing a cleverly disguised fake rabbit. Second, you're concerned with meaning in an objective, scientific sense. You realize that, as Quine (1960, p. 31) puts it, the relevant stimulus for the utterance of "Gavagai!" is "the pattern of chromatic irradiation of the eye" that the rabbit-sighting caused in the person you are observing—a pattern that might as easily have been caused by a fake rabbit. That stimulus, you recognize, is equally compatible with translating "Gavagai!" as "There goes a rabbit!", "There goes an undetached part of a rabbit!", or "There goes a temporal stage in a rabbit's life history!" (among many other candidates). And, from an objective, scientific viewpoint, the translation-relevant evidence includes only patterns of stimuli and verbal response. Thus, you conclude, there is no fact of the matter about which is *the* correct translation. All of the candidates are equally correct.

Can you pin down the meaning by making more empirical observations of the tribe-members' linguistic behavior? Initially, that might seem promising. Suppose you surmise that their expression "Bleeg" corresponds to the English expression "is the same as." You get the rabbit to scurry by a few more times, and you notice that they say "Bleeg Gavagai!" when it does. Could you then rule out that they mean "There goes a rabbit stage" by "Gavagai!"? Perhaps. After all, the rabbit stage you see this time is not the same rabbit stage that you saw before. But, on reflection, the very problem you tried to avoid now arises for "Bleeg." If you use only the objective evidence regarding stimulus and response as your guide, then you could equally translate "Bleeg" as "belongs with," for example. On reflection, you conclude, no further observations will solve the problem.

Quine uses considerations of that sort to conclude that meaning is indeterminate. That Quinean doctrine often goes under the heading of *the indeterminacy of translation*. But it is not just about translation or about unknown languages. It applies to all languages, including English. If the native speakers whose language you were studying tried to make a translation manual running from English to their language, they'd be led to exactly the same indeterminacy conclusions about English that you drew about their language. And, according to Quine and others, they (and you) would be right to draw those conclusions.

DISCUSSION

If linguistic meaning is indeterminate, then we ought to reject many propositions that we ordinarily take for granted. For example, ordinarily we do not think that what we refer to with our words is always indeterminate—as in the example noted above, where I seem to refer determinately to my friend Smith and the property of being tall with the words "Smith" and "is tall." But appearances can be deceiving, and in this case, according to Quine, they are.

Quine's indeterminacy doctrine has been highly influential. There has also been considerable push-back. Some criticize his argument. One well-known criticism is due to Noam Chomsky (1968). Quine's reasoning begins with a premise about underdetermination: the evidence you gather when you observe the tribe member's reaction to the rabbit doesn't determine which of your empirical hypotheses about the meaning of "Gavagai!" is correct. But, as Chomsky argues, from that premise, Quine's indeterminacy doctrine simply does not follow. Empirical hypotheses always go beyond the evidence. There are always multiple, inconsistent empirical hypotheses that are consistent with any set of observations. For example, there is an underdetermination by the evidence that physicists consider when they formulate empirical hypotheses. It does not follow that there is no fact of the matter regarding which hypothesis is correct. Likewise, according to Chomsky, in the case of linguistic meaning, Quine's premise—that the observable, empirical facts are consistent with multiple hypotheses about meaning—does not entail his indeterminacy of meaning doctrine.

In response, Quine could argue that Chomsky's objection assumes something that Quine rejects from the start: that there is something to the meaning of "Gavagai!" beyond the observable, objective facts concerning physical dispositions to respond to verbal stimuli. But some question the basis for Quine's rejection of that assumption.

A commonsense response to Quine's argument is to say, "Hey, I know what *my* words mean, at least sometimes." That response won't convince Quineans. They will complain that it assumes that meaning is at least partly a psychological matter, known by the speaker—and again, for Quine, meaning is not at all a psychological matter. Meaning is a matter of patterns of stimuli and response and is best understood from an objective, scientific viewpoint. You might well associate the words you use with psychological states you have. But those states do not figure directly in linguistic meaning. Instead, their linguistic role is only to produce responses to relevant stimuli.

Nevertheless, some (Searle 1983, Blackburn 1984, Glock 2003) defend versions of that commonsense response. For example, according to John Searle, Quine's argument is best regarded as a *reductio ad absurdum* (that is, a reduction to absurdity) of the assumptions on which it is based. As noted above (in the background section), Quine's argument begins with the behaviorist assumption that linguistic meaning is entirely a non-psychological matter, and instead concerns objective facts about physical dispositions to respond to external stimuli. Given that assumption, Quine's indeterminacy doctrine does indeed follow.

But that just shows that we should reject the assumption. If we accepted the indeterminacy doctrine, then distinctions that we know independently to be perfectly legitimate would be undermined. For example, we know independently that there is a difference between the tribe-member's meaning *rabbit* and her meaning *rabbit stage*. Yet, under Quine's behaviorist assumption, that difference disappears. Or at least the difference would not be even partly based, as it plainly is, on psychological facts about the person you observed saying "Gavagai!" and other native speakers of the language you're studying.

Quine (1969) recognizes that such consequences of his doctrine can seem absurd, especially when one applies it to one's own words. In response to that sort of worry, he appeals to another doctrine: the *relativity* of meaning and reference. In physics, a particle has a position and a velocity not in any absolute sense but only relative to a coordinate system. In Quine's view, the same is true of meaning and reference. As he puts it, "Reference *is* nonsense except relative to a coordinate system" (1969, p. 47), where a "coordinate system" is provided by a specific language, such as English. But does that analogy address the worry? In physics, the position and velocity of a particle consists entirely in its relations to a coordinate system. By contrast, there seems to be more to meaning than just the relations a term has to the language of which it is a part. Of course, which particular meaning a word has is relative to a language. For example, the word "gift" means present relative to English, but it means poison relative to German. Likewise, "rabbit" means rabbit only relative to English. But meaning itself does not seem to be language-dependent. When we ask whether there is a translation of "rabbit" into some other language, we are asking precisely whether there is a term in that other language with the same (language-independent) meaning.

Is rejecting behaviorism enough to undermine the case for Quine's indeterminacy doctrine? Many philosophers who reject behaviorism accept that doctrine, or something close to it. A prominent example is Donald Davidson. Although Davidson rejects behaviorism about mental states, he maintains a related view about semantics—that is, linguistic meaning. As he puts it, "The semantic features of language are public features" (1979/1984, p. 235). According to Davidson, no element of meaning can be a private matter, to which an individual speaker has privileged access—even when it comes to the words that she herself uses on a particular occasion. Instead, meaning (semantics) is a function of only publicly observable facts. And, plausibly enough, the publicly observable facts might not determine that when I say "rabbit" I mean rabbit rather than rabbit stage. But once again, that leaves us with a choice. We could accept that meaning and reference are indeterminate, and concede that this is true even of one's own words. Or we could take Davidson's reasoning to show that his starting assumption, that meaning is a function of only publicly observable facts, is false.

The choice has consequences. If we make the latter choice, rejecting the bases for Quinean indeterminacy doctrines, then we take the first-person perspective of individual speakers to play some vital role in determining meaning (Kripke 1977, Searle 1983). And it is not entirely clear what that role is. If we make the former choice, siding with Quine and Davidson, then different questions arise. Quine and Davidson do not simply accept indeterminacy and leave it at that. Their approach leads to positive projects. In light of indeterminacy, how can we attribute meaning to the words we and others use? Many who take a Quinean approach, including Quine himself, propose constraints on translation and interpretation, such as the principle of charity. Roughly, good translations should maximize agreement between us and the people whose language we are translating. David Lewis (1974) adds several other constraints, such as a rationalization principle: speakers should be interpreted as rational agents. And those are just a few of the consequences.

RECOMMENDED READING

CANONICAL PRESENTATION

Quine, Willard V. O. 1960. *Word and Object*. Cambridge, MA: MIT Press. (See Chapter 2.)

OVERVIEW

Khani, Ali Hossein. 2021. "The Indeterminacy of Translation and Radical Interpretation." *Internet Encyclopedia of Philosophy*. https://iep.utm.edu/indeterm/.

ADDITIONAL DISCUSSIONS

Blackburn, Simon. 1984. *Spreading the Word*. Oxford: Oxford University Press.
Chomsky, Noam. 1968. "Quine's Empirical Assumptions." *Synthese* 19: 53–68.

Davidson, Donald. 1979. "The Inscrutability of Reference." *Southwestern Journal of Philosophy* 10 (2): 7–19. Reprinted in *Inquiries into Truth and Interpretation*. New York: Oxford University Press, 1984: 227–41.

Glock, Hans-Johann. 2003. *Quine and Davidson on Language, Thought, and Reality*. Cambridge: Cambridge University Press.

Kripke, Saul A. 1977. "Speaker's Reference and Semantic Reference." *Midwest Studies in Philosophy* 2: 255–76.

Lewis, David K. 1974. "Radical Interpretation." *Synthese* 23: 331–44.

Putnam. Hilary 1974. "The Refutation of Conventionalism." *Noûs* 8 (1): 25–40

Quine, Willard Van Orman. 1969. "Ontological Relativity." In *Ontological Relativity and Other Essays*. New York: Columbia University Press.

Quine, Willard Van Orman. 1987. "Indeterminacy of Translation Again." *Journal of Philosophy* 84 (1): 5–10.

Searle, John. 1983. *Intentionality: An Essay in the Philosophy of Mind*. Cambridge: Cambridge University Press.

Soames, Scott. 1999. "The Indeterminacy of Translation and the Inscrutability of Reference." *Canadian Journal of Philosophy* 29 (3): 321–70.

Wright, Crispin. 1999. "The Indeterminacy of Translation." In Bob Hale and Crispin Wright (eds.) *A Companion to the Philosophy of Language*. Oxford: Wiley-Blackwell: Chapter 16.

SWAMPMAN

BACKGROUND

Many (perhaps all) mental states have representational content, also known as intentionality or aboutness (see Chapters 18 and 19). For example, consider Jones's belief that grass is green. Her belief is about grass and about being green. It also represents a proposition: the proposition that grass is green. That proposition is the representational content of her belief, in that her belief is true if and only if grass is, in fact, green. Why do mental states have the representational content they have? Why do they have representational content at all? This can seem mysterious, especially from a naturalistic perspective on which mental states are parts of the natural, physical world. For example, considered as a physical object, a photograph is nothing more than an arrangement of molecules, and molecules do not appear to be about anything. And, from a naturalistic perspective, the same would seem to be true of mental states. Teleological theories of content aim to dispel that mystery by showing how mental content derives from non-mental aspects of nature. According to such theories, mental content depends at least partly on functions of the things (or systems) that use or produce those contents. And such functions are usually understood in terms of natural selection (or a related process), roughly as what the thing in question was selected for. A classic source for this sort of view is Ruth Millikan's *Language, Thought and Other Biological Categories* (1984). One consequence of Millikan's view is that a subject's mental content depends on their evolutionary history. But what if a creature has no evolutionary history? Could it have mental contents? If so, how? And what would determine which contents they have?

THE CASE

Donald is an ordinary human being. Or rather, he was until one fateful day, when he was visiting a swamp that was struck by lightning. The lightning simultaneously caused two things to happen. It vaporized Donald's body and it transformed a nearby dead tree into an exact replica of him, known as Swampman. Swampman is physically and behaviorally indistinguishable from Donald. If you ask Swampman his name, or to explain his beliefs, he answers just as Donald would have. If you compare a scan of his brain at the moment he was created and a scan of Donald's brain a moment before he was vaporized, you will see no difference (other than the time stamp). Further, the remarkable similarity between Swampman and Donald is entirely a coincidence—an astronomically improbable coincidence, but that is exactly what happened.

Prior to the lightning bolt, Donald has the range of states with representational content that other normal human adults have, including beliefs, desires, perceptual experiences, and various other mental states. On teleological theories, his states have such content at least partly because of historical factors. Consider a simple example. Some of his mental states, such as his belief that grass is green, are about greenness. The explanation for this, according to teleological theories, is partly that he has experiences (or brain states) of a type that have historically co-varied with encounters with green-colored objects; such states have thus made contributions to human evolution. The details of such an explanation are complex and controversial. But, on all teleological theories, etiological/historical factors play a central role. And therein lies the problem posed by this thought experiment.

There would appear to be strong intuitive reasons to conclude that Swampman has mental states with content—for example, a belief that grass is green. If asked, he will say that grass is green. And if he tries to visualize green grass, his imaginative experience will feel just like Donald's would if Donald tried to visualize green grass. Intuitively, like Donald, Swampman has a belief, and his belief is about grass and greenness. But how could that be if teleological theories are correct? Unlike Donald, Swampman has no evolutionary history. No aspect of Swampman's mental life can be correctly described as having co-varied with encounters with green-colored objects (or with anything else). Factors that play a central role on teleological theories are absent. So, it is hard to see how those theories could be correct.

The Swampman case presents a similar challenge to a view about consciousness known as *representationalism* (also known as *intentionalism*). Earlier we noted that, at least from a naturalistic perspective, it can seem mysterious how mental states can represent (or be about) anything. We also noted that teleological theories of content promise to dispel that mystery, explaining mental representation in naturalistic (e.g., causal/historical) terms. Some suggest that those theories can also dispel another widely discussed mystery: how to explain the phenomenal, or "what it is like", aspect of conscious experience (Harman 1990, Dretske 1995, Tye 2000, Jackson 2003; and see Part I). These scholars' suggestion combines two ideas. The first is representationalism about phenomenal character, the view that a mental state's phenomenal character consists entirely in its representational character—that is, in how that state represents the world (this can include both representational content and the way that content is represented). The second is to apply teleological/co-variational theories to the representational character in which, according to representationalism, phenomenal character consists. The idea here is to explain this representational character in terms of naturalistic considerations about teleology and co-variation.

That suggestion might seem promising. Phenomenal character might not seem so baffling if it can be identified with a phenomenon that can be explained naturalistically. But again, the naturalistic explanation in question relies on teleological theories of mental content, and the Swampman example threatens to undermine those theories. Representationalists who accept teleological/co-variational accounts of representation would appear to be committed to denying that Swampman has phenomenal consciousness. In other words, their view seems to entail that Swampman does not feel anything—that there is nothing it's like for him to see green, for example. That might seem even more counterintuitive than the idea that Swampman has no beliefs.

DISCUSSION

The Swampman example first appeared in Donald Davison's 1987 article "Knowing One's Own Mind." But Swampman-like challenges to teleological theories had previously been discussed in the literature (Boorse 1976, Millikan 1984). Such challenges stem from the fact that, intuitively, having mental states with representational content seems compatible with the absence of the historical factors that teleological theories emphasize in their explanation of such content.

Some respond to the challenge by rejecting the historical/etiological component of such theories while retaining the teleological component (Schroeder 2004, Nanay 2014, Bauer 2017, Piccinini 2020). In other words, they explain representational content in functional terms, but give up on the attempt to explain a thing's function in terms of historical factors such as historical co-variation. For example, Bence Nanay proposes that, roughly put, a certain trait has a certain function F if and only if F would contribute to the relevant organism's fitness—whether or not F has served this function in the past (but see Artiga 2014, Garson 2019; and for other theories of representational content in which such historical factors do not play a central role, see Pautz 2021 and Siewert 1998).

Others respond to the challenge by rejecting the intuitive judgment that Swampman has mental states with content. Here the burden is to explain why we might naturally have the intuition in a way that is consistent with the intuitive judgment being false. Karen Neander (1991) tries to meet that burden by arguing that, even if our intuitions about real cases have some measure of reliability, the Swampman case is hypothetical and unrealistic. Neander (1996) and others, including Millikan (1996), also argue that our intuitions about Swampman might be no more trustworthy than analogous intuitions that have been proven false. For example, consider the proposition that there could be water without H_2O. It is widely accepted that there is no such possibility. Water could not exist without H_2O because water *is* H_2O (Kripke 1972, Putnam 1975). There could be a substance with all the superficial features of water—something that is indistinguishable from water if one does not examine it with a microscope, say.

But that would not be water. Similarly, Neander, Millikan, and others argue, although Swampman could exist, he would not have mental states with representational content. That is because what it *is* to have such states is (partly) to have states with a history of co-varying with certain environmental factors, features that his states lack. In other words, we should not expect intuition to reveal the true nature of representational content any more than intuition reveals the true nature of water. Swampman himself would probably be surprised to discover that his words don't refer to anything. But, according to Neander, Millikan, and others, that is true nonetheless.

Lastly, some argue that, on reflection, the possibility of Swampman existing with representational mentality is compatible with the teleological theories in question. For example, some argue that the relevant theories concern only actual cases, and so merely hypothetical cases are irrelevant (Papineau 2001). And some argue that the teleological theories in question make the historical account of representational content conditional on features that ordinarily obtain—features that are absent in Swampman cases. Michael Tye (2000) uses the latter strategy to defend representationalism about phenomenal content from a Swampman-type objection. He notes that representationalism's appeal to a causal co-variational account involves a *ceteris paribus* ("other things being equal") clause. Scientific generalizations often include such clauses, sometimes implicitly. For example, the generalization "Mixing an acid and a base produces salt" is not falsified by the fact that in non-optimal circumstances—e.g., the beaker containing the acid and the base is dropped before salt could be formed—mixing an acid and a base does not produce salt. Likewise, Tye argues, representationalism's co-variational account is not falsified by the fact that in non-optimal circumstances, such as in the Swampman case, one could have representational states that have no history of co-varying with what they are about. As Tye (2000, p. 137) writes, "In these cases, *ceteris* is not *paribus*."

RECOMMENDED READING

CANONICAL PRESENTATION

Davidson, Donald. 1987. "Knowing One's Own Mind." *Proceedings and Addresses of the American Philosophical Association* 60: 441–58.

OVERVIEW

Schulte, Peter, and Neander, Karen. 2022. "Teleological Theories of Mental Content." *The Stanford Encyclopedia of Philosophy* (Summer 2022 Edition), Edward N. Zalta (ed.), URL = <https://plato.stanford.edu/archives/sum2022/entries/content-teleological/>.

ADDITIONAL DISCUSSIONS

Dretske, Fred. 1995. *Naturalizing the Mind*. Cambridge, MA: MIT Press.
Harman, Gilbert. 1990. "The Intrinsic Quality of Experience." *Philosophical Perspectives* 4: 31–52.
Jackson, Frank. 2003. "Mind and Illusion." In A. O'Hear (ed.) *Minds and Persons: Royal Institute of Philosophy Supplement* 53. New York: Cambridge University Press: 251–71.
Kripke, Saul. 1972. "Naming and Necessity." In D. Davidson and G. Harman (eds.) *Semantics of Natural Language*. Dordrecht: Reidel: 253–5.
Millikan, Ruth. 1984. *Language, Thought and Other Biological Categories*. Cambridge, MA: MIT Press.
Millikan, Ruth. 1996. "On Swampkinds." *Mind and Language* 11 (1): 70–130.
Nanay, Bence. 2014. "Teleosemantics without Etiology." *Philosophy of Science* 81: 798–810.
Neander, Karen. 1996. "Swampman meets Swampcow." *Mind and Language* 11(1): 70–130.
Papineau, David. 2001. "The Status of Teleosemantics, or How to Stop Worrying about Swampman." *Australasian Journal of Philosophy* 79: 279–89.
Putnam, Hilary. 1975. "The Meaning of 'Meaning'." *Minnesota Studies in the Philosophy of Science*, 7. Reprinted in his *Mind, Language, and Reality: Philosophical Papers Volume 2*. New York: Cambridge University Press: 215–71.
Tye, M. 2000. *Consciousness, Color, and Content*. Cambridge, MA: MIT Press.

OTHER REFERENCES

Artiga, M. 2014. "The Modal Theory of Functions Is Not about Functions." *Philosophy of Science* 81: 580–591.
Bauer, M. 2017. "Ahistorical Teleosemantics: An Alternative to Nanay." *Southern Journal of Philosophy* 55 (2): 158–76.
Boorse, C. 1976, "Wright on Functions." *Philosophical Review* 85: 70–86.
Garson, J. 2019. "There Are No Ahistorical Theories of Function." *Philosophy of Science* 86: 1146–56.
Neander, Karen. 1991. "Functions as Selected Effects." *Philosophy of Science* 58: 168–84.
Pautz, Adam. 2021. *Perception*. Abingdon: Routledge.
Piccinini, G. 2020. *Neurocognitive Mechanisms*. Oxford: Oxford University Press.

Schroeder, T. 2004. "New Norms for Teleosemantics." In H. Clapin, P. Staines, and P. Slezak (eds.) *Representation in Mind: New Approaches to Mental Representation*. Amsterdam: Elsevier: 91–106.

Siewert, Charles. 1998. *The Significance of Consciousness*. Princeton: Princeton University Press.

TWIN EARTH AND ARTHRITIS MAN

BACKGROUND

Some mental states are *propositional attitudes*: attitudes (such as belief or doubt) toward propositions (such as the proposition that grass is green). One can believe that grass is green, hope that grass is green, desire that grass is green, etc. The relevant propositions are sometimes described as mental contents, which in turn are often described as containing concepts or notions, such as the concept of being green.

Features of one's environment often causally influence which propositions one believes, desires, etc. For example, seeing grass typically causes one to form beliefs about it. But do the contents that figure into one's propositional attitudes depend constitutively on one's environment? That is, are features of the environment part of the nature of one's propositional attitudes? According to *internalism* (also known as *individualism*), the answer is no. In principle, one might have exactly the same mental states even if one's external environment were radically different—indeed, even if it were some sort of illusion. Tyler Burge (1979, 1982) disagrees. He argues for *externalism* (his term for this view is "anti-individualism").

DOI: 10.4324/9781003179191-29

Externalism might seem easy to establish. Suppose at noon Alfred is looking at an apple. He believes it to be wholesome, and his belief is true: the apple is indeed wholesome. A minute later, when he looks away for a few seconds, the wholesome apple is replaced with a rotten one, which looks the same from the outside. Alfred turns back toward the apple but doesn't notice the change. We might describe him as having different belief contents at noon and at 12:01. After all, his earlier belief is true and his later belief is false. Even so, his internal states remain constant (in relevant respects). But, as Burge (1982) argues, Alfred could equally well be described as having the same belief content at both times, just applied (unwittingly) to two distinct apples. So, this case does not adequately establish externalism.

Burge's argument for externalism is more subtle. He appeals to two thought experiments. One is Twin Earth, a case originally devised by Hilary Putnam (1975) for a related purpose (Putnam was concerned with the reference of terms, whereas Burge is concerned with the contents of mental states). The other is Burge's own (1979) arthritis case.

THE CASES

Putnam (1975) imagines a near duplicate of our planet Earth, which he calls *Twin Earth*. There is one key difference: on Twin Earth, the liquid that runs through the rivers and faucets, and which is called "water" in the language some Twin Earth inhabitants call "English," is not H_2O. Their liquid has an entirely different chemical composition, XYZ—where X, Y, and Z are elements not presently known to us. Putnam claims that the liquid on Twin Earth is not water, despite the superficial similarity it bears to water. Burge agrees: it is what we might call *twin-water* instead. Putnam's and Burge's view about water and "twater" is widely shared. Water is a *natural kind*—a kind found in nature, which was not human-made. The fundamental nature of such a natural kind is determined not by superficial qualities, such as how it appears to humans, but rather by the underlying, more basic features, such as chemical composition.

Suppose Amari is an Earthling who doesn't know that water is H_2O. Now consider her Twin Earth counterpart, $Amari_{TE}$. Amari and $Amari_{TE}$ are duplicates in many respects. Their behavioral dispositions, their inner functional states, and their qualitative conscious states are indistinguishable. They are also physically indistinguishable, save for the fact that Amari's body contains water and Amari$_{TE}$'s contains twin-water. (As Burge notes, that last difference can be set aside since he could as easily have made the case about aluminum and twin-aluminum, mackerel, and twin-mackerel, etc.; and with those examples Amari and Amari$_{TE}$ would be fully physically indistinguishable.) In short, they are indistinguishable from the skin in, insofar as those features are described non-intentionally—that is, without reference to what their mental states represent.

What should we say about the mental states of Amari and Amari$_{TE}$? Suppose Amari and Amari$_{TE}$ have a belief that they might verbally express by saying: "I believe that water is refreshing." Amari's belief is about water, whereas Amari$_{TE}$'s belief is about twin-water. But do their beliefs have the same propositional content, just applied to different substances? Do they involve the same concepts? According to internalism, the answer is *yes*, for there is no relevant difference between individualistic features of Amari and her counterpart. According to Burge, the correct answer is *no*. Amari and Amari$_{TE}$ believe distinct propositions, which contain distinct concepts. The proposition Amari believes contains the concept of water, whereas the proposition Amari$_{TE}$ believes contains the concept of twin-water. Thus, Burge concludes, internalism is false.

The difference in mental content between Amari and Amari$_{TE}$ would seem to derive from differences in their *physical* environments. But Burge (1979) argues that mental content can constitutively depend on features of one's *social* environment as well. To show this, he considers a series of cases, one of which involves arthritis, a disease that can only occur in joints. Imagine someone who has a wide range of unsurprising attitudes about arthritis, such as the belief that the arthritis in his wrists and fingers is more painful than the arthritis in his ankles. But he also thinks that he has developed arthritis in his thigh—something his doctor might tell him is not possible since the thigh is not a joint. Derek Ball (2009) calls this fellow "Arthritis-man."

Now imagine a counterfactual situation in which Arthritis-man is the same as he actually is in all individualistic respects, just like Amari and Amari$_{TE}$. But, in the counterfactual situation, physicians, lexicographers, and informed non-experts apply the term "arthritis" not only to arthritis but also to various other ailments, some of which can occur in thighs. According to Burge, Arthritis-man and his counterpart have different mental contents. Arthritis-man's actual contents (the propositions he believes) contain the concept of arthritis. Yet, in the counterfactual situation, his contents contain a distinct concept—the concept of "tharthritis." Internalism is again refuted. But this time, the relevant environmental features are social.

In both the actual and counterfactual situations, Arthritis-man would describe what he means by "arthritis" in the same way (at least prior to when his doctor informs him that arthritis cannot occur in the thigh—something that would not happen in the counterfactual situation). Nevertheless, the concepts involved in the two situations are distinct. Initially, this might sound odd. How could one be mistaken about one's own concepts? But, on reflection, it isn't so odd. One can possess a concept incompletely, that is, without fully understanding what it does and does not apply to—a position many of us are in with respect to concepts like "fruit" and "vegetable" (which category should tomato go in?). Indeed, having incomplete mastery of our own concepts is quite common. Burge (2007) describes the idea that one might possess a concept without completely understanding it as the pivot on which his arthritis thought experiment turns. And if his analysis of that or the Twin Earth thought experiment is correct, then the content of one's mental states cannot be cleanly separated from specific features of one's environment in the way that internalism entails.

DISCUSSION

In the wake of Burge's argument, externalism has become widely held. But not everyone is convinced. Some critics respond by challenging Burge's argument. One move is to say that Arthritis-man's beliefs don't involve the concept of a disease that can't apply to a thigh condition (Crane 1991, Georgalis 1999, Wikforss 2001). Burge's mistake is merely linguistic: he falsely believes that the public-language term "arthritis" expresses *his* concept, rather than the more restrictive concept it actually expresses. Burge anticipates that move and gives several replies. For example, Arthritis-man and his doctor share some beliefs—such as the belief that he has arthritis in his ankles. And Burge argues that denying that Arthritis-man has the arthritis concept makes shared beliefs difficult to explain.

Other critics of Burge challenge his assumption that our reactions to thought experiments should carry as much weight as he suggests they should (Cummins 1991, Chomsky 1995). Still others raise problems concerning the distinction between "internal" and "external" properties—a distinction on which the debate about internalism rests. Brie Gertler (2012) argues that the standard ways of explicating that distinction all fail. For example, on one standard explication, the distinction is spatial: internal properties are properties instantiated within the subject's skin, brain, or head; and external properties are properties not instantiated within the subject's skin, brain, or head. But then what about Descartes? Descartes, a dualist, would deny that mental content depends only on such spatially internal properties, since he doesn't see mental contents as being specifiable in spatial terms. He therefore comes out as an externalist. But, as Gertler notes, Descartes is standardly regarded as the archetypal internalist, particularly in light of his famous "Evil Demon" thought experiment, according to which we might have all the same beliefs even if an Evil Demon was tricking us into thinking there was an external world. In Gertler's view, the situation is irremediable. She recommends abandoning the internalism/externalism debate.

Another common response is to distinguish between two kinds of content: *narrow* and *wide*. For example, the propositional attitudes of Amari and Amari$_{TE}$ share the same narrow content but differ with respect to wide content. On one version of this response (Fodor 1987), the narrow/wide distinction roughly corresponds to the distinction Burge draws when considering the example of Alfred's apples: the distinction between mental content itself and the application of that content to phenomena in one's environment (for criticisms of that version, see Burge 1982, Stalnaker 1989, Block 1991). But on other versions, the Twin Earth and Arthritis-man cases really do involve two kinds of mental content, as opposed to one kind, applied differently: the narrow kind, which all intrinsic duplicates share; and the wide kind, which is the kind Burge identifies—content that depends constitutively on extrinsic, environmental features. The narrow/wide distinction remains controversial. For example, Yli-Vakkuri and Hawthorne (2018) argue that there is no viable notion of narrow content.

The range of mental states to which externalism applies is also disputed. Burge argues that the range is considerable. Mental contents often contain concepts that are, as it is sometimes put, *Twin Earth-able*: concepts that pick out different things in different environments. Twin Earth-able concepts include at least concepts of many natural kinds (kinds found in nature, such as perhaps water, elm trees, and tigers), artifacts (human-made things), and much else. Arguably, not all concepts are Twin Earth-able. For example, it's hard to see how to tell a Twin Earth story about the concept of a friend or the concept of a philosopher. Another potential exception is the concept of phenomenal consciousness, such as pain (Burge 2003, Veillet 2012; but see Ball 2009, Tye 2009).

Externalism is interesting in itself. But it also might have significant implications for several philosophical issues, including mental causation, self-knowledge, and the mind–body problem, among others. Regarding mental causation: beliefs and desires, including those whose contents Burge's arguments concern, are commonly thought to play important roles in the causal explanation of action (see Chapter 12). But some argue that such causal explanations should appeal only to internal features of an individual. Environmental features would then seem to be irrelevant (Stich 1983, Pereboom 1995; but see Burge 1993, Dretske 1988). Regarding self-knowledge (see Chapter 47): if externalism is true, then how can we know the contents of our own beliefs and desires (Burge 1993)? For example, how does Amari know her belief contents concern water rather than twin-water? And, regarding the mind–body problem: some argue that externalism challenges important theories about the mental–physical relationship, such as the mind–brain identity theory. That is because, on that theory, mental states are construed as brain states, which are themselves understood as intrinsic features of individuals (Baker 1987; but see MacDonald 1990). And some argue that externalism has strong implications for widely discussed arguments against physicalism, such as the knowledge argument (Ball 2009, Tye 2009; but see Alter 2013 and Chapter 6).

RECOMMENDED READING

CANONICAL PRESENTATIONS

Burge, Tyler. 1979. "Individualism and the Mental." *Midwest Studies in Philosophy* 4: 73–121.

Burge, Tyler. 1982. "Other Bodies." In A. Woodfield (ed.) *Thought and Object: Essays on Intentionality*. Oxford: Clarendon: 97–120.

OVERVIEW

Rowlands, Mark, Lau, Joe, and Deutsch, Max. 2020. "Externalism about the Mind." *The Stanford Encyclopedia of Philosophy* (Winter 2020 Edition), Edward N. Zalta (ed.), URL = <https://plato.stanford.edu/archives/win2020/entries/content-externalism/>.

ADDITIONAL DISCUSSIONS

Block, Ned. 1991. "What Narrow Content Is Not." In B. Loewer and G. Rey (eds.) *Meaning and Mind: Fodor and His Critics*. Oxford: Blackwell: 33–64.
Burge, Tyler. 1988. "Individualism and Self-Knowledge." *Journal of Philosophy* 85: 649–63.
Burge, Tyler. 2007. "Postscript to 'Individualism and the Mental'". In his *Foundations of Mind*. New York: Oxford University Press: 151–81.
Fodor, Jerry A. 1987. *Psychosemantics: The Problem of Meaning in the Philosophy of Mind*. Cambridge, MA: MIT Press.
Georgalis, Nicholas 1999. "Rethinking Burge's Thought Experiment." *Synthese* 118 (2): 145–64.
Gertler, Brie. 2012. "Understanding the Internalism–Externalism Debate: What Is the Boundary of the Thinker?" *Philosophical Perspectives* 26 (1): 51–75.
Pereboom, Derk. 1995. "Conceptual Structure and the Individuation of Content." *Philosophical Perspectives* 9: 401–26.
Pessin, Andrew, and Goldberg, Sanford (eds.). 1996. *The Twin Earth Chronicles: Twenty Years of Reflection on Hilary Putnam's "The Meaning of 'Meaning'"*. Armonk, NY: Sharpe.
Putnam, Hilary. 1975. "The Meaning of 'Meaning'." In K. Gunderson (ed.) *Language, Mind, and Knowledge: Minnesota Studies in the Philosophy of Science, Volume 7*. Minneapolis: University of Minnesota Press: 139–93.
Stalnaker, Robert. 1989. "On What's in the Head." *Philosophical Perspectives* 3: 287–316.
Stich, Stephen. 1983. *From Folk Psychology to Cognitive Science: The Case Against Belief*. Cambridge, MA: MIT Press.
Yli-Vakkuri, Juhani, and Hawthorne, John. 2018. *Narrow Content*. Oxford: Oxford University Press.

OTHER REFERENCES

Alter, Torin. 2013. "Social Externalism and the Knowledge Argument." *Mind* 122: 481–96.
Baker, Lynn R. 1987. *Saving Belief: A Critique of Physicalism*. Princeton: Princeton University Press.

Ball, Derek. 2009. "There are No Phenomenal Concepts." *Mind* 118: 935–62.

Burge, Tyler. 1993. "Mind–Body Causation and Explanatory Practice." In J. Heil and A. Mele (eds.) *Mental Causation*. Oxford: Clarendon: 97–120.

Burge, Tyler. 2003. "Qualia and Intentional Content: Reply to Block." In M. Hahn and B. Ramberg (eds.) *Reflections and Replies: Essays on the Philosophy of Tyler Burge*. Cambridge, MA: MIT Press: 405–16.

Chomsky, Noam. 1995. "Language and Nature." *Mind* 104 (413): 1–61.

Crane, Timothy. 1991. "All the Difference in the World." *Philosophical Quarterly* 41 (162): 1–25.

Cummins, Robert. 1991. "Methodological Reflections on Belief." In. R. Bogan (ed.) *Mind and Common Sense*. Cambridge: Cambridge University Press: 53–70.

Dretske, Fred. 1988. *Explaining Behavior: Reasons in a World of Causes*. Cambridge, MA: MIT Press.

Macdonald, Cynthia. 1990. "Weak Externalism and Mind–Body Identity." *Mind* 99 (395): 387–404.

Tye, Michael. 2009. *Consciousness Revisited: Materialism without Phenomenal Concepts*. Cambridge, MA: MIT Press.

Veillet, Benedicte. 2012. "In Defense of Phenomenal Concepts." *Philosophical Papers* 41: 97–127.

Wikforss, Asa M. 2001. "Social Externalism and Conceptual Errors." *Philosophical Quarterly* 51 (203): 217–31.

OTTO'S NOTEBOOK

BACKGROUND

As we have seen in our discussion of Twin Earth and Arthritis Man (Chapter 25), philosophers who embrace externalism believe that our mental contents "extend" out into the world. According to externalism, which mental contents we have *depends constitutively* on what physical and social environment we are in—for example, whether the stuff that makes up our lakes and oceans is composed chemically of H_2O or some other chemical substance, such as XYZ. In the late 20th century, some philosophers began to embrace a more radical form of externalism on which the mental "extends" out into the world in a much stronger sense. Characterizing the externalism of philosophers such as Hilary Putnam (1975) and Tyler Burge (1979, 1982) as "passive," Andy Clark and David Chalmers (1998) put forth a more "active" externalist view on which the relevant worldly features come into play by driving—and even constituting—cognitive states and processes. The thought experiment discussed in this chapter aims to show that it is not just that mental content is constitutively determined by features of the external world: cognition itself sometimes resides in the external world. In other words, cognitive states themselves, such as memory states, can include external entities.

This claim is often referred to as *the extended mind thesis*. In recent years, the extended mind thesis has become associated with a larger research program known as *4E Cognition*—where the four E's stand for embodied, embedded, enactive, and extended.

THE CASE

Consider Inga, a resident of New York City. After hearing about a new exhibit at the Museum of Modern Art (MoMA), she is intrigued and decides to go see it. Having been to the Museum before, she pauses for a moment until she recalls that it is located on 53rd Street. She then heads in that direction.

Now, consider Otto, another resident of New York City. Otto is in the early stages of Alzheimer's disease, and he has developed various techniques to help him in his daily life. One such technique involves the use of a notebook where he writes down important information. He carries the notebook with him wherever he goes, is diligent about recording any new information in it, and consults it regularly throughout the day to look up information that he has already recorded in it. Like Inga, Otto is intrigued when he hears about the new exhibit at MoMA and decides to go see it. He pauses for a moment to consult his notebook, sees that the Museum is on 53rd Street, and therefore heads in that direction.

Both Inga and Otto want to go to the Museum. They also both believe that the Museum is on 53rd street. It's precisely because of this belief–desire pair that they each head in the relevant direction. But when did they acquire the belief about the location of the Museum?

With respect to Inga, the answer seems straightforward. She already had this belief prior to consulting her memory. The belief was not *occurrent*: she was not at that moment consciously thinking about its content. But at any given moment most of our beliefs are not occurrent. Presumably, most readers of this book have beliefs about who the current President of the United States is, or what city is the capital of France, or what kind of animal Dumbo is. But those beliefs were presumably not occurrent until you were prompted to call them to mind by reading this paragraph. Most of our beliefs remain stored in memory until they need to be accessed. They are *standing beliefs*. This is exactly how we would most naturally describe Inga's belief about the location of MoMA.

What about Otto? The process he goes through is, in most respects, exactly the same as Inga's. So, if we're prepared to grant that Inga believed that the Museum is on 53rd Street even before she consults her memory, why wouldn't we be prepared to grant that Otto believed that the Museum is on 53rd Street even before he consults his notebook? Sure, his belief wasn't occurrent at the time; but neither was Inga's. As Clark and Chalmers argue, the difference between Inga and Otto is not whether they had the belief, but in whether that belief is stored within the confines of skull and skin. Though Inga's beliefs are stored internally (note the "in" in "Inga"), Otto offloads his beliefs to external storage. Why should the location matter? The information that Inga stores in biological memory plays the same role for her that the information that Otto stores in his notebook plays for him. Remember, Otto is not merely a casual user of his notebook. He uses it consistently and relies on it completely. Insofar as we're inclined to accept that what makes something a belief is the causal-explanatory role that it plays in a cognitive system, it would be arbitrary to treat the case of Otto differently from the case of Inga. If something external to one's head, such as an inscription in a notebook, plays an appropriate causal-explanatory role, then, in Clark and Chalmers' view, it should qualify as a belief despite its location. It seems to follow that even before he consults his notebook, Otto believed that MoMA is on 53rd Street.

DISCUSSION

When Clark and Chalmers first published their theory, in 1998, smart devices were not yet in mass circulation. The first BlackBerry phones came out in 2002 and the iPhone followed in 2007. Our slavish reliance on these devices probably makes the case for the extended mind more compelling than it seemed two decades ago. When your sibling asks, "Do you know Mom's work number?" you might very well answer "yes" and pull out your phone to look it up in your contacts. In the 2020s, most of us no longer store our beliefs about phone numbers in our biological memory; rather, we store them in the non-biological memory of our phones. Just as Otto's mind extends out into the world to his notebook, our minds often seem to extend out into the world to our phones.

But at this point, a question arises. In light of the fact that we regularly carry our phones with us and use our phones the way that Otto uses his notebook, does that mean that *any* information contained on someone's phone counts as one of their beliefs? At any given time, someone could easily Google the population of Fresno or the recipe for figgy pudding. Does that mean that they count as having beliefs about these facts?

To guard against this kind of implausible result, Clark and Chalmers suggest four conditions that must be met in order for an external storage device to count as part of the mind and for the information stored in it to count as a standing belief. Where S is the subject and D is the relevant device:

1. D must be consistently and reliably available, and it must be typically called upon by S.
2. The information in D is easily accessible to S when it is needed.
3. S automatically endorses information from D.
4. The information is present in D because it was consciously endorsed by S in the past.

It's condition (4) that rules out newly Googled information counting as someone's standing belief. That information need not have ever been consciously endorsed by that individual.

The linchpin of Clark and Chalmers' argument consists in two claims. First is a claim often referred to as *the parity principle*: anything that plays the same causal-explanatory role as a standing belief is itself a standing belief. Second is a claim about Otto: the information in Otto's notebook plays the same causal-explanatory role as that played by standing beliefs stored within his brain. While the first claim is widely accepted (at least by those who endorse functionalism about belief; see Chapters 15 and 16), the second claim has frequently come under attack by critics.

In arguing against the second claim, critics often point to what seems like a salient difference between the information in Otto's notebook and standing beliefs stored in the brain: Otto accesses his notebook via perception; but he accesses standing beliefs by way of introspection. Other differences that also seem salient include the fact that Otto's notebook can easily be tampered with (much more easily than a brain can be tampered with), and the fact that Otto's notebook might be shared with someone else. Neither of those claims seems to hold of internal beliefs. In each case, Clark and Chalmers try to suggest that these differences are only "shallow" ones: Yes, they are differences, but they are not the kind of differences that make a difference to the causal-explanatory role played by the belief.

Another difference that can't be dismissed so easily concerns belief revision. Normally, when we learn new information, we adjust our other beliefs accordingly, and these adjustments happen automatically. But this doesn't seem true of the records in Otto's notebook. It's a fairly painstaking process to make all of the relevant adjustments each time he learns something new. We might put this point by saying that internal beliefs, unlike the notebook, are *informationally integrated* (see Weiskopf 2008).

A different way to attack Clark and Chalmers' conclusion has been proposed by Brie Gertler (2007). Though Gertler grants the claim that Otto's notebook might be seen as playing the same role as standing beliefs, she denies that standing beliefs are part of the mind. On her view, the mind consists only of occurrent states and conscious processes. Fundamental to her conception of mental states is their *introspectability*. In Gertler's view, standing states are not introspectable; when we introspect them, they become occurrent. She concludes that standing beliefs are, though internal, not part of the mind—and likewise for the records in Otto's notebook.

RECOMMENDED READING

CANONICAL PRESENTATION

Clark, Andy, and Chalmers, David J. 1998. "The Extended Mind." *Analysis* 58 (1): 7–19.

OVERVIEW

Menary, Richard (ed.). 2010. *The Extended Mind*. Cambridge, MA: MIT Press.

ADDITIONAL DISCUSSIONS

Burge, Tyler. 1979. "Individualism and the Mental." *Midwest Studies in Philosophy* 4: 73–121.

Burge, Tyler. 1982. "Other Bodies." In A. Woodfield (ed.) *Thought and Object: Essays on Intentionality*. Oxford: Clarendon: 97–120.

Clark, Andy. 2003. *Natural-Born Cyborgs: Minds, Technologies, and the Future of Human Intelligence*. New York: Oxford University Press.

Colombo, Matteo, Irvine, Elizabeth, and Stapleton, Mog (eds.). 2019. *Andy Clark and his Critics*. New York: Oxford University Press.

Farkas, Katalin. 2012. "Two Versions of the Extended Mind Thesis." *Philosophia* 40 (3): 435–47.

Gertler, Brie. 2007. "Overextending the Mind." In Brie Gertler and Lawrence Shapiro (eds.) *Arguing about the Mind*. Abingdon: Routledge: 192–206.

Heersmink, Richard. 2020. "Extended Mind and Artifactual Autobiographical Memory." *Mind and Language* 36: 1–15.

Krickel, Beate. 2020. "Extended Cognition, the New Mechanists' Mutual Manipulability Criterion, and the Challenge of Trivial Extendedness." *Mind and Language* 35 (4):539–61.

Putnam, Hilary. 1975. "The Meaning of 'Meaning'." In K. Gunderson (ed.) *Language, Mind, and Knowledge: Minnesota Studies in the Philosophy of Science, Volume 7*. Minneapolis: University of Minnesota Press: 139–93.

Rupert, Robert. 2009. *Cognitive Systems and the Extended Mind*. Oxford: Oxford University Press.

Tollefson, Deborah P. 2006. "From Extended Mind to Collective Mind." *Cognitive Systems Research* 7 (2–3): 140–50.

Weiskopf, Daniel A. 2008. "Patrolling the Mind's Boundaries." *Erkenntnis* 68 (2): 265–76.

THE BRAIN IN A VAT

BACKGROUND

Almost all of our knowledge of the external world comes from our senses. I know there is a computer in front of me because I feel it, see it, and hear the keys click as I type. Descartes famously realized that all of these experiences could be replicated in a dream, and he wondered how he could be sure he wasn't dreaming. Even if he were dreaming, he realized, dreams merely imitate what he experiences in waking life. So, even if he couldn't be sure he was sitting by his fireplace, he could still feel confident that he *had* experienced a fireplace, or at least the warmth and colors that compose his experience of the fireplace. He moved on to a more troubling source of doubt, however. Suppose there was an evil demon fooling him at every turn, generating the sensations of warmth and the crackling of the fire. There would be no guarantee in that case that he had ever experienced such things, or even the qualities involved: It could all be a trick of the demon.

Descartes' thought experiments are commonly thought to have an *epistemological* upshot. Because you can't know you aren't fooled by an evil demon, you can't know much of anything. At least when it comes to the world you know by your senses, you could be systematically deceived. If you are being systematically deceived, then you merely *think* you are sitting at a desk reading a book because you have a series of sense impressions caused by a deceptive demon. There is no book and no desk.

But there are other ways to view Descartes' thought experiments. Berkeley, for example, can be seen as drawing a different moral. Put very roughly, Berkeley (1713) argues that there is nothing more to the "external world" than sense impressions, and that, viewed a certain way, the evil demon world isn't really a *skeptical* scenario at all. It's merely a world with a different metaphysical foundation than we thought. Instead of tables and chairs being constituted by mind-independent matter, they are constituted by the very ideas we have of them. They are just collections of ideas. We might say that, for Berkeley, the demon involved isn't *evil*—it is God, who has no interest in tricking us. But the crucial move is the claim that we're not necessarily being tricked at all in this scenario—the world of desks and chairs is simply constituted differently than we thought. This sort of approach has been explored more recently in connection with Putnam's (1981) brain in a vat thought experiment.

THE CASE

Though I use my hands to feel and my eyes to see, my conscious awareness is a result of signals from my sense organs traveling to my brain. I could, presumably, have this same conscious awareness if my brain were simply stimulated in the right way. I could, in fact, be a carefully preserved brain in a vat, hooked up to a computer that stimulated the same brain regions that are now (presumably) stimulated by signals from my eyes, ears, and other senses. Things would appear exactly the same way to me if I were a brain in a vat—a *BiV* for short. I would seem to see my pen and my desk, but there would be no such things; there would only be stimuli coming from a powerful computer. Since the world where I am a BiV is, to me, indistinguishable from the world where I am not a BiV, it seems we have a traditional skeptical scenario: I can't know I'm not a BiV, so I don't know I'm actually sitting at a desk in front of a computer.

Hilary Putnam argued that there is an answer to the BiV skeptical worry based on the way terms gain their meaning. The word "desk" is just a group of letters or sounds that don't mean anything intrinsically.

If a constellation of stars happened to look like an inscription of the word "desk," that constellation wouldn't thereby refer to desks. Terms gain their meaning by holding a causal connection to things in the world. And the arrangement of stars bears no relevant causal relation to desks. This *causal theory of reference* complicates the BiV scenario. Suppose I am a BiV. My word "desk" is not caused by desks. It is caused by the outputs of a computer program. Similarly, my words "brain" and "vat" are not caused by brains and vats. My statement "I am a brain in a vat" is therefore not true—whatever the words refer to, they don't refer to brains and vats. So it appears that, in some sense, uttering the sentence "I am a BiV" is self-defeating.

So far Putnam's argument is about language and the way words refer. But, arguably, the case can be extended to thoughts as well. My thoughts about brains, vats, and other items in the external world are not intrinsically such that they refer to those things. As we saw in Chapter 25, when discussing Twin Earth, some philosophers take the content of our thoughts to be no less beholden to connections with the external world than our language is. On that view, if I am in fact a BiV, and so have had no perceptions of brains or vats, it seems to follow that I cannot even *think* that I am a brain in a vat. Since I can think that thought, skepticism can be rejected.

DISCUSSION

Many philosophers have noted that Putnam's argument does not provide a convincing answer to skepticism (Brueckner 1986), for, even if there are some BiV scenarios in which we couldn't think or express the hypothesis that we are brains in vats, there are many where we can. Suppose that I was envatted last night. That scenario cannot be ruled out as self-defeating, for, in that case, I would have had contact with brains and vats in the past, and my terms would refer just as they did before I was envatted. Still, even if Putnam's argument is not successful, the realization that the contents of what we are thinking and saying might not be the same if we were BiVs is an important one.

Many readers will recognize the similarity between the BiV hypothesis and the premise of the 1999 film *The Matrix*. In *The Matrix*, humans seem to experience the world just as you and I do. They go to work, dance at the club, and eat steak in fancy restaurants. As a matter of fact, though, humans have all been inside pods, floating in goo since birth. They are hooked up to "the Matrix," which generates a compelling virtual reality. Only a very few realize that they are in fact in the pods and that the world they knew was an illusion. How do we know we're not in the Matrix ourselves? Since our experiences in the Matrix would be indistinguishable from our experiences in the real world, it seems we can't know. *The Matrix* can therefore be seen as a skeptical scenario which threatens our knowledge of even the most mundane facts. If I'm in the Matrix, I'm not wearing shoes. So, since I can't know I'm not in the Matrix, I can't know I'm wearing shoes, etc.

But is the world in the Matrix an illusion? When Neo is in the Matrix and sits at his virtual desk in front of a virtual computer, is his belief that he is sitting at his desk false? David J. Chalmers (2005, 2022) thinks not. Tables and chairs exist in the Matrix. It's just that the underlying metaphysics is not exactly how we suppose it is. As a matter of fact, the underlying physics of the *actual world* is far from what we might suppose it is—it involves quantum particles, and perhaps even vibrations of multi-dimensional strings. This is very different than the idea that tables and chairs are made up of solid little pieces of tables and chairs. If the "bottom-level" story about tables and chairs is weirder than we realize, involving vibrating strings, are there no tables and chairs? Have we been wrong all along that there are such things? No, there are tables and chairs; they are just made of different stuff than we probably thought they were. The same is true, says Chalmers, of the Matrix. Under that scenario, everything we see, even the nature of spacetime, is a matter of computational processes. Desks are still desks—they are solid, are in spacetime, and are made of wood. It's only that the underlying basis of their solidity—the nature of the spacetime they occupy and the nature of wood itself—is ultimately different than it seems to be in the non-Matrix world.

Chalmers' argument is unlike Putnam's in that it doesn't use the causal theory of reference to argue that a skeptical scenario is self-defeating. Nevertheless, Chalmers' argument suggests important lessons about reference, mental content, and perception. To see this, suppose that the robotic overlords of the Matrix allow a couple of humans, Dave and Dan, to be raised outside the machine as pod-custodians, cleaning up leaky goo and fixing loose wires. These two often rest by sitting at their desks and discussing philosophy. Dan says, "Those poor dupes in the Matrix think they're at their desks, doing their work; but as a matter of fact it's all an illusion." Dave demurs, insisting that their desks are perfectly real. Dan disagrees. "Desks," he says, knocking on his, "are like this: solid, three dimensional, heavy. There is nothing like this in the Matrix." Who is right? It appears Dan has a point. There is nothing like his desk in the Matrix. Desks outside the Matrix are not underwritten by computational processes, so they are quite different. And perhaps that difference is enough for Dan to say, correctly, that there are no desks in the Matrix. But Dave is right too. When those people in the Matrix believe they are sitting at desks, they are correct. How can they both be right? Plausibly, what Dan and Dave mean when they think of desks is different from what the denizens of the Matrix mean. So, again, what thoughts and words are about is determined in part by the nature of the world we are in. The things in the Matrix are real, and most of the beliefs the inhabitants of the Matrix have about the world around them are true. But they aren't exactly the beliefs we have—*if* we reside outside the Matrix, that is.

RECOMMENDED READING

CANONICAL PRESENTATIONS

Chalmers, David J. 2005. "The Matrix as Metaphysics." In Christopher Grau (ed.) *Philosophers Explore the Matrix*. Oxford: Oxford University Press: 132ff.

Putnam, Hilary. 1981. *Reason, Truth and History*. Cambridge: Cambridge University Press.

OVERVIEWS

Hickey, Lance P. n.d. "The Brain in a Vat Argument." *Internet Encyclopedia of Philosophy*. https://iep.utm.edu/brain-in-a-vat-argument/.

McKinsey, Michael. 2018. "Skepticism and Content Externalism." *The Stanford Encyclopedia of Philosophy* (Summer 2018 Edition), Edward N. Zalta (ed.), URL = <https://plato.stanford.edu/archives/sum2018/entries/skepticism-content-externalism/>.

ADDITIONAL DISCUSSIONS

Berkeley, George. 1713. *Three Dialogues between Hylas and Philonous*. London: Printed by G. James for Henry Clements.

Brueckner, Anthony L. 1986. "Brains in a Vat." *Journal of Philosophy* 83 (3):148–67.
Chalmers, David J. 2022. *Reality+: Virtual Worlds and the Problems of Philosophy*. New York: Norton.
Wright, Crispin. 1992. "On Putnam's Proof that We Are Not Brains in a Vat." *Proceedings of the Aristotelian Society* 92 (1): 67–94.

PUZZLING PIERRE

BACKGROUND

It's a curious fact that "Hesperus" is the Greek name of the evening star and "Phosphorus" is the Greek name of the morning star. As a matter of fact, the heavenly body people used these names for is just one thing—the planet Venus. Suppose Caroline does not know that fact. Given this, when she sincerely asserts "Hesperus is not Phosphorus," what is she believing? Despite the fact that the morning star and evening star are both Venus, to many it seems incorrect to say that Caroline is believing the contradictory claims that Venus is not Venus, Hesperus is not Hesperus, or Phosphorus is not Phosphorus. Caroline is not irrational, so none of those things seems to capture what she is thinking. Gottlob Frege introduced this sort of case to reject the "Millian" principle—named after John Stuart Mill—that co-referring names can be substituted for one another in a sentence without changing the proposition expressed by the sentence. Instead, the proposition expressed by the assertion "Hesperus is bright" is— or at least can be—different from the proposition expressed by the assertion "Phosphorus is bright." According to Frege (1892), although "Hesperus" and "Phosphorus" have a single reference—Venus—they have different "senses" that constitute part of their meaning. Such

DOI: 10.4324/9781003179191-32

senses can be expressed using definite descriptions. Perhaps Hesperus has the sense "the heavenly body that appears in the evening" and Phosphorous has the sense "the heavenly body that appears first in the morning." Millians deny this, and therefore need a response to Frege's anti-Millian argument. Kripke (1979) provides one, based on his puzzle about belief.

THE CASE

Consider a Frenchman named Pierre who, growing up in rural France, knows no English. He has seen nice postcards of the capital of England, and so readily and sincerely assents to the sentence "Londres est jolie." Whatever we might think of his evidence, it seems clear that Pierre believes London is pretty. That's just what the French sentence means: he speaks French fluently, and he assents to it. A little later in life, Pierre moves to an unattractive part of London. While there, he picks up English from those around him (rather than by translation) and, naturally enough, comes to know that the English call this city "London." Because he never leaves his bad neighborhood, Pierre comes to sincerely assent to the sentence "London is not pretty." It seems clear that Pierre believes London is not pretty. That's just what the sentence means: he speaks English fluently, and he assents to it. Nevertheless, and here's the twist, Pierre never realizes the city in the postcard was the city he lives in now. He still unhesitatingly assents to the sentence "Londres est jolie." The belief expressed by that sentence didn't change. But now we have a puzzle. Pierre, who is perfectly rational, seems to believe at one and the same time that London is pretty and that London is not pretty.

Pierre seems to be in the same position as Caroline: we seem forced to describe him as having contradictory beliefs, even though he is not irrational. But this time rejecting the Millian principle doesn't help, since the puzzle doesn't depend on the claim that co-referential names can be substituted for one another. Instead, this puzzle seems to depend on independently plausible and less contentious claims. One is a simple fact about translation: "London is pretty" is a translation of "Londres est jolie," and so those sentences express the same proposition. The other is an unobjectionable view about belief ascription: when a subject assents to a sentence "S" and understands what "S" means—namely S—then the subject believes S. It seems we often use these principles implicitly. Suppose John, an English-speaker, sincerely assents to the sentence "London is pretty." It looks like we should say John believes London is pretty. Suppose Jacques, a French-speaker, sincerely asserts to the sentence "Londres est jolie." It seems we should say Jacques also believes London is pretty. Following the same sorts of principles in the Pierre case leads to the puzzling fact that Pierre believes both that London is pretty and that London is not pretty.

There are at least two lessons we can take from Kripke's example. First, it's a puzzle: what exactly does Pierre believe? Something seems to have gone wrong here; but what? Second, since it seems puzzles of this sort can be generated without the Millian principle; we might think again about our inclination to reject that principle because of Hesperus/Phosphorus cases: they appear to be very similar to the Londres/London cases, after all, which don't depend on the Millian principle. If the puzzle raises a general problem for belief ascription, it's not clear the Millian principle is to blame in Hesperus/Phosphorus cases after all.

DISCUSSION

Although the literature on Kripke's puzzle is voluminous and the solutions often technical, responses to his puzzle fall into two general camps. In the first camp are those who tend to accept that Pierre, while rational, has contradictory beliefs: he believes London is pretty and he believes London is not pretty. This response denies that belief ascriptions are governed by norms about what an agent can or cannot rationally believe. While this solution does, in a sense, divorce what is believed from the rational significance of the belief for the agent, defenders can claim that rational significance is captured by the *way* that propositions are believed, not by the propositions themselves. So, for example, while Pierre does believe the propositions that London is pretty and that London is not pretty, he believes them in ways, or under guises, that hide the inconsistency. His rationality is governed by the way he believes propositions, not the propositions he believes. While philosophers who take this stance needn't accept the Millian principle, they often do, taking the same stance in traditional Hesperus/Phosphorus cases. (Although their views differ in important ways, this view is defended by Braun (1998), Salmon (1986), Soames (2002), and others.)

In the second camp are those who want to hold onto the intuition that belief ascriptions should capture the cognitive significance of the belief for the subject. We needn't ascribe contradictory beliefs to Pierre. In general, these philosophers argue that, while it is true that "London is pretty" is a translation of "Londres est jolie," and they both mean that London is pretty, Pierre is still thinking about London in two different ways. So far this is consistent with the strategy taken by philosophers in the first camp; but the crucial difference is that philosophers in the second camp believe these "ways of thinking" make a difference to the content of Pierre's beliefs. Perhaps (at least part of) the content of the belief Pierre expresses by "Londres est jolie" is that the city in the postcard is pretty, and (at least part of) the content of the belief he expresses by "London is not pretty" is that the city he lives in is not pretty (Sosa 1996, Bach 1997).

A twist on this strategy holds that there is more than one dimension of content, and so, in effect, Pierre's belief can't be fully captured by a single proposition. Pierre does believe two incompatible propositions: London is pretty and London is not pretty. There is, however, another layer of content that captures the significance of the belief for Pierre, just as it was suggested above. This is ultimately a version of the Fregean strategy in that it provides a level of content that includes something like a term's sense and another that includes its referent. Which of the two dimensions of content we employ when we ascribe beliefs—that is, when we say such things as "Pierre believes London is pretty," or "Pierre believes London is not pretty," or "Pierre believes London is pretty and he believes that it's not pretty"—will depend in part on context. If we want to highlight the city he is thinking about, we will be inclined to ascribe the referential content; but when we want to highlight the way in which he is thinking about these cities, we will ascribe the content more closely aligned with a "sense" (Stalnaker 1987, Crimmins and Perry 1989, Chalmers 2002).

RECOMMENDED READING

CANONICAL PRESENTATION:

Kripke, Saul A. 1979. "A Puzzle about Belief." In A. Margalit (ed.) *Meaning and Use*. Dordrecht: Reidel: 239–83.

OVERVIEW

McGlone, Michael. 2009. "Understanding Kripke's Puzzles about Belief." *Philosophy Compass* 4 (3): 487–514.

ADDITIONAL DISCUSSIONS

Bach, Kent. 1997. "Do Belief Reports Report Beliefs?" *Pacific Philosophical Quarterly* 78 (3): 215–41.

Braun, David. 1998. "Understanding Belief Reports." *Philosophical Review* 107 (4): 555–95.

Chalmers, David. 2002. "The Components of Content." In David J. Chalmers (ed.) *Philosophy of Mind: Classical and Contemporary Readings*. New York: Oxford University Press.

Crimmins, Mark. 1992. *Talk About Beliefs*. Cambridge, Ma: MIT Press.

Crimmins, Mark, and Perry, John. 1989. "The Prince and the Phone Booth: Reporting Puzzling Beliefs." *Journal of Philosophy* 86 (12): 685_711.

Frege, Gottlob. 1892/1960. "On Sense and Reference/Über Sinn und Bedeutung." In P. Geach and M. Black (eds.) *Translations from the Philosophical Writings of Gottlob Frege*. Oxford: Blackwell: 56–78.

Lewis, David K. 1981. "What Puzzling Pierre Does Not Believe." *Australasian Journal of Philosophy* 59 (3): 283–9.

Marcus, Ruth Barcan. 1981. "A Proposed Solution to a Puzzle about Belief." *Midwest Studies in Philosophy* 6 (1): 501–10.

Recanati, François. 1993. *Direct Reference: From Language to Thought*. Oxford: Blackwell.

Richard, Mark. 1990. *Propositional Attitudes: An Essay on Thoughts and How We Ascribe Them*. Cambridge: Cambridge University Press.

Salmon, Nathan U. 1986. *Frege's Puzzle*. Cambridge, MA: MIT Press.

Saul, Jennifer Mather. 2007. *Simple Sentences, Substitution, and Intuitions*. Oxford: Oxford University Press.

Schiffer, Stephen. 1987. "The 'Fido'-Fido Theory of Belief." *Philosophical Perspectives* 1: 455–80.

Schiffer, Stephen. 1992. "Belief Ascription." *Journal of Philosophy* 89 (10): 499–521.

Soames, Scott. 2002. *Beyond Rigidity: The Unfinished Semantic Agenda of Naming and Necessity*. New York: Oxford University Press.

Sosa, David. 1996. "The Import of the Puzzle about Belief." *Philosophical Review* 105 (3): 373–402.

Stalnaker, Robert. 1987. "Semantics for Belief." *Philosophical Topics* 15 (1): 177–90.

Taschek, William W. 1998. "On Ascribing Beliefs." *Journal of Philosophy* 95 (7): 323–53.

THE SHOPPING LIST

BACKGROUND

When we say "Sally believes that her mother will send money," we ascribe to Sally an attitude towards a proposition, or something that could be true or false. In this case, Sally believes the proposition that her mother will send money. But Sally can have other attitudes towards the same proposition. Sally could desire that her mother send money. What makes one state a belief and the other a desire? Can anything general be said about the difference, beyond simply repeating that one is a belief and the other is a desire? Elizabeth Anscombe (1957) suggests (or at least has been taken to suggest) that a key difference is what she calls "direction of fit." Her famous case of the shopping list illustrates this concept.

THE CASE

Imagine a man walking through a grocery store with a shopping list. The list says: cheese, bread, chocolate, grapes .... Following him is a detective who writes her own list, based on what the man bought. Her list says: cheese, bread, chocolate, grapes ....These lists are in some sense exactly the same—they name the same items. But they also differ. The shopper's list guides the shopper's actions—to make the list accurate, he must fill his cart with the listed items. The items should match the list. The detective's list, on the other hand, is meant to reflect what the shopper bought. The list should match the items. So, suppose that the man gets home and finds that instead of grapes he bought grappa. The shopper can't fix his mistake by crossing "grapes" off the list and replacing it with "grappa." This would miss the point of the list—to fix the mistake he needs to go back and trade the grappa for the grapes. If the detective, on the other hand, has "grapes" on her list when the man bought grappa, she can fix the mistake by correcting her list. The point can be glossed by the idea that the lists have different *directions of fit*. The detective's list has to fit the way the world turns out to be. The shopper has to make the world fit the list. Anscombe's suggestion, then, is that mental states differ in the same way as the lists. Beliefs are like the detective's list: they aim at matching the way the world is. Desires are like the shopper's list: they aim at making the world match the agent's representation of it. Beliefs and desires are characterized by these differences in direction of fit. Other states seem to differ in this way as well. Perceptions aim to fit the world, but intentions aim to make the world fit them.

DISCUSSION

Though there is clearly something suggestive about Anscombe's example and the resulting notion of directions of fit, it has proved to be a little difficult to spell out. One famous interpretation and application of direction of fit comes from Michael Smith (1994), who uses it to provide a functionalist account of beliefs and desires. On Smith's model, somewhat roughly: a belief is that p is a state that tends to go out of existence when there is a perception that not-p, while a desire is that p is a state that endures despite that perception, and leads the subject to try to bring it about that p (see also Velleman 2000, p. 115.). This is a descriptive account of what makes beliefs and desires the states that they are. But there are a number of worries about this account, not least that beliefs don't always go out of existence in the face of disagreeing perceptions. Some beliefs are stubborn. For example, a mother might believe her son is innocent despite mountains of evidence that he is not. And some perceptions are properly disregarded.

For example, the (illusory) perception that the stick in water is bent has no effect on my belief to the contrary (Sobel and Copp 2001, Frost 2014).

A natural suggestion here is that the direction of fit contrast is not meant to capture how beliefs and desires as a matter a fact behave, but how they should behave. Anscombe's presentation of the case suggests that she might have something normative like this in mind. Crudely, one might say a subject's beliefs should represent the world—a subject should believe p only if it is true. And desires make normative demands on how the subject should interact with the world—if S desires that p, S should try to bring it about that p. (This is suggested but not exactly endorsed by Searle 1983, pp. 7–8. See also Platts 1979, pp. 256–7, Zangwill 1998.) Put in this crude way, something is clearly wrong: just because S desires p doesn't always mean S should bring p about. Mark could want to murder his sister; but the existence of that desire doesn't mean he should (Frost 2014)! Furthermore, does p's simply being the case mean S should believe p? What if S has no evidence p is the case, or even has evidence against it?

There are, of course, refinements of these views in light of such objections. But it is worth asking, what hangs on the issue? Aside from the hope of a theoretically satisfying distinction between beliefs and desires, some philosophers such as Smith think that the direction of fit analysis vindicates a Humean picture of motivation that sees the motivation to act as provided only by desires—you can believe giving your son a gift will make him happy; but, unless you have the desire to make him happy, you won't be motivated to give him a gift. The direction of fit intuition potentially explains why beliefs are motivationally inert. If beliefs are only characterized by their disposition to reflect the world, getting information about the world will lead to a change of beliefs but never a motivation to change what they are about. It is desires, with their particular direction of fit, that lead subjects to change the world (Smith 1994, p. 116). However, that argument seems to assume that there are no states that are both belief-like, in that they are meant to represent the way the world is, and that have a motivational direction of fit, in that they lead the subject to change the world to fit the belief. That assumption could be questioned. The belief that it is good to make children happy might be something that reflects a fact about the world but that also leads one to give gifts to children. So might the belief that I promised to pick you up from the airport, which is what leads me to pick you up (Schueler 2013). Perhaps there are other arguments to bolster the Humean view (Smith 1994, pp. 118–21; though see Coleman 2008). But the sorts of observations Anscombe makes about direction of fit aren't likely to get us all the way there.

RECOMMENDED READING

CANONICAL PRESENTATION

Anscombe, G. E. M. 1957. *Intention*. Oxford: Blackwell.

OVERVIEW

Schueler, G. F. 2013. "Direction of Fit." In Hugh LaFollette (ed.) *International Encyclopedia of Ethics*. Oxford: Blackwell: 1362–6

ADDITIONAL DISCUSSIONS

Archer, Avery. 2015. "Reconceiving Direction of Fit." *Thought: A Journal of Philosophy* 4 (3): 171–80.
Coleman, Mary Clayton. 2008. "Directions of Fit and the Humean Theory of Motivation." *Australasian Journal of Philosophy* 86 (1): 127–39.
Frost, Kim. 2014. "On the Very Idea of Direction of Fit." *Philosophical Review* 123 (4): 429–84.
Humberstone, I. Lloyd. 1992. "Direction of Fit." *Mind* 101 (401): 59–83.
Platts, Mark de Bretton. 1979. *Ways of Meaning: An Introduction to a Philosophy of Language*. Cambridge, MA: MIT Press.
Schueler, G. F. 1991. "Pro-Attitudes and Direction of Fit." *Mind* 100 (400): 277–81.
Searle, John R. 1983. *Intentionality: An Essay in the Philosophy of Mind*. Cambridge: Cambridge University Press.
Smith, Michael. 1994. *The Moral Problem*. Oxford: Blackwell.
Sobel, David, and Copp, David. 2001. "Against Direction of Fit Accounts of Belief and Desire." *Analysis* 61 (1): 44–53.
Tenenbaum, Sergio. 2006. "Direction of Fit and Motivational Cognitivism." In Russ Shafer-Landau (ed.) *Oxford Studies in Metaethics*. Oxford: Oxford University Press: 235–64.
Velleman, David. 2000. *The Possibility of Practical Reason*. Oxford: Oxford University Press.
Zangwill, Nick. 1998. "Direction of Fit and Normative Functionalism." *Philosophical Studies* 91 (2): 173–203.

PART IV

PERCEPTION, IMAGINATION, AND ATTENTION
INTRODUCTION

Much of philosophy of mind concerns big-picture questions—for example, questions about the nature of mind or about the nature of consciousness. But philosophers of mind also devote considerable attention to more specific questions concerning various mental states and mental capacities. We have already explored some questions of this more specific sort, particularly in connection with belief. In Part IV, we explore a series of specific questions that arise in connection with perception, imagination, and attention.

We start with three issues that trace back to the 17th and 18th centuries. In Chapter 30, we consider a thought experiment first proposed by William Molyneux in a letter to John Locke. This thought experiment explores the relationship between perception in different sensory modalities—for example, between visual perception and tactile perception. In particular, we are asked to consider a person blind from birth whose sight is restored. While blind, the person could use their sense of touch to identify various three-dimensional objects such as cubes and spheres. Now with sight restored, would the individual be able to identify such objects purely by sight, without touching them?

In Chapter 31, we consider a thought experiment owing to David Hume that explores the limits of imagination and sheds light on the debate about whether all of our concepts trace back to experience. Suppose that a person has seen all the shades of blue that humans can distinguish except one—call it blue$_{76}$. Could that person successfully imagine that shade of blue without having had any prior experience of it?

Chapter 32 also takes up questions about the limits of imagination. Here we consider a thought experiment proposed by René Descartes that explores the extent to which imagination can represent fine-grained content. For example, can our imaginings distinguish between a 100-sided figure and a 1000-sided figure, or is that a difference that can only be represented by some other kind of mental capacity? A related issue arises in the thought experiment of the speckled hen discussed in Chapter 33: Can your mental image discriminate between an image of a hen with 72 speckles and a hen with 73 speckles?

The remaining chapters in Part IV take up more contemporary issues. In Chapter 34 we consider a thought experiment that puts pressure on our standard taxonomy of mental states. This thought experiment seems to suggest that we need to accept a new category of mental states, called *aliefs*, that have a different kind of content from both beliefs and imaginings. In Chapter 35, we consider several thought experiments that have been put forth to suggest that perception represents not just low-level features such as shape and color but also higher-level features such as being a particular kind of tree.

The other chapters in Part IV don't concern thought experiments, but rather puzzle cases drawn from real life. In Chapters 36–38, we consider three puzzling phenomena relating to perception: synesthesia, change blindness, and blindsight. For people who are synesthetes, a sensory stimulation typically associated with one perceptual modality will automatically prompt or trigger an experience in another perceptual modality. So, for example, a synesthete might experience different shapes as having distinctive tastes or experience different sounds as having distinctive colors. Blindsight is a phenomenon that occurs in some cases when an individual's visual cortex has been damaged. Though the individual will report having a part of the visual field in which they can't see anything, when forced to make guesses about objects in that area of the visual field, they are able to do so with an accuracy rate that's greater than chance. Unlike these first two phenomena, change blindness is a condition that affects us all. Sometimes when we look first at one stimulus and then another, we fail to notice any difference between the two—even when the difference should be a glaring one. In developing theories of consciousness, philosophers have taken these puzzling phenomena to have important consequences.

MOLYNEUX'S PROBLEM

BACKGROUND

In *An Essay Concerning Human Understanding* (1694), John Locke distinguishes between ideas that were particular to a particular sense and ideas that can be acquired by more than one sense. Color, for example, is particular to vision—someone without vision could not acquire the idea of color. Shape, on the other hand, appears to be an idea we can get both from vision—by seeing the outline of a body—and from touch—by feeling the edges of a body. Relatedly, Aristotle held that some qualities are perceivable only by a single sense—again, only vision perceives color, only hearing perceives sound, etc.—while other qualities are "common sensibles" and can be perceived by multiple senses; again, shape is a paradigm case, but size, number, and motion are arguably others. What, though, is the relationship between the different sensory representations of these common sensibles? What is the relationship between the visual perception of shape and the tactile perception of shape? This is the issue that gives rise to Molyneux's problem.

THE CASE

Suppose someone has been blind since birth. Through touch, they learn how to distinguish between a cube and a sphere. They feel the corners of the cube and its six faces. They notice the stark contrast between that and the smooth feeling of the sphere. Now, suppose they are suddenly given sight and are presented with the cube and the sphere. Could they know, by sight alone, which one was the cube and which one was the sphere?

This question was initially proposed to John Locke in a letter from William Molyneux in 1688, though there are historical antecedents in both Lucretius and Ibn Tufayl (Ferretti and Glenney 2021, Scalas 2021, Goodman 2021). Throughout the many centuries of discussion, a number of modifications and refinements have been made to Molyneux's problem (Van Cleve 2007). Diderot suggested it would be better to ask if the subject could visually identify a circle versus a square to avoid problems of depth perception. Leibniz suggested that the subject be told that one of the items being displayed is the cube and the other is the sphere, and be given time to work out which is which. As this suggests, there are really two different questions one might ask: first, whether the person could know *immediately* by sight alone which was the cube and which the sphere; and, second, whether the information provided by sight, combined with the information recalled from touch, could be used to reason to the correct conclusion. The various refinements and interpretations of the problem have led some philosophers to divide it into a group of sub-problems (Matthen and Cohen 2020). For example, there are questions about the relationship between the way sensory modalities represent space more generally, as well as questions about how vision and touch represent shape (Evans 1985). There are also questions about the relationships between the properties represented by touch and by vision—whether they are in fact the same property.

DISCUSSION

In its original presentation, Molyneux's problem was considered a thought experiment, to be answered by philosophical theories of perception and the source of ideas. But the question he asked Locke seems to be an empirical one that can potentially be answered by experiment. Though these approaches are related, we'll focus on the philosophical approaches first, and then consider some of the empirical results.

Very generally, philosophers of an empiricist bent who believe that our ideas and concepts stem from sensory experience alone tend to answer Molyneux's question in the negative. Because visual and tactile experiences of shape are distinct, and the newly sighted person hasn't learned to associate the visual experience of shapes with tactile experiences of shapes, they would not be able to identify which object was a cube and which was a sphere. Molyneux himself thought this, and Locke and Berkeley agreed. Rationalists like Leibniz, however, answered in the affirmative: given the ability to reason about the sensations, the newly sighted person could tell which object was which. Reid in some ways splits the difference. Though the visual and tactile sensations themselves do not resemble each other (or the objects they represent), they give rise to ideas that can be seen to relate to one another (see Van Cleve 2007).

More recently, philosophers such as Gareth Evans (1985) and John Campbell (2005) have argued for affirmative answers. According to Evans, both visual and tactile concepts share an egocentric representation of space, depicting things as oriented around the subject, and so a subject should be able to make the transition between them. According to Campbell, our experiences are externally individuated—that is, experiences are the same or different based on the properties they represent in the world (see Chapters 19 and 20); and so, if two experiences really were of the same property, they would share a way of appearing.

Empirical results were brought to bear on Molyneux's problem surprisingly early. In the early 18th century, William Cheselden wrote about a cataract patient whose sight was restored. According to Cheselden (1728), once vision was restored the patient was unable to distinguish shapes visually, suggesting a negative answer to Molyneux's question. Much more recently, a negative answer has been suggested by Project Prakash, documented by Held et al. (2011), in which five congenitally blind children had their sight restored. The children were unable to visually identify differently shaped Lego blocks they had previously known by touch. Though these empirical results seem to point to an unequivocal negative answer to Molyneux's problem, they have been called into question by a number of critics. Those critics argue, for example, that, because the visual systems of the patients aren't immediately fully functioning, we cannot tell whether the failure is due to the difference between visual and tactile representations of space or, more simply, the inadequacy of the patient's visual system immediately after surgery (Toribio 2021).

RECOMMENDED READING

CANONICAL PRESENTATIONS

Locke, John. 1694. *An Essay Concerning Human Understanding* (second edition). London: Printed by Eliz. Holt for Thomas Bassett. (See Book II, Chapter ix, Section 8.)

Molyneux, W. 1688. "Letter to John Locke, 7 July." In *The Correspondence of John Locke, vol. 3*, edited by E. S. de Beer. Oxford: Clarendon, 1978: No. 1064.

OVERVIEWS

Degenaar, Marjolein. 1996. *Molyneux's Problem: Three Centuries of Discussion on the Perception of Forms*. Dordrecht: Kluwer.

Degenaar, Marjolein, and Lokhorst, Gert-Jan. 2021. "Molyneux's Problem." *The Stanford Encyclopedia of Philosophy* (Winter 2021 Edition), Edward N. Zalta (ed.), URL = <https://plato.stanford.edu/archives/win2021/entries/molyneux-problem/>.

Glenney, Brian. 2012. "Molyneux's Question." *Internet Encyclopedia of Philosophy*. https://iep.utm.edu/molyneux/.

ADDITIONAL DISCUSSIONS

Campbell, John. 2005. "Information-Processing, Phenomenal Consciousness and Molyneux's Question." In José Luis Bermúdez (ed.) *Thought, Reference, and Experience: Themes From the Philosophy of Gareth Evans*. Oxford: Clarendon.

Cheselden, W. 1728. "An Account of Some Observations Made by a Young Gentleman, Who Was Born Blind, Or Lost His Sight So Early, that He Had No Remembrance of Ever Having Seen, and Was Couch'd between 13 and 14 Years of Age." *Philosophical Transactions of the Royal Society of London* 35: 447–50.

Cohen, Jonathan, and Matthen, Mohan. 2021. "What Was Molyneux's Question a Question About?" In G. Feretti and B. Glenney (eds.) *Molyneux's Question and the History of Philosophy*. New York: Routledge: Chapter 20.

Eilan, Naomi M. 1993. "Molyneux's Question and the Idea of an External World." In N. Eilan, R. A. McCarthy, and B. Brewer (eds.) *Spatial Representation: Problems in Philosophy and Psychology*. Oxford: Blackwell: 236–55.

Evans, Gareth. 1985. "Molyneux's Question." In *Collected Papers*, edited by J. McDowell. New York: Oxford University Press.

Ferretti, Gabriele, and Glenney, Brian (eds.). 2021. *Molyneux's Question and the History of Philosophy*. New York: Routledge.

Goodman, Lenn E. 2021. "Molyneux, Mysticism, Empiricism and Independent Thinking." In G. Feretti and B. Glenney (eds.) *Molyneux's Question and the History of Philosophy*. New York: Routledge: Chapter 2.

Held, R., Ostrovsky, Y., de Gelder, B., Gandhi, T., Ganesh, S., Mathur, U., and Sinha, P. 2011. "The Newly Sighted Fail to Match Seen Shape with Felt." *Nature Neuroscience* 14: 551–3.

Levin, Janet. 2008. "Molyneux's Question and the Individuation of Perceptual Concepts." *Philosophical Studies* 139 (1): 1–28.

Matthen, Mohan, and Cohen, Jonathan. 2020. "Many Molyneux Questions." *Australasian Journal of Philosophy* 98 (1): 47–63.

Scalas, Giulia. 2021. "Epicureanism and Molyneux's Question." In G. Feretti and B. Glenney (eds.) *Molyneux's Question and the History of Philosophy*. New York: Routledge: Chapter 1.

Toribio, Josefa. 2021. "Molyneux's Question and Perceptual Judgments." In G. Feretti and B. Glenney (eds.) *Molyneux's Question and the History of Philosophy*. New York: Routledge: Chapter 16.

Van Cleve, James. 2007. "Reid's Answer to Molyneux's Question." *The Monist* 90 (2): 251–70.

THE MISSING SHADE OF BLUE

BACKGROUND

Where do our various ideas and concepts come from? Where do we get the concept of dinosaurs, Barack Obama, goodness, or God? Many of them are surely derived from experience. For example, it would be surprising if someone was born with the concept of dinosaurs. Some ideas, though, are more difficult to trace to experiences. This has led some philosophers, at least as early as Plato, to claim that some of our concepts are innate. Plato argued that we have ideas we couldn't have gotten from experience—we've likely never experienced perfectly round circles, but we have the idea of them and know what properties they must have. It's therefore hypothesized that we were born with these concepts, and they were only triggered by experiences of imperfect objects. Philosophers of a more empiricist bent tend to argue, on the other hand, that even those concepts come from experience—perhaps aided by the mental activity of abstraction.

John Locke famously argued that the mind was a *tabula rasa*, a blank slate: whatever ideas we have in our minds come from experience. Several decades later, David Hume adopted a version of this principle, claiming that every idea in the mind is just a copy of some previous sense impressions. Our idea of having pain comes from experiences of pain; our idea of redness comes from experiences of red. This principle drives much of Hume's later skepticism about causality, substance, and the self. Consider causation, for example. Though we can experience a succession of events, we cannot experience the causal relations among them. In cases like these, where we cannot locate a sense impression corresponding to our idea, we must conclude that our idea is somehow flawed. We don't have a sense impression corresponding to our idea of a substance, for example; but only have sense impressions of the qualities a substance is supposed to have. So, we should recognize that our idea of substance is flawed. In an interesting twist, however, Hume himself came up with a counterexample to this strict empiricism about ideas. This is the case of the missing shade of blue.

THE CASE

Suppose someone with good vision has experienced a large array of colors for the first 30 years of their life. They have experienced many different shades of blue, red, etc. They have not, however, experienced a particular shade of blue, S. Now, imagine they are presented with a color spectrum from light blue (A) to dark blue (Z), corresponding to all the colors they have experienced. There is a gap somewhere in the spectrum—between R and T, perhaps. Despite the fact that they have never seen S, Hume suggests they can nevertheless look at R and T and imagine the shade in between them. At this point they gain an idea of S, even though they have never experienced it. This seems to be a clear counterexample to the claim that every idea must be derived from a corresponding sensation.

DISCUSSION

Oddly enough, Hume himself doesn't even attempt to resolve the problem posed by the missing shade of blue. This might seem to discredit his entire enterprise (Prichard 1950, p. 177). If we can come up with a shade of blue without experiencing it, why can't we have a concept of necessary connection, substance, or self without experiencing those phenomena? To the degree that Hume relies on the principle that an idea is flawed if we can't trace it to some corresponding sensation or group of sensations, his influential skeptical arguments seem to be in trouble.

One might try to save the Humean enterprise by pointing out that Hume only thought that *simple* ideas (that is, ideas that are not combinations of other ideas) need to trace back to particular impressions. We can easily imagine a unicorn despite never seeing one, simply by conjoining our ideas of a horse and a horn. Color theory tells us that colors are not simples, but are combinations of hue, value, and saturation. Perhaps a Humean can make use of this idea to resolve the puzzle—the missing shade of blue is built up out of ideas of hue, value, and saturation that correspond to experiences the subject has had. It's not clear, though, that the puzzle can't be recast, involving missing saturations, hues, or values. Further, even if the complexity of color experience does help, it cannot help Hume himself, since he seemed to believe particular color shades were simples (Hume 1740/1978, p. 637).

Nevertheless, even if one believes that ideas and impressions of particular shades of color are simple, this doesn't rule out the existence of resemblance relations between them. These resemblance relations give us a grasp of the missing shade of blue. Though we can't trace an idea of that shade to a particular impression of that shade, we can explain it in respectable (and Humean) empiricist terms. We can trace it to our impressions of other colors and the resemblances between them (Fogelin 1984, Garrett 1997). This might also help address the concern about Hume's skeptical arguments regarding the ideas of substance, necessary connection, etc. Perhaps those ideas can also be explained in respectable, empiricist terms. But how to do this is not obvious. For example, unlike the case of color, the necessary connection between causal relata not only doesn't stem from a simple impression, but also doesn't stem merely from resemblances among simple impressions.

The missing shade of blue is not just of historical interest. The issue has arisen in recent debates about *phenomenal concepts*. Phenomenal concepts are concepts of the particular "what it's likeness" of conscious states, and they seem deeply tied to our having those conscious states (Stoljar 2005; see also Chapters 6 and 8). While I might gain a concept of pain from seeing someone hopping around saying "ouch," I gain a different concept of pain by having it. The latter concept is a phenomenal concept. Phenomenal concepts are often discussed in contemporary debates about consciousness. For example, recall Frank Jackson's (1982) knowledge argument, which we discussed in Chapter 6.

Recall that Mary learns all the physical truths there are about color vision without ever seeing in color; she lives in a black-and-white room and gains all her knowledge from black-and-white books and videos. Then she leaves and finally sees red for herself. It is often said that seeing colors enables her to know that seeing red is like *this*, where *this* indicates the use of a phenomenal concept. Some conclude that possession of phenomenal concepts of a property depends on experiences of that property. If so, this might seem to undermine Jackson's claim that Mary would not be able to figure out, from within her room, what it's like to see red. If we can imagine the missing shade of blue without seeing that shade, then maybe Mary can imagine what it's like to see red without seeing it (Dennett 2007, Mandik 2010, Kind 2019).

But the matter is contested. Imaginatively extrapolating the missing shade is one thing; imaginatively extrapolating from black and white to color is quite another. And Torin Alter (2008) argues that the knowledge argument is not committed to the claim that every phenomenal concept can be traced to a corresponding experience. The argument implies that we cannot deduce certain truths involving phenomenal concepts from truths involving only physical concepts (such as concepts of motion and space). But that is a much weaker principle, which is not threatened by the missing shade of blue case.

In addition to connecting with contemporary debates about phenomenal concepts, the missing shade of blue case also connects with contemporary debates about the limits of imagination. In discussions of Nagel's bat case (see Chapter 5), it is often suggested that we cannot imagine what it is like to be a bat because a bat's echolocation experiences are too different from our experiences—that the differences are too great for us to make the appropriate extrapolations. But how different is too different? Although that question remains open, philosophers have recently begun to focus more on the nature of the imagination. And that has implications for our understanding of its limits. For example, Amy Kind (2020) suggests that, because imagination is a skill, there might be skilled imaginers that are able to draw on prior experiences to imaginatively extrapolate to alien experiences to a surprising extent—quite a lot farther than recreating the missing shade of blue.

RECOMMENDED READING

CANONICAL PRESENTATION

Hume, David. 1740/1978. *A Treatise of Human Nature*, edited by L. A. Selby Bigge, revised by P. H. Nidditch. Oxford: Clarendon.

OVERVIEW

Garrett, Don. 1997. *Commitment and Cognition in Hume's Philosophy*. New York: Oxford University Press.

ADDITIONAL DISCUSSIONS

Alter, Torin. 2008. "Phenomenal Knowledge without Experience." In E. Wright (ed.) *The Case for Qualia*. Cambridge, MA: MIT Press: 247–67.
Cummins, Robert. 1978. "The Missing Shade of Blue." *Philosophical Review* 87: 548–65.
Dennett, Daniel C. 2007. "What RoboMary Knows." In Torin Alter and Sven Walter (eds.) *Phenomenal Concepts and Phenomenal Knowledge: New Essays on Consciousness and Physicalism*. New York: Oxford University Press: 15–31.
Fogelin, Robert J. 1984. "Hume and the Missing Shade of Blue." *Philosophy and Phenomenological Research* 45: 263–72.
Jackson, Frank. 1982. "Epiphenomenal Qualia." *Philosophical Quarterly* 32: 127–36.
Kind, Amy. 2019. "Mary's Powers of Imagination." In Sam Coleman (ed.) *The Knowledge Argument*. Cambridge: Cambridge University Press: 161–79.
Kind, Amy. 2020. "The Skill of Imagination." In Ellen Fridland and Carlotta Pavese (eds.) *The Routledge Handbook of Philosophy of Skill and Expertise*. Abingdon: Routledge: 335–46.
Mandik, Pete. 2010. "Swamp Mary's Revenge: Deviant Phenomenal Knowledge and Physicalism." *Philosophical Studies* 148 (2): 231247.
Morreall, John. 1982. "Hume's Missing Shade of Blue." *Philosophy and Phenomenological Research* 42 (3): 407–15.
Prichard, H. A. 1950. *Knowledge and Perception*. Oxford: Oxford University Press.
Stoljar, Daniel. 2005. "Physicalism and Phenomenal Concepts." *Mind and Language* 20: 469–94.
Stroud, Barry. 1977. *Hume*. London: Routledge & Kegan Paul.
Williams, William H. 1992. "Is Hume's Shade of Blue a Red Herring?" *Synthese* 92 (1):83–99.

IMAGINING CHILIAGONS

BACKGROUND

Consideration of the many thought experiments explored in this book shows us that imagination is an important philosophical tool. Our engagement with these thought experiments seems to proceed via imagination. But what is imagination? In most of the chapters, our effort to imagine a given scenario aims at teaching us something about the scenario under consideration. In this chapter, by contrast, we focus on our effort to imagine a given scenario with the aim of teaching us something about imagination itself. The imagined scenarios in question come from Descartes' *Meditations on First Philosophy* 1641/2017), where he explores the difference between imagination and what he calls *pure understanding*. This latter mental exercise is typically referred to as *conceiving* in contemporary philosophy, and that's how we'll refer to it here. To help explain the difference between these two mental activities, Descartes asks us to engage in several mental exercises that involve consideration of various geometrical figures: triangles, pentagons, myriagons, and chiliagons. Though most readers are probably familiar with the fact that triangles have three sides and that pentagons have five sides, these other figures may be less familiar, so it's worth noting that myriagons have 10,000 sides and chiliagons have 1000 sides.

THE CASE

First, think of a triangle. Try to bring it before your mind. Spend a moment reflecting on your mental act and what it is like. Next, think of a chiliagon. Try to bring it before your mind. Again, spend a moment reflecting on your mental act and what it is like.

In Descartes' view, these two mental activities proceed differently. In the first case, when he thinks of a triangle and tries to bring it before his mind, he is able to "see" the triangle, all three sides of the bounded figure, in what he calls his *mind's eye*. He takes his activity to be similar experientially to perceiving, and it's this kind of activity that he takes to be imagining. In the second case, however, when he thinks of a chiliagon and tries to bring it before his mind, Descartes reports that he doesn't do quite the same thing. Just as he understands that a triangle has three sides, he understands that a chiliagon has 1000 sides. But he reports that he is unable to see all 1000 sides of the chiliagon before his mind's eye. Yes, he might produce some kind of "confused representation of some figure," but that figure is not necessarily a chiliagon, and there's nothing to distinguish it from the kind of representation that he would produce were he to try to bring a myriagon before his mind. In his view, his consideration of the chiliagon does not proceed by way of imagination, but rather by way of pure understanding. As contemporary philosophers would say, he *imagines* the triangle but *conceives* of the chiliagon.

What's the difference? Descartes explains it by reflecting on what we might do when calling a pentagon to mind. As he notes, he can understand what a pentagon is, just as he can understand what a chiliagon or a myriagon is—understanding that proceeds without the employment of imagination. But, he adds, he can do something else with the pentagon. He can imagine it by applying his mind's eye to its shape, to its five sides and the area that is contained within their boundaries. From these series of reflections, he draws a conclusion about the nature of imagination—namely, that it "requires a peculiar effort of mind which is not required for understanding" (1641/2017, p. 51). It seems natural to take this peculiar effort of mind to involve mental imagery.

DISCUSSION

Though Descartes' examples are all visual in nature, a similar point can be made about imaginings in other sensory modalities. Just as you might call a triangle to mind by seeing it in your mind's eye, you might call the happy birthday song to mind by hearing it in your mind's ear. Philosophers working on imagination tend to use the notion of mental imagery in an expanded sense so that we can just as easily refer to auditory or gustatory imagery as we can refer to visual imagery.

Even prior to Descartes, the view that imagination should be understood in terms of mental imagery was prevalent among philosophers, and it remained the dominant view for several centuries thereafter (see Brann 1991). In the early 20th century, however, the rise of behaviorism led this view to fall out of favor. Though philosophers have long recognized a tight connection between mental states and behavior, and though it is common to take behavior to be a manifestation of our inner mental states, behaviorists took the connection to be even tighter. On their view, behavior is not a manifestation of a mental state; rather, all that it is to be in a mental state is to exhibit (or be disposed to exhibit) the relevant behavior. To suppose that we have inner mental states is to fall victim to a confusion—a confusion that they often referred to as "Descartes' myth" or as "the myth of Cartesianism"; and the acceptance of mental imagery is simply a further perpetuation of this alleged myth. In one influential effort to overthrow Cartesianism, Gilbert Ryle (1949) advanced a behavioristic theory of mind that eliminated mental images entirely. Toward this end, he developed an analysis of imagination that takes it to be identical with pretending, an activity that can be understood non-imagistically. On Ryle's view, to imagine a triangle is to pretend to see a triangle; and to imagine a world containing philosophical zombies is just to pretend that a world of philosophical zombies exists (see Chapter 7).

Though behaviorism is no longer a popular view among philosophers, the imagery-based view of imagination has not returned to its former dominance. Even philosophers who are perfectly willing to countenance the existence of mental imagery deny that it is an essential component of imagining, and it is commonly accepted that imagining can occur without imagery (see, e.g., Walton 1990, White 1990, Van Leeuwen 2013). Motivating this view are two broad classes of examples. First, there are cases of imaginings where it's hard to see how imagery could play a role. For example, someone who is reading Tolkien's *Lord of the Rings* might imagine that elves live forever. But, as Neil Van Leeuwen claims, this proposition can't be imagined using mental imagery; in his words, "It would take too long!" (2013, p. 222). Second, there are cases of imaginings where it's hard to see how imagery could distinguish one imagining from another. Consider, for example, a case where we imagine a young child emerging from the ocean and scrambling up the shore. How could a mental image differentiate this from where it's the young child's identical twin who is emerging from the ocean (White 1990)?

In response to these kinds of cases, proponents of an imagery-based account of imagining note that the cases only seem to raise worries because of overly demanding conceptions of the role that imagery would have to play in imagining. For example, Amy Kind (2001) suggests that we can assign mental imagery an essential role in imagining without requiring that it distinguish one imagining from another. Likewise, we might assign mental imagery an essential role in imagining without requiring that every aspect of the imagining has to be "read off" from the image.

How exactly we are to understand imagining, and how it is related to other speculative mental activities such as conceiving, also proves important for attempts to ascertain the epistemic value of these mental activities. As we have seen throughout this book, we frequently draw inferences about what's possible based on what we imagine or what we conceive. Is one of these mental activities better suited for this philosophical role than the other? In attempting to answer these questions, some philosophers interpret imagining as a special kind of conceiving (Chalmers 2002), while others differentiate the two activities. For example, Magdalena Balcerak Jackson (2016) sees both imagining and conceiving as forms of perspective-taking; but, while she sees imagining as a form of *experiential* perspective-taking, she sees conceiving as a form of *rational* perspective-taking.

Before closing our discussion, it's worth noting that not everyone has the same kind of experience when calling a triangle to mind as the one that Descartes himself has. There seem to be vast individual differences among people with respect to their capacity for mental imagery. This kind of variation has been observed at least since the time of Francis Galton (1880), but recent studies have brought it prominently into the limelight (Zeman et al. 2015). Individuals with what's now referred to as *aphantasia* have a severely decreased capacity for mental imagery, with some such individuals reporting that they are completely unable to produce mental imagery voluntarily. Sometimes this deficit appears in just a single sensory modality, but sometimes it appears in multiple sensory modalities. Indeed, some aphantasics report that they do not even experience *involuntary* mental imagery. More specifically, they do not even experience mental imagery when they dream.

RECOMMENDED READING

CANONICAL PRESENTATION

Descartes, Rene. 1641/2017. *Meditations on First Philosophy with Selections from the Objections and Replies*, edited by John Cottingham. Cambridge: Cambridge University Press.

OVERVIEWS

Liao, Shen-yi, and Gendler, Tamar. 2019. "Imagination." *The Stanford Encyclopedia of Philosophy* (Spring 2019 Edition), Edward N. Zalta (ed.), URL = <https://plato.stanford.edu/archives/spr2019/entries/imagination/>.

Kind, Amy. 2016. "Introduction: Exploring Imagination." In Amy Kind (ed.) *The Routledge Handbook of Philosophy of Imagination*. Abingdon: Routledge: 1–11.

ADDITIONAL DISCUSSIONS

Balcerak Jackson, Magdalena. 2016. "On the Epistemic Value of Imagining, Supposing, and Conceiving." In Amy Kind and Peter Kung (eds.) *Knowledge Through Imagination*. Oxford: Oxford University Press: 41–60.

Brann, Eva. 1991. *The World of Imagination*. Lanham, MD: Rowman & Littlefield.

Chalmers, David J. 2002. "Does Conceivability Entail Possibility?" In Tamar Szabo Gendler and John Hawthorne (eds.) *Conceivability and Possibility*. Oxford: Oxford University Press: 145–200.

Galton, Francis. 1880. "Statistics of Mental Imagery." *Mind* 5: 301–18.

Kind, Amy. 2001. "Putting the Image Back in Imagination." *Philosophy and Phenomenological Research* 62: 85–109.

Ryle, Gilbert. 1949. *The Concept of Mind*. Chicago: University of Chicago Press.

Van Leeuwen, Neil. 2013. "The Meanings of 'Imagine' Part I: Constructive Imagination." *Philosophy Compass* 8 (3): 220–30.

Walton, Kendall. 1990. *Mimesis as Make-Believe*. Cambridge, MA: Harvard University Press.

White, Alan. 1990. *The Language of Imagination*. Oxford: Blackwell.

Zeman, Adam, Dewar, M., and Della Sala, S. 2015. "Lives without Imagery: Congenital Aphantasia." *Cortex* 73: 378–80

33

COLOR SWATCHES AND SPECKLED HENS

BACKGROUND

Although perception is perhaps the most fundamental way we can know about the world outside the mind, our senses can clearly lead us astray. There are everyday cases of misperception—as when a drinking straw in a glass of water looks bent or when orange juice tastes foul after brushing your teeth. There are also more extreme scenarios where we can be in error. You could be hallucinating a hedgehog, or could be fooled about all external appearances by an evil demon who systematically deceives you. Even though we can be very wrong in these cases, it seems there is something we cannot be wrong about: the way things seem to us. The straw *seems* bent and there *seems* to be a hedgehog. This epistemological point slides naturally into a metaphysical view: though we might be wrong about there being a pink elephant, we nonetheless have an internal image of a pink elephant. Internal states such as images determine how things seem to us. As such, if such internal states seem a certain way, they are that way. Some philosophers put the point in terms of there being a "common factor" between perceptions and misperceptions. There is something mental in common between a hallucination of a hedgehog and a perception of a hedgehog: the sense impression or internal image of a hedgehog. While we can be wrong about there really being a hedgehog, we can't be wrong about the image of a hedgehog. We can call this *the theory of seemings*. The theory of seemings typically has two parts, one metaphysical and one epistemological: (1) when something seems like F to you, there is a mental image or a "seeming" that is F; and (2) you cannot be wrong about whether that seeming is F. The cases we consider in this chapter challenge the theory of seemings, and thereby also challenge the common factor view.

THE CASE

Suppose there is a series of 100 color swatches, S1 to S100, ranging from blue to green (Putnam 1999). The transition between swatches is very gradual—so much so that any two consecutive swatches seem indistinguishable to you. We can imagine the following case. If you look at S1 and S2 together, they appear indistinguishable, and the same is true for S2 and S3. But if you look at S1 and S3 side by side, they seem different. Though this is a common enough case, it poses a problem for the theory of seemings. According to that theory, when you look at S1, S2, and S3 you have seemings S★1, S★2, and S★3. Since in this case seemings are how the swatches seem, and S★1 and S★2 are indistinguishable, S★1 and S★2 are qualitatively identical. So then are S★2 and S★3. But there is a problem: S★1 and S★3 are distinguishable, so they are not qualitatively identical. But if S★1 is qualitatively identical to S★2 and S★2 is qualitatively identical to S★3, then, by the transitivity of identity, S★1 must be qualitatively identical to S★3. But, since you can distinguish between them, they aren't qualitatively identical. So we have a contradiction: S★1 is qualitatively identical to S★3 by the transitivity of identity, but, since they are distinguishable, they are not qualitatively identical. The theory of seemings therefore must be wrong: there cannot be internal states defined by how things seem. This suggests that the view that there is an internal common factor between perceptions and misperceptions—a common factor that explains how things seem—is incorrect.

DISCUSSION

One concern about the swatches argument is that it seems to assume that a swatch seems the same across contexts. But the defender of seemings will probably deny this (Jackson and Pinkerton 1973). It could be that how a particular swatch seems depends on what else is seen with it. When S1 is side by side with S2, they seem the same, and both S1 and S2 generate qualitatively identical seemings. The same is true when S2 is seen next to S3. But there is no single way S2 seems. When S2 is compared to S1, it generates the seeming S★2 (which is qualitatively identical to S★1), but when it is compared to S3 it generates the seeming S★★2 (which is qualitatively identical to S★2). This line of reasoning, which we can call the *contextual seemings view*, blocks the argument because there is no single seeming that is qualitatively identical with S★1 and S★3.

Despite its success in blocking the swatches argument, the contextual seemings view might be unsatisfying to some. The problem is that the seemings don't really seem to change from context to context. S2 itself arguably doesn't seem to change from context to context—we don't feel we are looking at a slightly different color depending on what it is compared to. Perhaps we just don't notice the shift in seemings, but then it turns out that we are fallible about those seemings after all. That's not necessarily a problem for the view—the theory of seemings can drop the claim that all judgments about seemings are infallible.

The idea that we have seemings but have fallible access to them receives support from another thought experiment (Chisholm 1942). Suppose you are looking at a speckled hen with 40 speckles. You can clearly be wrong, at least at a glance, about whether there are 40 speckles. But, according to the theory of seemings, you have an image of a speckled hen that you can't be wrong about. Now consider your image: how many speckles are in your image? Even if you counted or were willing to hazard a guess as to the number of speckles in your image, it seems clear that you could easily be wrong. The theory of seemings is therefore false: there are no mental images or seemings you cannot be wrong about. On the one hand, this is an epistemological conclusion about what we can know by introspection. But it could be seen as making a metaphysical point as well: there are no internal seemings. If there were, then when it seemed to you that the hen had 40 spots, there would be an image, a seeming, that had 40 spots. But, even if you had such an image, you could be wrong about it—it could seem to you the image had 41 spots when it had 40. It can, in other words, seem to you that there are 40 spots without there being anything—in the world or in your mind—that has 40 spots. It seems to you that things are a certain way, but there is no seeming. If we don't need seemings to explain how things seem in this case, this undermines the case for positing them in the first place.

The problem of the speckled hen isn't as easily resolved by the context-dependence solution that we discussed above in connection with the swatches case. One can hold the context fixed, focusing on just one image, and it seems clear that one doesn't know how many speckles there are. It is tempting to say that this isn't really a problem for the theory of seemings because it doesn't seem to you that there are, say, 39 speckles. It doesn't seem to you that there is any particular number of speckles at all. But this leads to counterintuitive results: it suggests that there can be seemings, or mental images, with speckles but no determinate number of speckles. This initially seems implausible (Chisholm 1942). One can presumably know in a case like this that there are more than two or three speckles and fewer than 100. But how could there be between three and 100 speckles without there being either 4, or 5 or ... 99? Indeed, it is likely that the image of the hen seems to have a determinate number of speckles—you could count them if you liked. (Though, even if one did, one could easily be wrong.)

Is it so strange, though, to say that our representation of the hen is indeterminate? Munton (2021) argues that this only seems strange because we are implicitly accepting a pictorial model of perception, according to which our representation of a scene is like a photograph of it. On this model, it makes sense to represent redness only by, say, representing a particular instance of red in all its determinacy. But, Munton insists, representation is not always like that. We can hope that our team wins without hoping for a particular score. I can remember that I caught a fish on my seventh birthday without remembering the particular kind or size of fish. Perceiving the speckled hen—or really anything complex—is more like this than it is of possessing a mental picture of the hen. If this is plausible, it provides an elegant resolution of the puzzle.

Some philosophers prefer to retain the metaphysical portion of the theory of seemings—perhaps along with the implicit pictorialism—but reject its strong epistemological claim (Fantl and Howell 2003). There are determinate mental images on this view, but we can be wrong about their properties. In the case of the hen, we represent it as having a determinate number of speckles, but we're fallible about certain features of our representations. This fallibilist position offers a solution to the swatches puzzle as well. S★1 and S★2 are in fact qualitatively distinguishable, but we are fallible about slight qualitative differences in our sensory representations.

It might seem, though, that this solution flies in the face of the intuitions that made us posit "seemings" in the first place. How can we be wrong about how our seemings seem? Either two things seem the same or they don't. It is very odd sounding to say that we have mental images that account for how things seem, but that we are wrong about how they seem.

But defenders of the solution argue that this criticism equivocates on two different notions of "seems" (Jackson 1977, Fantl and Howell 2003). We might say that there is a *phenomenal* sense of "seems," which captures the qualitative nature of our conscious states, and a *cognitive* sense of "seems," which reflects the judgments we are inclined to make. We can have seemings in the sense that there is something that it is like to see a 39-speckled hen, and this is qualitatively different from what it is like to see a 40-speckled hen; but we cannot form a reliable judgment about that phenomenology. It thus seems a certain way in that we have a certain determinate conscious state; but, because our judgments about that phenomenology are distinct from the phenomenology itself, we can be wrong about how things seem phenomenally (see Chapter 32.) As introduced above in the background section, the theory of seemings had two parts, one epistemic and the other metaphysical. This argument suggests they might stem from an ambiguity in the use of "seems" and that they can be, and perhaps should be, divorced from one another.

RECOMMENDED READING

CANONICAL PRESENTATIONS

Armstrong, D. M. 1968. *A Materialist Theory of the Mind*. New York: Routledge.
Chisholm, Roderick. 1942. "The Problem of the Speckled Hen." *Mind* 51 (204): 368–73.

OVERVIEW

Silins, Nicholas. 2021. "Perceptual Experience and Perceptual Justification." *The Stanford Encyclopedia of Philosophy* (Winter 2021 Edition), Edward N. Zalta (ed.), URL = <https://plato.stanford.edu/archives/win2021/entries/perception-justification/>.

ADDITIONAL DISCUSSIONS

Chuard, Philippe. 2010. "Non-Transitive Looks and Fallibilism." *Philosophical Studies* 149 (2): 161–200.

Fantl, Jeremy, and Howell, Robert J. 2003. "Sensations, Swatches, and Speckled Hens." *Pacific Philosophical Quarterly* 84 (4): 371–83.

Fara, Delia Graff. 2001. "Phenomenal Continua and the Sorites." *Mind* 110 (440): 905–35.

Fumerton, Richard. 2005. "Speckled Hens and Objects of Acquaintance." *Philosophical Perspectives* 19 (1): 121–38.

Jackson, Frank. 1977. *Perception: A Representative Theory*. Cambridge: Cambridge University Press.

Jackson, Frank, and Pinkerton, R. J. 1973. "On an Argument against Sensory Items." *Mind* 82 (326): 269–72.

Markie, Peter. 2009. "Classical Foundationalism and Speckled Hens." *Philosophy and Phenomenological Research* 79 (1): 190–206.

Munton, Jessie. 2021. "Visual Indeterminacy and the Puzzle of the Speckled Hen." *Mind and Language* 36 (5): 643–63.

Pace, Michael. 2010. "Foundationally Justified Perceptual Beliefs and the Problem of the Speckled Hen." *Pacific Philosophical Quarterly* 91 (3): 401–41.

Pautz, Adam. 2021. *Perception*. Abingdon: Routledge.

Putnam, Hilary. 1999. *The Threefold Cord: Mind, Body, and World*. New York: Columbia University Press.

34

THE SKYWALK

BACKGROUND

Folk psychology provides us with a categorization of distinct mental state types: belief, desire, imagination, hope, fear, intention, and so on. Over the centuries, this categorization has remained fairly stable. But in recent years various challenges have arisen that call the traditional categorization into question. Some of these challenges raise the question of whether all of these attitudes are really distinct from one another; perhaps instead some of them should be seen as being on a spectrum. For example, perhaps belief and imagination are not as different from one another as we have traditionally thought, but are instead continuous with one another (see, e.g., Schellenberg 2013, Block 2023). Other challenges raise the question of whether there are attitudes that we have previously failed to recognize but that need to be included in our categorization. The case we consider in this chapter poses this latter kind of challenge.

To understand how such a challenge arises, it will be useful to consider how philosophers differentiate mental states and attitudes from one another. Take a claim like "There are some brownies in the kitchen." It's possible for us to take many different mental attitudes towards that same content. We might believe that there are some brownies in the kitchen, hope that there are some brownies in the kitchen, fear that there are some brownies in the kitchen, and so on. When trying to explain the difference between these various attitudes, philosophers of mind tend to rely heavily on their different functional profiles. Believing that there are brownies in the kitchen will bring about different behavior from that brought about by fearing that there are brownies in the kitchen; and it also has different connections to other mental states. Occasionally, cases arise in which we see a person behaving in ways that don't match the expected functional profile of the mental states that we would typically see them as having. How should such cases be accounted for? Though sometimes we might be able to account for the behavior by reassessing which beliefs and desires (and other traditionally recognized mental states) the person has, sometimes this does not seem adequate. Faced with that inadequacy, another option would be to explore the addition of a new mental state category to our traditional taxonomy.

THE CASE

At the west rim of the Grand Canyon, on the Hualapai Reservation in Peach Springs, Arizona, is a remarkable glass bridge that was erected in 2007. This bridge, the Grand Canyon Skywalk, consists of more than 1 million pounds of steel and 83,000 points of glass, and in total it weighs 1.2 million pounds. Its foundation is strong enough to support approximately 71 million pounds. At 4000 feet high, Skywalk is more than twice as tall as New York's One World Trade Center and Taipei 101 in Taiwan, and considerably taller than the 2717-foot Burj Khalifa in Dubai, currently the world's tallest building.

As advertised on the Grand Canyon's website:

> Unparalleled views of one of the world's Seven Natural Wonders await you at Grand Canyon West on Skywalk. This breathtaking 10-foot wide, horseshoe-shaped glass bridge extends 70 feet out over the rim of the Grand Canyon, giving you a clear view 4,000 feet to the Canyon floor below. There's simply no thrill like stepping out on glass thousands of feet in the air, yet there's no need to be nervous—Skywalk is strong enough to hold seventy fully loaded 747 passenger jets.
>
> (https://grandcanyonwest.com/things-to-do/skywalk/)

In the first five years after its opening, more than 1.8 million people visited Skywalk, and in January 2020 attendance hit the 10 million visitor mark. Presumably, visitors to Skywalk believe it is safe. They have read the statistics, and they see all the people safely walking across it. And it's hard to believe that anyone would step out onto a bridge that high if they really had any doubt that they were in danger. Yet it is not at all uncommon for people to hesitate before stepping out. Some end up refusing to go through with the experience, despite having paid a hefty admission fee. And even those who do manage to make it to the center of the bridge are likely to feel a rush of vertigo as they do so. Despite their belief that everything is safe, it's as if there's some inner voice yelling at them "Danger! Danger! Really high! Long way down! Get back!"

But why are people at Skywalk in this kind of state, given their firm belief that everything is safe? Why do they hesitate? As Tamar Gendler (2008a) puts it, there is a belief–behavior mismatch, and this presents us with a puzzle. And the case of Skywalk is not the only situation where this kind of puzzle arises. Empirical studies have shown that people are uncomfortable eating fudge that has been formed in the shape of dog poop, that they are hesitant to eat soup out of a brand-new bedpan, and that they are disinclined to drink sugar water that has been labeled "poison." In the empirical literature, phenomena such as these are often treated as cases of "sympathetic magic" (Rozin et al. 1986). Let's flesh out the details of the last example.

Study participants saw an experimenter open a commercially labeled box of sugar and pour some of it into two clean, empty bottles. They were then given two labels—one that said "sucrose" and one that said "sodium cyanide, poison"—and instructed to stick one to each bottle. The participants watched while water from the same source was poured into two glasses, and they also saw some powder from the bottle marked "poison" mixed into one glass and some powder from the bottle marked "sucrose" mixed into the other glass. Following all of this, participants were asked to rate how willing they were to take a sip from each glass, and the results showed a significant preference for the bottle that was labeled "sucrose"—even though participants acknowledged that they knew there was no poison in either glass, and that both glasses contained the same sugar water (Rozin et al. 1986).

How do we account for these cases? It doesn't look like an instance of contradictory beliefs. People at Skywalk don't seem to have the belief "It's not safe" alongside their belief "It's safe." And it's hard to see how people in the sugar water experiment would believe "There's poison in this glass." Do they merely imagine that Skywalk is unsafe or that there's poison in the glass? The problem with this suggestion is that imaginings tend to be quarantined off from real-life belief and action. As Gendler puts it, imagination is like Las Vegas—what happens in imagination stays in imagination (2008b, p. 568).

DISCUSSION

In Gendler's view, the best way to resolve the puzzle is to postulate the existence of a novel mental state—what she calls *alief*. Alief is a state that is associative, automatic, and arational. It is not reducible to belief or other mental states/attitudes. In fact, it is both developmentally and conceptually antecedent to these related mental states/attitudes. Moreover, aliefs are action-generating and affect-laden. In the Skywalk case, for example, we can explain the visitors' reluctance to step out onto the glass bridge in terms of their alief with the representational–affective–behavioral content that includes "the visual appearance as of a cliff, the feeling of fear and the motor routine of retreat" (Gendler 2008a, p. 641).

In fact, Gendler thinks aliefs can be invoked to explain a whole host of other phenomena as well. Why does a soccer fan watching a replay of an earlier match yell at the players to pass, or to shoot, or to run faster? Why does a committed antiracism activist exhibit preferences for Caucasian faces over Black faces when taking the Implicit-Association test? Why does a movie-goer watching a horror film startle and shriek when the monster appears out of nowhere to claim a new victim? In all of these cases, Gendler thinks the behavior is best explained by attributing a certain alief to the relevant individual.

Not everyone agrees that we need to invoke aliefs to explain the belief–behavior mismatch in cases like the Skywalk. Eric Mandelbaum (2013) has posed a dilemma to Gendler: either the content of an alief is propositional or it is associative. If the content is propositional–of the sort "this is a dangerous situation," say—then it's not clear why aliefs are really any different from beliefs. But if the content is associative—of a sort that is not accessible for truth or falsity—then it's not clear that aliefs can really play the explanatory role that Gendler needs them to play. (For a response to Mandelbaum's worry, see Danón 2021.)

A related criticism has been raised by Greg Currie and Anna Ichino (2012), who argue that the kinds of cases that prompt Gendler to postulate the novel category of alief can all be accounted for in terms of mental-state types that we already countenance. Consider the sports fan or the sugar water study participant. When watching the match replay, the fan might be vividly imagining that they are present at the match. When faced with the option of drinking from a glass labeled "poison," the study participant might be vividly imagining that the glass contains poison. Moreover, though imagination is *often* quarantined off from belief, it is not always so—as Gendler herself has argued in other work (2006). In many cases when we engage with fiction or games of pretend, our imaginings are not cordoned off from what we believe, but are integrated in various ways with that content. In reality, what happens in Vegas doesn't always stay there either.

A different kind of criticism arises from Gendler's characterization of alief as having a novel kind of content that combines representational, affective, and behavioral elements all in one. Some have charged that alief seems best understood as an amalgam of different kinds of mental state types rather than as single, unified mental-state type of its own (Doggett 2012). Though the different components of alief may tend to be co-activated, that doesn't entail that there is any greater unity to the phenomenon, and certainly not the kind of unity that generates the postulation of a *sui generis* mental-state type.

RECOMMENDED READING

CANONICAL PRESENTATIONS

Gendler, Tamar Szabó. 2008a. "Alief and Belief." *Journal of Philosophy* 105 (10): 634–63.

Gendler, Tamar Szabó. 2008b. "Alief in Action (and Reaction)." *Mind and Language* 23 (5): 552–85.

OVERVIEW

Gendler, Tamar Szabó. 2010. *Intuition, Imagination, and Philosophical Methodology*. Oxford: Oxford University Press. (See pp. 1–17, "Introduction," especially Section 4.)

ADDITIONAL DISCUSSIONS

Brownstein, Michael, and Madva, Alex. 2012. "The Normativity of Automaticity." *Mind and Language* 72 (4): 410–34.

Currie, Greg, and Ichino, Anna. 2012. "Aliefs Don't Exist, Though Some of their Relatives Do." *Analysis* 72 (4): 788–98.

Danón, Laura. 2021. "The Content of Aliefs." *Synthese* 198 (9): 8503–20.

Doggett, Tyler. 2012. "Some Questions for Tamar Szabó Gendler." *Analysis* 72 (4): 764–74.

Kwong, Jack M. C. 2012. "Resisting Aliefs: Gendler on Belief-Discordant Behaviors." *Philosophical Psychology* 25 (1): 77–91.

Leddington, Jason. 2016. "The Experience of Magic." *Journal of Aesthetics and Art Criticism* 74 (3): 253–64.

Mandelbaum, Eric. 2013. "Against Alief." *Philosophical Studies* 165 (1): 197–211.

Nagel, Jennifer. 2012. "Gendler on Alief." *Analysis* 72 (4): 774–88.

OTHER REFERENCES

Block, Ned. 2023. *The Border between Seeing and Thinking*. New York: Oxford University Press.

Gendler, Tamar Szabó. 2006. "Imaginative Contagion." *Metaphilosophy* 37 (2): 183–203.

Rozin, Paul, Millman, L., and Nemeroff, Carol. 1986. "Operation of the Laws of Sympathetic Magic in Disgust and Other Domains." *Journal of Personality and Social Psychology* 50: 703–12.

Schellenberg, Susanna. 2013. "Belief and Desire in Imagination and Immersion." *Journal of Philosophy* 110: 497–517.

PINE TREES AND CYRILLIC TEXT

BACKGROUND

Many philosophers take perceptual experiences to represent things—that is, to have representational content. For example, visual experiences can represent colors, such as the black color of the letters printed on this page. Here "represent" could be understood in terms of *accuracy conditions*—that is, conditions under which your experience is or is not accurate (or more or less accurate). If your current experience represents the presence of blackness, then your experience is accurate if and only if something you are seeing is black. Your experience is inaccurate if, for example, the page is blank but you are hallucinating. What sort of properties does perception represent? Most agree that visual perception represents colors, shapes, depth, and illumination. But what about high-level properties, such as *being a table* or *being a horse*? Are those ever represented in visual perception? Some think the answer is no: the categories of being a table and being a horse are not part of your visual perceptual content, which is limited to representing low-level properties such as color and shape (e.g., Dretske 1995, Tye 1995, Clark 2000). According to this view, high-level categories are introduced only after perceptual processing is completed, by a different part of your cognitive system. Susanna Siegel (2006, 2010) disagrees. According to what she calls *the Rich Content View*, high-level properties can, and often do, figure into perceptual content. Siegel's main argument for that view appeals to examples of perception, including one involving pine trees and one involving Cyrillic text.

THE CASES

First example: you've been hired to cut down all the pine trees in a grove that contains many different sorts of trees. You don't know what pine trees look like. Fortunately for you (though not for the pines), someone points out which trees are pines, and your ability to recognize pine trees improves over the following weeks. Eventually, you can spot them almost immediately.

Second example: you look at a page filled with Cyrillic text, but you can't read Russian. To you, what's on the page are just meaningless squiggles and squoggles. Then you go about learning to read Russian, and eventually you succeed. The same page, with the Cyrillic text unaltered, looks notably different to you than it used to. When you started to learn, you had to attend to each letter separately, but now it actually takes effort to do that. You perceive the symbols as meaningful words and sentences.

Both examples involve a sort of experiential shift: a marked change in *what it's like* for you to perceive the same thing (a pine tree or some Cyrillic writing). How should that be explained? According to Siegel, the answer is provided by the Rich Content View. Before you learned how to recognize pine trees by sight, the property of *being a pine tree* was not part of the representational content of your visual experience of seeing a pine tree. But that property is part of that content now that you're an expert pine-tree spotter. That, Siegel argues, is what explains the perceptual change. Likewise, the change in how Cyrillic looks to you now, as compared to when you couldn't read it, is explained by which properties your visual experiences represent. After, but not before, you learned how to read Russian, your experiences represented semantic properties of the Cyrillic symbols (*semantic* properties are properties concerning meaning). In both cases, there is a striking experiential shift, which Siegel calls a *phenomenal contrast*. That, in brief, is Siegel's argument for the Rich Content View: we should believe it because it explains the phenomenal contrasts.

The examples of the pine trees and the Cyrillic text are not exotic or unusual. The sort of perceptual change they illustrate is common. Charles Siewert (1998, ch. 7) provides several other examples, such as the fact that a person might look different to you after you've gotten to know them, and the fact that your neighborhood might look different to you after you've lived there for a while. Also, the focus on cases involving vision is not essential. For example, there is a marked difference in what it's like to *hear* a foreign language before and after learning it (Block 1995, p. 234). According to Siegel, the Rich Content View explains such facts about perception.

DISCUSSION

Can the phenomenal-contrast cases Siegel discusses be explained without appeal to the Rich Content View? There have been attempts to provide alternative explanations. For example, Casey O'Callaghan (2011) denies that the difference in how a foreign language sounds to you before and after you learn it is best explained by saying that you hear the meanings of words (that is, by saying that your auditory contents represent semantic properties). A better explanation, he argues, is that, when you learn, you come to hear phonological (not semantic) features specific to that language (cf. Prinz 2006; but see Brogaard 2018). Other parts of Siegel's argument are also in dispute, and positive arguments for the view that she opposes have been advanced (O'Shaughnessy 2000, ch. 17). But both the Rich Content View and Siegel's argument for it remain influential; and, further, more empirically based arguments for the Rich Content View (or something close to it) have also been developed (Block 2023).

The Rich Content View relates to a host of philosophical issues (Siegel 2010, pp. 7–11). Some concern specific high-level properties. For example, consider the Humean claim that one can perceive the succession of events but not causal relations among events (see Chapter 31). Assuming causation is a high-level property, that Humean claim might lose some of its motivation if the Rich Content View is true. The Rich Content View also relates to general issues concerning mental representation, including, for example: why are any mental states *about* anything, and why do particular mental states have the representational contents they do (see Chapters 23 and 24)? The Rich

Content View puts constraints on theories intended to answer those questions. If the Rich Content View is true, then the explanation had better allow for the fact that perceptual contents represent high-level features. According to Siegel (2010, pp. 11–13), the Rich Content view also relates to various issues in psychology and neuroscience.

To mention one more related philosophical issue: can we draw a clean distinction, in the philosophy of science, between observation and theory? Siegel's main argument for the Rich Content View, if sound, complicates that distinction. According to her argument, expertise can influence what experience represents. If so, then if a distinction between observation and theory can be drawn at all, it "will not align with the representation of low-level properties, on the one hand, and high-level properties on the other" (Siegel 2021, sec. 4.3).

Both proponents and opponents of the Rich Content View assume that perceptual experiences have representational contents, and that assumption is controversial. But, as Siegel observes, the Rich Content View and her argument for it could be framed without it. For example, according to one alternative view about perception, known as *relationalism* or *naïve realism*, in veridical perception one's experience is partly constituted by a perceived object and its properties, rather than representations thereof (Campbell 2002, p. 116). But in that case the issue will simply be recast as concerning whether the relevant properties include high-level properties.

RECOMMENDED READING

CANONICAL PRESENTATIONS

Siegel, Susanna. 2006. "Which Properties Are Represented in Perception?" In T. S. Gendler and J. Hawthorne (eds.) *Perceptual Experience*. Oxford: Oxford University Press: 481–503.

Siegel, Susanna. 2010. *The Contents of Visual Experience*. New York: Oxford University Press. (See Chapter 4.)

OVERVIEWS

Siegel, Susanna. 2021. "The Contents of Perception." *The Stanford Encyclopedia of Philosophy* (Fall 2021 Edition), Edward N. Zalta (ed.), URL = <https://plato.stanford.edu/archives/fall2021/entries/perception-contents/>. (Section 4, esp. 4.3.)

Connolly, Kevin. 2017. "Perceptual Learning." *The Stanford Encyclopedia of Philosophy* (Summer 2017 Edition), Edward N. Zalta (ed.), URL = <https://plato.stanford.edu/archives/sum2017/entries/perceptual-learning/>. (Section 3, esp. 3.1.)

ADDITIONAL DISCUSSIONS

Block, Ned. 1995. "On a Confusion about a Function of Consciousness." *Behavioral and Brain Sciences* 18 (2): 227–47.

Block, Ned. 2023. *The Border between Seeing and Thinking*. New York: Oxford University Press.

Brogaard, Berit. 2018. "In Defense of Hearing Meanings." *Synthese* 195 (7): 2967–83.

Campbell, John. 2002. *Reference and Consciousness*. Oxford: Oxford University Press.

Clark, Austen. 2000. *A Theory of Sentience*. Oxford: Oxford University Press.

Dretske, Fred. 1995. *Naturalizing the Mind*. Cambridge, MA: MIT Press.

Masrour, Farid. 2011. "Is Perceptual Phenomenology Thin?" *Philosophy and Phenomenological Research* 83 (2): 366–97.

Nanay, Bence. 2011. "Do We See Apples as Edible?" *Pacific Philosophical Quarterly* 92 (3): 305–22.

O'Callaghan, Casey. 2011. "Against Hearing Meanings." *Philosophical Quarterly* 61 (245): 783–807.

O'Shaughnessy, Brian (ed.). 2000. *Consciousness and the World*. Oxford: Oxford University Press.

Peacocke, Christopher. 1992. *A Study of Concepts*. Cambridge, MA: MIT Press.

Prinz, Jesse J. 2006. "Beyond Appearances: The Content of Sensation and Perception." In T. S. Gendler and J. Hawthorne (eds.) *Perceptual Experience*. Oxford: Oxford University Press: 434–60.

Siewert, Charles. 1998. *The Significance of Consciousness*. Princeton: Princeton University Press.

Tye, Michael. 1995. *Ten Problems of Consciousness*. Cambridge, MA: MIT Press.

SYNESTHESIA

BACKGROUND

In cases of synesthesia, a sensory stimulation typically associated with one perceptual modality will automatically prompt or trigger an experience in another perceptual modality (cross-sensory synesthesia) or a different type of experience in the same sensory modality (intrasensory synesthesia). Two of the most common types of synesthesia are chromesthesia and grapheme-color synesthesia. When someone has chromesthesia, also known as *colored hearing*, certain sounds will trigger certain color experiences; for example, the sound of a C sharp being played on the piano might trigger an experience of the color blue. When someone has grapheme-color synesthesia, the numeral 2 might appear to be red in color or the letter D might appear to be green in color. Though the colors associated with particular letters and numbers vary from one synesthete to another—so the number 2 might appear red to one synesthete and blue to another—they stay constant for a given synesthete over time. If the number 2 appears red to a synesthete, it will always appear red to that synesthete. Among the many other varieties of synesthesia, there is also taste-tactile association, taste-color association, olfactory-tactile association, and visual-olfactory association. Sometimes cases are classified as forms of synesthesia even when the trigger is not sensory in nature, as when days of the week are taken to be colored or months are taken to have locations in space. In this chapter, we will focus on the sensory cases.

Although references to the phenomenon of synesthesia can be found as far back as the 17th century, and though it was discussed by Francis Galton in the late 19th century, it did not generate much sustained attention until the 1980s. Estimates vary widely about what percentage of people have synesthesia, from well below 1% of the population to as high as 15%, though one especially well-regarded study reports the prevalence of synesthesia to be 4.4% (Simner et al. 2006; for discussion see Johnson et al. 2013). The condition seems to be more common in females than in males, though some recent studies have demonstrated otherwise (e.g., Simner et al. 2006). Synesthesia seems to run in families and seems to be an inherited condition; but there are also some cases of acquired synesthesia, sometimes due to neurological conditions and sometimes due to the use of hallucinogenic drugs. Moreover, some cultures, such as the Ancient Mayan and other Mesoamerican peoples, seem to have put great emphasis on the cultivation of cross-modal experiences like those associated with synesthesia—an emphasis that is revealed throughout their art, architecture, and other cultural practices (see Houston and Taube 2000).

THE CASE

Consider a typical synesthete whom we'll call Cyndi. Cyndi has chromesthesia. For her, making breakfast is a very colorful experience. When she puts the bacon into the pan and hears the sizzle, she has a sensation of red. When she cracks an egg, she has a sensation of blue. And when she pours orange juice into a glass, she has a sensation of green.

How are we to characterize these color experiences? Are they perceptual in nature? If so, should we say that Cyndi is *seeing* green or *hearing* green? Neither of these options seems satisfactory.

On the one hand, given that colors are typically discriminated visually, it may seem tempting to say that Cyndi is seeing green as she's pouring the orange juice. But there is nothing green in her visual field. Her eyes may even be closed while she is having the relevant experience. Moreover, given that her color experience is caused by an auditory stimulus, it may seem odd to characterize her perceptual experience as something that's visual in nature. One way that we distinguish auditory experiences from visual experiences is in terms of the kinds of inputs that generate the relevant experience. In Cyndi's case, there is not the kind of input typical of visual experiences. In this case, the input is auditory in nature.

That suggests that we should say she is hearing the color. And in fact, this is how synesthesia is often described, as in neurologist Richard Cytowic's 1998 book titled, *The Man Who Tasted Shapes* (see also Brang and Ramachandran 2011). But it's not clear how we are to make sense of the claim that colors can be heard. Given the nature of colors, they are not the kinds of experiences that can be discriminated from one another by way of auditory perception. All of their properties are visual in nature (hue, brightness, etc.). They do not have auditory properties (volume, tone, etc.).

So, it's hard to know how to classify Cyndi's perceptual experience. Shall we just say that her senses have gotten cross-wired? Though the description may seem apt, it doesn't provide us with much of an explanation of what's going on, but rather seems simply to re-describe the case.

Perhaps instead we should deny that Cyndi's experience is perceptual in nature. Perhaps we should say that she's merely imagining green. But this too seems implausible. Typically, imagination is voluntarily produced, but Cyndi would deny that her experience of green is something that she's voluntarily producing. Also, we can usually tell when we're imagining and when we're perceiving; but it doesn't feel to Cyndi like she's imagining. Moreover, tests reveal that her experience of the sound of pouring orange juice and the sensation of green are stably coordinated for her over a long period of time. The connection between the sound and the color seems to be too tight and too immediate for it to be simply an imaginative association or some other learned association of ideas. And there's nothing special about Cyndi. Tests on other synesthetes reveal similar results. For example, consider a typical color-grapheme synesthete whom we'll call Jade. For Jade, the number 2 appears red (see Ramachandran and Hubbard 2001). She is presented with an array of numbers printed in green ink. All of them are 5s except for a few 2s that are scattered throughout the array. When asked to point out the 2s, Jade can almost instantly locate them. She can locate them in the same amount of time it takes for non-synesthetes to do so when the 5s are printed in black and the 2s are printed in some other bright color). As Jade tells the researchers, because the 2s appear red to her, they "pop out" from the 5s. Her performance on these tests suggest to the researchers that the triggered colors must be genuinely perceptual in nature—that is, they are being processed by her visual system.

DISCUSSION

Among the many puzzles that synesthesia presents, one concerns the nature of sense perception and the individuation of the senses. How can we make sense of an experience's being visual in nature rather than auditory or rather than tactile? Some philosophers try to distinguish the senses by way of the sensory organ used; some try to distinguish them in terms of typical (and often proprietary) stimuli. But both of these ways of doing so are challenged by the case of synesthesia. Cyndi need not be using her eyes to "see" red when the bacon sizzles. Moreover, the stimulus she actually senses (the sound of sizzling bacon) is proprietary to audition, while color is proprietary to vision.

In response to this puzzle, some researchers have suggested that we need to rethink the way we differentiate the senses from one another. Generally speaking, for example, discussions of the senses treat them as relatively discrete systems. As noted by Brian Keeley, "it is common to assume that the different senses are significantly separate and independent of one another" (2002, p. 25). Synesthesia calls this assumption into question. If we were to drop this assumption, then synesthesia would no longer be as puzzling. Dropping this assumption would also enable us to provide a better account of other puzzling phenomena, such as the McGurk effect—a phenomenon in which the same syllable is heard differently depending on the visual input one is having. For example, when one looks at a face making the typical mouth movements associated with "Fa," one will hear the syllable "Ba" as "Fa". On this kind of response to the puzzle of synesthesia, rather than thinking of synesthesia as a case where the senses have gotten "cross-wired," perhaps we should conceive of the senses as not being separately wired in the first place.

In addition to presenting a puzzle about the individuation of the senses, synesthesia has also been thought to raise challenges for functionalist theories of mind (Gray, 2004). On a functionalist view, mental states are defined in terms of their functional roles, and states that have different functional roles are thus classified as states of different types (see Chapters 15 and 16). A state's functional role is specified partly in terms of its cause, and so the functional role of a color experience will be specified partly in terms of the stimulation of the visual system (perhaps more specifically, the stimulation of the retina). For example, when Cyndi sees a red apple and has a red experience, her retina is stimulated. But Cyndi claims to have the same experience of red—an experience that feels the same to her as the one she has when she sees a red apple—when she hears bacon sizzling. In this case, there is a complete absence of the relevant stimulation of the visual system. As we noted earlier, Cyndi's eyes may even be closed. Thus, even though these two experiences of red are experientially the same, because they have different functional roles, functionalism cannot classify them as the same kind of experience. In response to these worries, various defenses of functionalism have been proposed. Some have argued that more sophisticated versions of functionalism can escape the challenge from synesthesia (Macpherson 2007), while others have argued that we should treat synesthetic experience as a malfunction, and thus not take it to shed any light on a given mental state's *typical* functional role (Gray 2001).

Other philosophers have used related considerations to raise worries about representationalist views of consciousness—that is, the view that phenomenal character is nothing over and above representational content (see, e.g., Wager 1999, Rosenberg 2004; see Chapters 19 and 20). Here the problem seems to arise from the fact that mental states can be the same representationally without being the same phenomenally. When a non-synesthete hears bacon sizzling and when Cyndi hears bacon sizzling, the thought goes, the experiences have the same representational content (of bacon sizzling), but Cyndi's experience has "extra" phenomenal content. In response, however, the representationalist might try to find differences between the representational contents of the two experiences (see, e.g., Alter 2006).

Finally, synesthesia might be seen to raise worries about the reliability of introspection. Generally speaking, we are deferential to individuals when they are reporting their experiences. Even if introspective reports are not infallible, we tend to think that people themselves are the best judges of what kinds of experiences they are having. With respect to synesthesia, however, some philosophers and other researchers have worried about the accuracy or completeness of individuals' introspective reports. Take synesthetes with grapheme-color synesthesia and, in particular, someone like Jade, for whom the number 2 appears red. When looking at a page with the number 2 printed on it, the synesthete can accurately report what color ink was used (black, say). So, the number must also appear black to them. As Fiona Macpherson argues, it is hard to make sense of how this could be—that is, how the number could appear both (wholly) red and (wholly) black to someone like Jade. Could there really be experiences that represent two colors to be (wholly) in the same place at the same time? Could the red experience really be just like the red experience Jade has when looking at an apple? On Macpherson's view, more work is needed to untangle and understand the introspective reports of synesthetes and the phenomenal nature of synesthetic experience.

RECOMMENDED READING

CANONICAL PRESENTATION

Cytowic, Richard. 1998. *The Man Who Tasted Shapes*. Cambridge, MA: MIT Press.

OVERVIEWS

Allen-Hermanson, Sean, and Matey, Jennifer. 2012. "Synesthesia." *Internet Encyclopedia of Philosophy*. https://iep.utm.edu/synesthe/.

Hubbard, Edward M., and Ramachandran, Vilayanur S. 2006. "Hearing Colors, Tasting Shapes." *Scientific American* 16 (3s): 76–83. doi:10.1038/scientificamerican0906-76sp.

ADDITIONAL DISCUSSIONS

Alter, Torin. 2006. "Does Synesthesia Undermine Representationalism?" *Psyche* 12 (5). https://journalpsyche.org/files/0xab04.pdf.

Brogaard, Berit. 2014. "Varieties of Synesthetic Experience." In Richard Brown (ed.) *Consciousness Inside and Out: Phenomenology, Neuroscience, and the Nature of Experience*. Dordrecht: Springer: 409–12.

Gray, Jeffrey. 2004. *Consciousness: Creeping Up on the Hard Problem*. Oxford: Oxford University Press. (See especially Chapter 10.)

Gray, Richard. 2001. "Cognitive Modules, Synaesthesia and the Constitution of Psychological Natural Kinds." *Philosophical Psychology* 14 (1): 65–82.

Johnson, Donielle, Allison, Carrie, and Baron-Cohen, Simon. 2013. "The Prevalence of Synesthesia." In Julia Simner and Edward Hubbard (eds.) *The Oxford Handbook of Synesthesia.* Oxford: Oxford University Press: 3–22.

Keeley, Brian. 2002. "Making Sense of the Senses: Individuating Modalities in Humans and Other Animals." *Journal of Philosophy* 99 (1): 5–28.

Macpherson, Fiona. 2007. "Synaesthesia, Functionalism, and Phenomenology." In Massimo Marraffa, Mario De Caro, and Francesco Ferretti (eds.) *Cartographies of the Mind: Philosophy and Psychology in Intersection.* Dordrecht: Springer: 65–80.

Ramachandran, Vilayanur S., and Hubbard, Edward M. 2001. "Psychophysical Investigations into the Neural Basis of Synaesthesia." *Proceedings of the Royal Society of London B* 268: 979–83.

Rosenberg, G. 2004. *A Place for Consciousness: Probing the Deep Structure of the Natural World.* New York: Oxford University Press.

Sagiv, Noam, and Frith, Chris D. 2013. "Synesthesia and Consciousness." In Julia Simner and Edward Hubbard (eds.) *The Oxford Handbook of Synesthesia.* Oxford: Oxford University Press: 924–40.

Segal, Gabriel. 1997. "Synaesthesia: Implications for Modularity of Mind." In Simon Baron-Cohen and J. Harrison (eds.) *Synaesthesia: Classic and Contemporary Readings.* Cambridge, MA: Blackwell: 211–23.

Wager, A. 2001. "Synaesthesia Misrepresented." *Philosophical Psychology* 14 (3): 347–51.

OTHER REFERENCES

Brang, David, and Ramachandran, Vilayanur S. 2011. "Survival of the Synesthesia Gene: Why Do People Hear Colors and Taste Words?" *PLoS Biology* 9 (11): 1–6.

Houston, Stephen, and Taube, Karl. 2000. "An Archaeology of the Senses: Perception and Cultural Expression in Ancient Mesoamerica." *Cambridge Archaeological Journal* 10 (2): 261–94.

Simner, Julia, Mulvenna, Catherine, Sagiv, Noam, Tsakanikos, Elias, Witherby, Sarah A., Fraser, Christine, Scott, Kirsten, and Ward, Jamie. 2006. "Synaesthesia: The Prevalence of Atypical Cross-Modal Experiences." *Perception* 35 (8): 1024–33.

37

CHANGE BLINDNESS

BACKGROUND

We tend to think of conscious visual perception on the model of a color photograph (or video)—as capturing the colors and shapes in one's visual field in remarkably rich detail. No doubt, things in front of our eyes have features to which we are oblivious. For one thing, there's a "blindspot" in the visual field, corresponding to where the optic nerve attaches to the retina. For another, unless we're wearing special goggles or something, we don't see infra-red light. But, within the range of humanly visible light, we usually see pretty much everything that a color photograph would capture (the blindspot area notwithstanding). Or so we tend to assume. Some philosophers challenge that assumption on the basis of a psychological phenomenon called *change blindness*, which is the failure to notice something markedly different about a display.

THE CASE

You're first shown drawing A, then drawing B. They seem identical (though in fact they are not). You look again. Still nothing. Then you look a third time, and finally you see it: in drawing B, someone's glasses are missing. This is an example of change blindness. Change blindness is common, and it has been demonstrated in the lab and in the field. In one study (Simons and Levin 1998), an experimenter asks an unsuspecting pedestrian for directions. While the pedestrian is busy pointing at a map and explaining the directions, two people carrying a door pass between them—so for a moment the person asking directions is behind the door—and the experimenter slyly changes places with one of the people carrying the door. About half of the pedestrians in the study didn't notice that, after the door passed by, they were talking with a different person, dressed entirely differently from the first person. Both cognitive scientists and philosophers have reflected on what change blindness shows about perceptual experience and consciousness more generally.

Consider the first example, and think about the first time you looked at drawing A. Did you see the glasses? Were they part of your conscious, visual experience? Consider another example (Dretske 2007). Sarah looks at seven people gathered around a table, each of whom is clearly visible to her. She looks at them for several seconds, and then briefly looks away. While she looks away, an eighth person, Sam, joins the group. He too is clearly visible. When Sarah looks back, she doesn't notice the difference. Does Sarah see Sam?

Several philosophers and cognitive psychologists say the answer to both questions is *no*. Sarah didn't see Sam, and you didn't see the glasses (until you looked the third time). Those "no" answers reflect the view that *perceptual consciousness is sparse*. That is, conscious perception is more informationally impoverished than we tend to assume it is. We do *not* see pretty much everything that a color photograph would capture (the blindspot area notwithstanding). A photograph of the eight people in Sarah's field of vision would depict Sam. Sarah's visual experience does not. Visual experience isn't nearly as rich as we tend to think.

Proponents of that conclusion also cite other evidence, such as the related phenomenon known as inattentional blindness. This happens when we fail to notice something that we would normally notice because our attention is directed elsewhere. A striking example of inattentional blindness goes like this (Simons and Chabris 1999). Subjects are shown a video in which six people are passing basketballs. Half are wearing white and half are wearing black. Subjects are instructed to count how many times the players wearing white pass the ball. After the video, they are first asked to report on the number they counted. Then they are asked, "Did you see the gorilla?" They are asked that second question because, in the middle of the video, someone in a gorilla suit walks into plain view, beats their chest, and leaves. About half of the subjects report that they did *not* see the gorilla!

Inattentional blindness and change blindness aren't identical. Only change blindness need involve the subject comparing a display with what they remember about an earlier one. But clearly, the two phenomena are related, and some take both to support the view that perceptual consciousness is sparse. On this view, the reason half the people who see the basketball video deny having seen the gorilla is simple: they didn't see the gorilla, even though it was there to be seen.

If perceptual experience is sparse, then why do we tend to assume otherwise? Proponents of the sparse experience have an explanation. If you even wonder whether you're seeing something in your visual field, you turn your attention to it, and *then* you see it. Our false assumption is an instance of *the refrigerator-light illusion*: thinking the light is always on because it's on every time you open the fridge door. We see things in our visual field only when we attend to them. Otherwise, they're only potentially seen.

DISCUSSION

Does change blindness (or inattentional blindness) really show that perceptual experience is sparse? Some think so (Blackmore et al. 1995, Rensink et al. 1997, Simons 1997, O'Regan and Noë 2001, Tye 2009). But others do not (Dretske 2007, Block 2007, 2012). How can we decide?

Some issues can be resolved empirically. For example, consider experimental results such as the following (Fernandez-Duque and Thornton 2000). Subjects are first shown pairs of pictures that look identical to them (in the way drawings A and B look to you at first). Then they do a forced-choice task of selecting those pairs where there is a change. In other words, they are told to choose which pairs aren't identical, even though they say all pairs look identical. They successfully identify the non-identical pairs at above-chance levels. This indicates that it's probably incorrect to say that your visual system doesn't register or represent the things in the visual that you don't notice. And so it's probably misleading to say, without qualification, that you're literally blind to those things—that, for example, Sarah doesn't visually perceive Sam in any sense.

But that doesn't settle the issue of whether Sarah *consciously* perceives Sam. It's consistent with the results of the forced-choice experiments that Sarah perceives Sam unconsciously, and that to see him consciously would require her focusing attention on him—at least enough for her to ask "Who (or what) is that?" Michael Tye defends that position. In his view, consciously seeing is less like taking a photograph than like drawing a picture. He writes: "At a conscious level, a constructive process operates that is something like drawing a picture. ... It is not like taking a clear, color photograph. It leaves things out" (2009, p. 167).

So, although Tye believes that "our visual fields do not have gaps in them" (because we unconsciously perceive things we don't notice), he maintains that *conscious* perception is sparse. Others deny that claim, holding instead that conscious perception is rich—roughly as rich as is common to assume. When you first see drawing A, you *do* see the glasses, and Sarah *does* see Sam—consciously, in both cases. You just don't *notice* that you do. On this view, consciousness requires neither attention nor access (at least not in the ways Tye and others think).

One proponent of that alternative view is Fred Dretske (2007). According to Dretske, Sarah sees Sam because she can know things about him by the way he looks. For example, she knows that no one gathered around the table was wearing a clown suit. If Sam had not been dressed normally (say, normally for a dinner party rather than a circus), then Sarah might not have been able to know that. Sarah saw Sam. She just didn't notice that she did. Dretske fleshes out that idea using a different example. Suppose you're shown an image of gray brick walls, with bricks missing in various, random places. Then you're shown an image that's the same except that there's one extra brick, in the middle somewhere, which Dretske names "Sam" (the same name he gives to the person that Sarah didn't notice in his other example). You don't see the difference. But had Sam been black instead of gray or tilted instead of straight, you would have seen the difference pretty much immediately. According to Dretske, you know some things about Sam: you know that Sam isn't black or tilted. Moreover, you know those things on the basis of how Sam looks. So, you see Sam. You just didn't notice that you did.

Dretske's argument can be resisted. For one thing, one could grant everything Dretske says but deny that you *consciously* see Sam. Instead, Sam's color and spatial orientation is detected on an unconscious level. For another, one could distinguish your knowing based on how the bricks look to you *collectively* and knowing based on how each brick in the collection looks to you *individually* (Tye 2009, p. 180). But even if Dretske's argument can be resisted, his conclusion might be true. There are ways to explain change blindness that are consistent with the view that conscious perception is rich. For example, one might suggest that change blindness involves (or can involve) what Ned Block (2012) calls *phenomenal overflow*: the subject has conscious experiences but cannot access them (or the information they provide) in ways one usually can.

Ned Block (1995) has argued that other experimental results support the existence of phenomenal overflow. In one study he describes, by Georg Sperling (1960), subjects are shown groups of letters, for example, in 3×4 arrays, for brief periods (e.g., 50 milliseconds). Subjects usually report that they can see all (or at least most) of the letters, but they can report only about half of them (see Chapter 38). Sperling then varied the experiment, playing a tone right after the display. A high tone meant that the subjects were to report the top row, a medium tone meant the middle row, etc. Subjects then were able to report the letters in the row indicated by the tone, but not the other letters. Block suggests that this case might involve phenomenal overflow: the subjects consciously saw all (or most) of the letters in the whole array but did not have access to all of the detailed information that their conscious experiences represented. If Block is right about that, then perhaps the same sort of thing happens in change blindness: the experience is rich, but the access is poor (Block 2012; see Chapter 28).

RECOMMENDED READING

CANONICAL PRESENTATION

O'Regan, J. Kevin, and Noë, A. 2001. "A Semsorimotor Approach to Vision and Visual Consciousness." *Behavioral and Brain Sciences* 24: 883–975.

OVERVIEW

Simons, Daniel J., and Rensink, Ronald A. 2005. "Change Blindness: Past, Present, and Future." *Trends in Cognitive Sciences* 9 (1): 16–20.

ADDITIONAL DISCUSSIONS

Block, Ned. 2007. "Overflow, Access, and Attention." *Behavioral and Brain Sciences* 30: 530–48.

Block, Ned. 2012, "Perceptual Consciousness Overflows Cognitive Access." *Trends in Cognitive Sciences*: 15 (12): 567–75.

Dretske, Fred. 2007. "What Change Blindness Teaches about Consciousness." *Philosophical Perspectives* 21: 215–30.

Rensink, Ronald A., O'Regan, J. Kevin, and Clark, James J. 1997. "To See or Not to See: The Need for Attention to Perceive Changes in Scenes." *Psychological Science* 8: 368–73.

Simons, Daniel J. 1997. "Change Blindness." *Trends in Cognitive Sciences* 1: 261–7.

Tye, Michael. 2009. *Consciousness Revisited: Materialism without Phenomenal Concepts.* Cambridge, MA: MIT Press. (See especially Chapter 7.)

OTHER REFERENCES

Blackmore, Susan J., Brelstaff, Gavin Nelson, Katherine, and Trosciano, Tom. 1995. "Is the Richness of Our Visual World an Illusion? Transsaccadic Memory for Complex Scenes." *Perception* 24 (9): 1075–81.

Block, Ned. 1995. "On a Confusion about a Function of Consciousness." *Behavioral and Brain Sciences* 18: 227–47.

Fernandez-Duque, Diego, and Thornton, Ian. 2000. "Change Detection without Awareness: Do Explicit Reports Underestimate the Representation of Change in the Visual System?" *Visual Cognition* 7 (1–3): 323–44.

Simons, Daniel J., and Chabris, Christopher F. 1999. "Gorillas in Our Midst: Sustained Inattentional Blindness for Dynamic Events." *Perception* 28: 1059–74.

Simons, Daniel J., and Levin, Daniel T. 1998. "Failure to Detect Changes to People during a Real-World Interaction." *Psychonomic Bulletin & Review* 5: 644–9.

Sperling, Georg. 1960. "The Information Available in Brief Visual Presentations." *Psychological Monographs: General and Applied* 74 (11): 1–29.

BLINDSIGHT, DISTRACTED DRIVING, AND PNEUMATIC DRILLS

BACKGROUND

We all think we know what it is to be conscious. It's the difference between being awake and aware and being in a coma or a dreamless sleep. It's arguably not so simple, however. Studies of patients with damage to their visual cortex, as well as reflections on more mundane cases, suggest that consciousness might be a "mongrel concept" involving distinct functions and properties (Block 1995; see Chapter 4).

THE CASES

Patients with damage to their visual cortex often have "blindspots" in their visual fields, where they report seeing nothing at all. There's an odd twist, though. When forced to "guess" about features of objects in their blindspot, they are surprisingly accurate. So, for example, if an experimenter moves an object (perhaps a cursor on a screen) across the blindspot, the patient says they see nothing. If, however, they are asked to guess whether it is moving to the right or to the left, they can do so quite reliably. Paradoxically, they seem to be able to perceive something even though they are not aware of perceiving it. This phenomenon is dubbed *blindsight* (Weiskrantz 2009).

What is going on in cases of blindsight? Although there are a number of relatively early philosophical discussions of the import of blindsight (Van Gulick 1989 and Searle 1992, for example), Ned Block's (1995) discussions are probably the most influential. For Block, blindsight suggests that two distinct sorts of consciousness can come apart. He argues for a distinction between *phenomenal consciousness* and *access consciousness*. A phenomenally conscious state is in the "what it's like sense" (see Chapters 4–6). The state is experiential and comes with a particular "feel" for the subject—there is something it is like to taste chocolate, see red, feel pain, etc. Blindsighters seem to lack this phenomenal consciousness of things in their blindspots. According to Block, in addition to phenomenal consciousness, though often intertwined with it, is *access consciousness*. A state is access conscious, roughly, when the state provides information to the subject that can be used in reasoning and action—information that is readily accessible to them. Blindsight can help us see that these two can come apart: the blindsighters seem to have access to the "blind" contents of their visual fields, but nevertheless lack phenomenal consciousness with respect to those contents.

The inference from the existence of blindsight to the separability of phenomenal consciousness and access consciousness is not entirely straightforward. Because blindsighters have to "guess" about the contents of their visual fields, and do so only when prompted, it is not clear that the information those contents contain is *readily available* to them for use in reasoning and action. But, according to Block, we can imagine "super-blindsighters" who can prompt themselves and who can thereby know about the relevant items in their blindspots without having any conscious experience of those items. These super-blindsighters would have access consciousness without phenomenal consciousness, even if the same is not true of actual blindsighters. Block does not, and need not, deny that in typical subjects, access and phenomenal consciousness go together. Arguably, they do: when I perceive the donkey, I get usable information about the donkey, *and* there is something it is like for me to see the donkey. Block's point is that access and phenomenal consciousness *can* come apart. And, if they can, even if they typically do not, then they are distinct features. If they are distinct features, then we shouldn't think that an explanation of one will necessarily explain the other.

Consider a more ordinary case. Imagine that you are driving late at night on a cross-country road trip. Your mind wanders—you start to think about that incident at work and worry about whether or not you've left enough food for the cat. After a while you snap out of this meandering and realize that you've been driving for some time without being aware of what you were seeing or doing (Armstrong 1981, p. 59). There is some sense in which you were conscious of the road and the scenery you were passing. It's not as though you were blind. As Block would say, you were access conscious of these things. But it might seem there is another sense in which you weren't aware of the flow of dotted lines on the road or the well-lit billboards you were passing. As Block would say, you were not phenomenally conscious of the road. Cases like this seem to add further support to his claim that the two sorts of consciousness he distinguishes can come apart and might require different explanations.

If there can be access consciousness without phenomenal consciousness, what about vice versa? Can there be cases when we have phenomenal consciousness without access consciousness? Block suggests a somewhat ordinary case. Suppose that, in the middle of a deep conversation, you realize there is a pneumatic drill pummeling the pavement outside your office. Block thinks it plausible that you were hearing it all along. It's not as though you were selectively deaf. Nevertheless, you weren't consciously aware of the sound in the sense of having access consciousness of it—it wasn't in a position to guide action or speech.

DISCUSSION

There are a number of ways to interpret what is going on in all of these cases. In the case of blindsight, there continues to be fruitful scientific research and challenging philosophical debate. Campion et al. (1983) argue that in blindsight cases there is reason to believe that the patients are phenomenally conscious of the stimuli, at least to some extent. For one thing, normal subjects show similar behaviors when a stimulus is very dim, near the threshold for detection, suggesting that the blindsight patients might merely have a very dim perception. In addition, blindsight subjects could be responding to light scattered from the "unseen" object to other parts of the retina.

Perhaps most seriously, the experiments are plagued by what's known as *response bias*. In particular, in blindsight experiments there are two different metrics being used. One is a yes/no question: "Are you aware of anything?" The blindsight patient says "no." The other is a forced choice in which the patient has to commit to something happening in the visual field: for example, "Is the cursor moving left or right?" The blindsighter often answers this question correctly. The difference between these procedures raises the possibility that the patient is dimly conscious of the stimulus in both cases, but the types of questions prompt the use of different criteria in responding. In the first case there is a conservative bias to deny there is awareness; but in the case when the patient has to commit, they are forced to draw on even the slight conscious signal they have (Phillips 2016).

Finally, there is the potential that, in the case of blindsight, there is phenomenal consciousness without access consciousness. To put the point without fully committing to Block's distinction, we might say that there is phenomenal consciousness without verbal reportability (Phillips 2016). Perhaps there's something it is like for the blindsighter when they are presented with items that lie in their blindspot, but the problem is that they can't report on what they've seen. This is the opposite of the original explanation of the phenomenon, but the experiments don't seem to rule out either explanation. (For discussion of many of these issues as well as relevant experimental results, see Cowey 2010.)

There are also varying interpretations of the cases involving the pneumatic drill and the distracted driver. According to Block, the pneumatic-drill case illustrates the possibility of having phenomenal consciousness without access consciousness. But one might instead describe the case as illustrating a different possibility: the possibility of having a conscious state but not attending to it (Tye 1995, 2000; see Chapter 37). On this interpretation, you *do* have access consciousness of the drill's sound. You just don't attend to it. Relatedly, it could be that, in the distracted-driver case, there is phenomenal consciousness of the stimuli, but not higher-order awareness—you lack awareness of your awareness of the stimuli. The distracted driver *is* phenomenally conscious of the road. He just isn't, in some sense, perceiving that he's perceiving (see Armstrong 1981, Dretske 1995).

RECOMMENDED READING

CANONICAL PRESENTATIONS

Armstrong, David M. 1981. "What Is Consciousness?" In John Heil (ed.) *The Nature of Mind*. New York: Cornell University Press.

Block, Ned. 1995. "On a Confusion about a Function of Consciousness." *Brain and Behavioral Sciences* 18 (2): 227–47.

OVERVIEWS

Cowey A. 2010. "The Blindsight Saga." *Experimental Brain Research* 200 (1): 3–24. doi:10.1007/s00221-009-1914-2 [correction appears in *Experimental Brain Research* 202 (2): 527].

Weiskrantz, Lawrence. 2009. *Blindsight: A Case Study Spanning 35 Years and New Developments*. Oxford: Oxford University Press.

ADDITIONAL DISCUSSIONS

Azzopardi, Paul, and Cowey, Alan. 1997. "Is Blindsight Like Normal, Near-Threshold Vision?" *Proceedings of the National Academy of Sciences* 94 (25): 14190–94.

Brogaard, Berit. 2015. "Type 2 Blindsight and the Nature of Visual Experience." *Consciousness and Cognition* 32: 92–103.

Campion, John, Latto, Richard, and Smith, Y. M. 1983. "Is Blindsight an Effect of Scattered Light, Spared Cortex, and Near-Threshold Vision?" *Behavioral and Brain Sciences* 6 (3): 423–86.

Dretske, Fred. 1995. *Naturalizing the Mind*. Cambridge, MA: MIT Press.

Mazzi, Chiara, Bagattini, Chiara, and Savazzi, Silvia. 2016. "Blind-Sight vs. Degraded-Sight: Different Measures Tell a Different Story." *Frontiers in Psychology* 7: 901. doi: 10.3389/fpsyg.2016.00901.

Michel, Matthias, and Lau, Hakwan. 2021. "Is Blindsight Possible under Signal Detection Theory? Comment on Phillips (2021)." *Psychological Review* 128 (3): 585–91.

Overgaard, M., Fehl, K., Mouridsen, K., Bergholt, B., and Cleeremans. A. 2008. "Seeing without Seeing? Degraded Conscious Vision in a Blindsight Patient." *PLoS ONE* 3 (8): e3028. doi.org/10.1371/journal.pone.0003028.

Overgaard, Morten. 2011. "Visual Experience and Blindsight: A Methodological Review." *Experimental Brain Research* 209: 473–9.

Phillips, Ian. 2016. "Consciousness and Criterion: On Block's Case for Unconscious Seeing." *Philosophy and Phenomenological Research* 93 (2): 419–51.

Phillips, Ian. 2021. "Blindsight Is Qualitatively Degraded Conscious Vision." *Psychological Review* 128 (3): 558–84.
Searle, John R. 1992. *The Rediscovery of the Mind*. Cambridge, MA: MIT Press.
Tye, Michael. 1995. *Ten Problems of Consciousness*. Cambridge, MA: MIT Press.
Tye, Michael. 2000. *Consciousness, Color, and Content*. Cambridge, MA: MIT Press.
Van Gulick, Robert. 1989. "What Difference Does Consciousness Make?" *Philosophical Topics* 17 (1): 211–30.
Vision, Gerald. 1998. "Blindsight and Philosophy." *Philosophical Psychology* 11 (2): 137–59.
Wright, Wayne. 2005. "Distracted Drivers and Unattended Experience." *Synthese* 144 (1): 41–68.

PART V

PERSONS, PERSONAL IDENTITY, AND THE SELF
Introduction

This section concerns several related problems about persons that are often grouped together under the heading of *the problem of personal identity*. One such problem concerns the nature of persons: What makes something a person? Another such problem concerns personal identity over time: What makes person A at a given time the same person as person B at another time? Connected with these questions about the nature of persons are also questions about selfhood and the nature of the self.

As we saw in the introduction to Part I, contemporary discussions of the mind–body problem in the western tradition often trace to Descartes. In contrast, contemporary discussions of the problem of personal identity in the western tradition tend to trace to a different philosopher living in the 17th century, John Locke. On Locke's view, a person is "a thinking intelligent being, that has reason and reflection, and can consider itself as itself." This definition leads him to a view of personal identity over time that focuses on continuity of psychology, and, in particular, on continuity of memory. Locke motivates his *memory theory* of personal identity by way of a body-swapping thought experiment. If, via a mysterious body swap, the memories of the prince were to come to reside in the body of the cobbler, and vice versa, which person is which? We discuss this thought experiment, and what it shows us about personal identity over time, in Chapter 39.

Just as Descartes' discussion of the mind–body problem did not come out of nowhere, Locke's discussion of the problem of personal identity did not come out of nowhere. Some precedents come from earlier in the western tradition. For example, the 6th-century Roman philosopher Boethius had defined personhood in terms of the notion of "a rational nature." Other precedents come from non-western traditions. One important discussion takes place in *The Questions of King Milinda* (*The Milinda Pañha*), a Buddhist text that is thought to have been written between 100 BCE and 200 CE. In a conversation between King Milinda and a monk named Nagasena, this text presents an argument that there is really no such thing as the self. In connection with this no-self view, however, the text also explores questions relating to a person's endurance through time. This exploration, centered on thought experiments involving chariots and candles, is discussed in Chapter 40.

The remaining chapters in Part V take up related themes. The thought experiments discussed in Chapters 41–43 raise various challenges to Locke's memory theory. Some of these challenges might be met by broadening from a theory about continuity of memory to a theory about continuity of psychology. But other challenges run deeper, and many philosophers have suggested that we would do better to abandon psychologically based theories of personal identity and instead adopt physical theories. We explore some of the considerations in favor of a physical theory in Chapter 41 by returning to a pair of thought experiments involving body-swaps. In Chapter 42, we explore related issues by considering a thought experiment in which a person's mind is uploaded to a computer. In Chapter 43, we consider a thought experiment about a statue and the clay out of which it is made in an effort to better understand the relationship between persons and bodies.

Chapter 44 explores the phenomenon of split brains, a real-life condition that results from a surgical procedure in which the brain's two hemispheres are disconnected from one another. As this chapter discusses, this puzzle case has important ramifications for personal identity and the unity of consciousness. We continue exploration of the unity of consciousness in Chapter 45, which explores a thought experiment that suggests that thoughts and minds might be shared by more than one person. Chapter 46 returns to issues that arose in connection with the Buddhist no-self view discussed in Chapter 40; in particular, it explores a puzzle about our ability to have introspective access to the self. Chapter 47 turns from questions about self-introspection to questions about self-reference, objectivity, and self-awareness.

The final three chapters in this section turn to questions about the essence of persons and the self. Chapter 48 considers a thought experiment designed to show that the origins of a person are essential to that person's identity. Chapter 49 considers which kinds of characteristics are especially salient towards making a person the person that they are. Finally, Chapter 50 explores how cases involving transformative decisions raise problems for a person's ability to stay true to themselves.

THE PRINCE AND THE COBBLER

BACKGROUND

Although philosophers have been grappling with issues relating to personal identity at least as far back as Plato, these issues came in for renewed scrutiny in the 17th century via the work of John Locke. Addressing the topic in a chapter entitled "Of Identity and Diversity" in his *An Essay Concerning Human Understanding* (1689), Locke took up two inter-related questions: First, what is the nature of persons? And, second, what accounts for a person's identity over time? Our interest in this chapter is the second question, and the issue of personal identity over time is now often referred to as *the problem of personal identity*. Philosophers working on this problem have typically split into three broad camps. Those who defend *the soul theory* suggest that a person's identity over time consists in the continued existence of the same soul. Those who defend *the psychological theory* suggest that a person's identity over time consists in psychological facts. Those who defend *the physical theory* suggest that a person's identity over time consists in physical facts. Locke falls into the second camp, and the particular psychological facts on which he focuses are facts about memory. Suppose we have a person we'll call A existing at a certain time t1, and a person we'll call B existing at some later time t2. On Locke's view, B is the same person as A if and only if B remembers an experience had by A.

The thought experiment we'll consider in this chapter is put forth to support this view.

THE CASE

Consider two men living very different lives in the same town. The first is a wealthy prince. He resides in a grand palace with the rest of the royal family, and his every need is catered to by a coterie of servants. He spends his days eating lavish meals, engaging in various leisure activities, and making occasional public appearances where he is applauded by his loyal subjects. The second is a poor cobbler. He resides in a ramshackle cottage and, together with his wife, he is raising several children. He spends his days working hard to repair shoes, and has almost no time for leisure activities. Money is tight, and the family typically has barely enough to eat. One night, in a mysterious twist, the prince's consciousness somehow comes to inhabit the body of the cobbler. The individual who wakes up in the cobbler's bed has no idea where he is. His surroundings are completely unfamiliar to him. He doesn't recognize the woman sleeping beside him, or the young children sleeping in a cramped second room. The threadbare and uncomfortable sleeping garment he finds himself wearing is completely different from the luscious dressing gown that he had been wearing when he went to bed. He can remember being brought up in the palace, eating delicacies at every meal, and being waited on hand and foot. He's still having the same kinds of princely thoughts he's always had, but everyone around him takes him to be the cobbler. They address him by a name that isn't his, and no one seems to believe him when he says that he's the prince. They all think he must be joking, and they chide him for being late for work.

So, who has woken up in the cobbler's bed? Is it the prince or the cobbler? According to Locke, the answer is obvious. Though the individual has the cobbler's body, he is clearly the same person as the prince.

DISCUSSION

Locke uses the prince and the cobbler case as support for what contemporary philosophers have referred to as *the memory theory* of personal identity (though see Behan 1979 for an argument that the interpretation of Locke as a memory theorist is mistaken). What makes an individual at one time the same person as an individual at another time is not a soul or a body, but rather the continuity of consciousness that enables the individual at the later time to remember the experiences of the individual at the earlier time. Even having the same soul (without any memories accompanying it) is not enough. If we discovered that the prince somehow had the same soul as Nestor of Troy but didn't remember anything about Nestor's experiences or about Troy, we should not identify the prince as the same person as Nestor. Likewise, though it might not be immediately apparent to those who interact with the cobbler's body that they are really interacting with the prince, when we consider the fact that the cobbler's body now has all the memories of the prince and none of the memories of the cobbler, we are not inclined to identify the individual as the same person as the cobbler.

In the centuries since Locke's time, similar hypothetical scenarios have often turned up in works of fiction and film, and our judgments about them seem generally to accord with Locke's judgment about the prince and cobbler case. To give just one example, consider the 2003 film *Freaky Friday*, in which a mother and a teenage daughter are depicted as swapping bodies after reading their fortunes from a magic fortune cookie. Somehow, the mother's psychology emanates from the teenage body and the daughter's psychology emanates from the older body. After the swap, viewers find it natural to identify the person in the teenage body as the mother and the person in the older body as the daughter.

Despite the intuitive appeal of the memory theory, it has often come in for criticism. One influential criticism, offered in the 18th century by Thomas Reid (1785), proceeds by way of a thought experiment involving a brave army officer. While fighting in an important campaign, this officer saves his entire unit and is awarded a prestigious medal. Though the officer is now highly respected, he was something of a miscreant as a young boy. In particular, he remembers an incident in which he stole some apples from his neighbor's tree. As the officer ages, he becomes a general, and then retires. In retirement, he gradually becomes more and more senile, and, at a certain point, the retired general can remember winning the medal but can no longer remember stealing the apples or anything else from that time of his life. As Reid notes, Locke's theory now gives us a paradoxical result. To simplify, let's refer to the retired general as RG, the army officer as AO, and the young boy as YB. Since RG can remember experiences of AO, RG is identical to AO. Since AO can remember experiences of YB, AO is identical to YB. According to the transitivity of identity, if A is identical to B and B is identical to C, then A is identical to C. Putting this together with the two prior claims, we get the result that RG is identical to YB. But, since RG has no memories of the experiences of YB, and since Locke's memory theory requires such memory connections for personal identity, we also get the result that RG is not identical to YB. Thus, Locke's memory theory seems to result in a contradiction. RG cannot be both identical to YB and not identical to YB.

To address Reid's criticism, we might revise the Lockean theory so that it does not require *direct* connections of memory between two individuals in order for them to be identical. Rather, what matters is that we have *continuity* of memory between them, or overlapping chains of memory between them. When RG remembers something that AO experienced and AO remembers something that YB experienced, there is continuity of memory between RG and AO even if there are no direct memory connections between them. But even the revised memory theory faces problems. For example, some have worried that the notion of memory presupposes personal identity, and thus cannot explain it (Butler 1736; for a response see Perry 1975). Take a case where you recount an incident in which you told a particularly funny joke. Were we to discover that someone else other than you was the one who told the joke, we would deny that you really remember the incident that you recounted; rather, you only *seem* to remember it. If you weren't the one who told the joke, then you can't have a genuine memory of having done so. But this suggests that facts about memory depend on facts about personal identity. So, it would then be circular to claim that facts about personal identity depend on facts about memory.

With worries like this in mind, in contemporary times many philosophers have broadened the theory to consider other kinds of psychological connections over and above memory. We are connected to our future selves by means of intentions, for example. My current self forms an intention to go to the store, and then my future self acts on that intention. And we also have continuing psychological connections in virtue of our desires, beliefs, habits, and other personality traits. Thus, the psychological theory claims that B is the same person as A if and only if there is psychological continuity between B and A.

But even the broader psychological theory is not immune to criticism. First, it's not clear that it really solves the worry about circularity. Just as the notion of memory might seem to presuppose personal identity, so too might the notion of intention—and likewise for other psychological states. But, second, the broader psychological theory faces a major issue concerning what's become known as the *problem of reduplication*. (Note that the original memory theory would also face this problem.) Identity is a relation that holds 1:1. An individual at time t1 can only be numerically identical to a single individual at time t2. But psychological continuity does not seem to be a relation that holds 1:1, since it seems possible that an individual at time t1 can be psychologically continuous with many individuals at time t2. Consider the kinds of teletransportation depicted in science fiction. When the transporter is functioning normally, it scans an individual on one planet, dematerializes that individual, and then re-materializes the individual on another planet. But, in cases of transporter malfunction, the individual on the original planet might not be dematerialized, or they might be re-materialized on multiple planets. There could be an individual on Mars and an individual on Jupiter, both of whom are psychologically continuous with the individual who entered the transporter on Earth (Parfit 1984). Reduplication worries can also be generated by considering cases of uploading one's consciousness to a computer, a topic we'll consider in Chapter 42.

Another kind of worry for the psychological theory arises from the fact that we don't seem to have psychological continuity with our fetus selves, especially when we consider early fetuses who lack psychological states altogether. In fact, even infants don't seem to have adequate psychological states to support the kinds of psychological connections typically invoked by those who accept the psychological theory. Thus, the psychological theory seems to rule out the possibility that we were once fetuses (Olson 1997). And some consider that a flaw in the theory.

To turn to one last worry, consider contemporary research that suggests that memory and other psychological states are considerably more embodied than Locke seems to have thought. In cases of severe trauma, for example, memory does not seem to be purely a psychological state. Traumatic flashbacks are often experienced as bodily states. When we consider this kind of case, we're led to the conclusion that memories reside in the body; one might even be inclined to say that the body remembers the trauma (Brison 2002). Thus, the notion that we can wholly separate psychological facts from physical facts as the psychological theory suggests has struck many as implausible.

RECOMMENDED READING

CANONICAL PRESENTATION

Locke, John. 1689/1974. "Of Identity and Diversity." In *An Essay Concerning Human Understanding*, edited with an introduction by A.D. Woozley. New York: New American Library: 206–20.

OVERVIEWS

Kind, Amy. 2015. *Persons and Personal Identity*. Cambridge: Polity Press. (See Chapter 2, "The Psychological Approach to Personal Identity.")
Noonan, Harold W. 2019. *Personal Identity*, third edition. Abingdon: Routledge. (See Chapter 2, "Locke.")

ADDITIONAL DISCUSSIONS

Baker, Lynne Rudder. 2012. "Personal Identity: A Not-So-Simple Simple View." In Matthias Stefan (ed.) *Personal Identity: Simple or Complex*. Cambridge: Cambridge University Press: 179–91.
Behan, David P. 1979. "Locke on Persons and Personal Identity." *Canadian Journal of Philosophy* 9 (1): 53–75.
Brison, Susan. 2002. *Aftermath: Violence and the Remaking of a Self*. Princeton: Princeton University Press.
Butler, Joseph. 1736/2008. "Of Personal Identity." In John Perry (ed.) *Personal Identity*, second edition. Berkeley: University of California Press: 99–105.
Olson, Eric. T. 1997. "Was I Ever a Fetus?" *Philosophy and Phenomenological Research* 57 (1): 95–110.
Parfit, Derek. 1984. *Reasons and Persons*. Oxford: Oxford University Press.
Perry, John. 2008. "Personal Identity, Memory, and the Problem of Circularity." In John Perry (ed.) *Personal Identity*, second edition. Berkeley: University of California Press: 135–55.
Reid, Thomas. 1785/2008. "Of Mr. Locke's Account of Our Personal Identity." In John Perry (ed.) *Personal Identity*, second edition. Berkeley: University of California Press: 113–18.

Rorty, Amélie Oksenberg (ed.). 1976. *The Identities of Persons*. Berkeley: University of California Press.

Swinburne, Richard. 1973–4. "Personal Identity." *Proceedings of the Aristotelian Society, New Series* 74: 231–47.

Wilkes, Kathleen. 1988. *Real People: Personal Identity without Thought Experiments*. Oxford: Oxford University Press.

THE CHARIOT AND THE CANDLE

BACKGROUND

It is a central tenet of Buddhist metaphysics that there is no self. We are encouraged to draw up an inventory of all that we find in experience. When we do, we will discover that there is nothing unchanging that endures throughout our changing experiences, and that there is nothing underneath our experiences that has them (see Chapter 46). For the Buddhists this is not merely an arcane philosophical point: letting go of the notion of self is essential to freeing ourselves from suffering and reaching enlightenment. Many, though, find this no-self view, or *anatta*, counterintuitive. We seem to be committed to a self by our language and concepts—some of our names and pronouns surely refer to something, and what do they refer to if not a self? Further, the no-self view seems to fly in the face of the Buddhist view of reincarnation as well as the more mundane view that we persist through time. How could I be born in another life if there is no I? In what sense do I survive from day to day if there is no I? The chariot and candle cases we consider in this chapter attempt to motivate the no-self view and show how these questions can be answered.

DOI: 10.4324/9781003179191-46

THE CASES

In *The Questions of King Milinda*, the King meets a monk and asks his name. The monk replies that everyone calls him "Nagasena," but he is careful to note that "Nagasena" is just a "convenient designator, a mere name," and that in fact there is no person there. There is indeed a collection of parts corresponding to Nagasena—feelings, thoughts, body parts, etc.—but none of these alone is Nagasena; nor are all these things taken as a whole. Naturally, this bewilders King Milinda. It seems to him that he is talking to Nagasena, that Nagasena is speaking, and if there is no Nagasena, no one can be talking to him; nor is there someone to receive alms, which would be too bad for a Buddhist monk. If there is no Nagasena, the claim "Nagasena receives alms" is not only false, but arguably meaningless: if the name doesn't designate anything, it appears to be merely an empty sound.

Nagasena replies with an analogy. Both Nagasena and the King agree that the King arrived in a chariot. But the chariot is not the axle, or the wheels, or the yoke, etc. Nor is it all those parts taken as a collection—put all these parts in a bag and you still don't have a chariot. So, there appears to be no chariot; and, contrary to what the King himself believed, he must not have arrived in a chariot. But, of course, he did, and "chariot" is not just an empty sound. Instead, Nagasena explains, in both the case of the chariot and the person, we use words to designate certain arrangements of parts. But there is no further thing that is the chariot beyond that changeable arrangement of parts, and there is no further thing that is a person or self over and above the changing parts of the body and mind. Using the words "chariot" or "Nagasena" is a helpful way to designate those parts, but we shouldn't be misled into believing that there is something behind those phenomena that the words refer to.

This no-self view raises important questions about a person's endurance over time. This question is particularly pressing for the Buddhists who believe in reincarnation. Reincarnation seems to consist in one person's dying and then being reborn in another body. For the Buddhists, this has an ethical dimension—one's actions generate karma that determines the quality of rebirth, and one strives to reach the perfected state of the Buddha, who will not be reborn. How can there be one person who dies and is then reborn, whose karma determines the nature of their later incarnation, if there is no self in the first place? Even if we're not concerned with reincarnation or karma, we might wonder whether an adult is the same person they were as a child or that they will be in later years. According to Nagasena, the adult is not the same person as the child; but nor are they someone else—since there is no person there in the first place. Despite this, Nagasena admits that there is a sense in which the adult is the same as the child. If there weren't, he says, there could be no mothers, since a mother has to have given birth to a child. If there were no sense in which someone endures through time, no person has ever given birth to anyone!

Again, Nagasena appeals to an analogy. It is possible to light a lamp and have it shine all night. Is the flame at midnight the same as the flame at dusk? In a sense it certainly is—the flame never went out. On the other hand, there is no thing that is the flame, shining from hour to hour. The flame at a time is just a set of molecules vaporizing and oxidizing, and new molecules (from the fuel) continually replace the old ones. There is no thing there from time to time. Nevertheless, there is a causal process that continues, each combustion leading to the next, and this is what it means to say that there is a single flame all night long. A person's surviving from day to day, throughout a lifetime, is just like the lamp's burning all night. There is no single thing that continues throughout a lifetime; rather, there are causal interactions that give rise to conscious states, and from moment to moment those states change, but there is nonetheless a continuous causal chain throughout a life. Reincarnation is then a special instance of this, but it is akin to a candle being lit from another candle. The flame passes from candle to candle, in a sense, but there is no thing—the flame—that goes from one to the other. Similarly, in reincarnation there would be a causal process from one body to another such that there is a causal connection between the mental states of one and those of another, despite there being no single self or mind that passes from body to body.

DISCUSSION

Does the self exist, according to the Buddhist? Does the chariot? Though Buddhists are famous for holding that there is no self, the answer is more complicated than a simple "no." The statements "the self exists" and "the chariot exists" are *conventionally true*. That is, it is a matter of convention to call a certain assemblage of matter a chariot and another assemblage of matter and mental states a self. Calling one of these things "chariot" and the other "self" is helpful, but these truths don't reflect ultimate reality. You can't read metaphysics off the truth of such statements. It is conventionally true, but not *ultimately true*. Consider an analogy: my weather app says "The sun rises at 8 am." Indeed, dawn is at 8 am, so what the weather app said was true. But it is only true in a conventional sense since the sun doesn't really rise at all. The sun is staying in one place and the Earth is turning. It would be silly and pedantic to correct everyone who talked about the sunrise. Still, if you want to know what is really going on you have to recognize that, though that statement is conventionally true, it is ultimately false. Similarly, "the self exists" is conventionally true, but ultimately false. Really, ultimately, the self doesn't exist, and neither does the chariot (Siderits 2021).

There are some worries about this way of putting things. In some sense, all language is conventional: our word "tree" refers to trees not by some magic nature of the look or sound of the word, but because we have decided to use it that way. Given this, all statements are in some sense conventionally true—including statements the Buddhists say are ultimately true. It might be more helpful to move away from the linguistic explanation and argue that some ways of conceptualizing the world are merely helpful for humans but other ways carve nature at its joints, getting at the real, mind-independent essence of things (Quine 1969). Whether or not something is or isn't a sundial, for example, is probably not a deep fact about the world—many things can be used to tell time using shadows cast by the sun. Is a mountain peak in a clearing a sundial? It probably depends more on what we decide to say than about the way the world really is in a mind-independent sense. That might not be true of electrons or more fundamental items. Electrons are not merely groupings of items for practical purpose. They exist independent of convention, and if we didn't think of the world in terms of electrons, we would be missing something about the constitution of the world. We can perhaps say that things like sundials are conventional kinds and things like electrons are natural kinds. Perhaps the right thing to say, then, is that selves and chariots are like sundials: it's *helpful* to conceptualize things in this way—to think of the world as containing those items—but doing so doesn't get at the basic nature of things. It's still true to say that there are selves, just as it's true that there are sundials. But that truth doesn't reflect anything deep about the world—only about our way of conceptualizing it.

Given the distinction between natural and conventional kinds, the analogy of the chariot suggests a couple of ways to resist the Buddhist no-self view. One is to deny that the cases are analogous—that perhaps the chariot isn't a natural kind but the self is. The other is to grant they are analogous, but to also say that, in any sense that matters, they both exist.

One way to get at the idea that the self is different from the chariot is to say that what constitutes a chariot is conventional in a way the self is not (Van Inwagen 1990, Merricks 2001). So, for example, is a car a chariot? What if it is pulled by horses? Suppose you remove a chariot's wheels—is it still a chariot? What if you replace the wheels with hovering drones? Suppose you lash two chariots together and combine parts. At any point are they one chariot? In cases like these, it's tempting to say that there is no deep fact of the matter: what counts as a chariot is purely conventional. Is the same thing true of a self? Suppose you cut your hair. Is there still a self there? Suppose you forget how to ride a bike, get a tumor resected, and lose your arms and legs. Is there still a self there? (Note the question is not the question we discuss in Chapter 39 about whether you are the *same* self or person before and after these events; the question is whether there is a self there at all.) What if you are shot in the head and lose life and consciousness? If you have a surgeon stitch you to your best friend, is there one self there or two? Here it might seem the answers are not a matter of convention. Except in the case where you are shot in the head, there is still a self there. When you are sewn to your friend, assuming your brains aren't mixed together, there are still two selves there. If someone argued that there was only one self, or that there was no self when you cut your hair, they would simply be wrong. Unlike the case of the chariot, the case of the self is not conventional.

Another option is to say that the chariot and the self both exist in the same sense, and there is no good sense in which either one does not exist (Thomasson 2007). Perhaps one is a natural kind and the other isn't; but just because something isn't a natural kind doesn't mean that it doesn't exist, or exists in any lesser sense. This strategy is apt to reject a crucial premise in the Buddhist's argument. The Buddhist argues that, in both the case of the chariot and the self, there is merely an assemblage of parts organized in a certain way. But why think that means only the parts exist and not the whole made of the parts? The chariot *just is* parts arranged in this way, and the self *just is* parts arranged in this way. The Buddhists seem inclined to disagree because they are committed to *mereological nihilism*, the view that there are no objects composed of parts—if you put two parts together, you still just have the parts (Unger 1979). While this is counterintuitive, there are interesting arguments to that end, related to the considerations in the previous paragraph. It can be a vague matter of whether or not parts constitute a whole or whether the whole survives changes in its parts. Whether or not parts actually compose a thing, or whether the thing survives changes of its parts, might therefore seem to be a matter of convention rather than some objective matter of fact. Many philosophers resist mereological nihilism, but the Buddhists have plenty of contemporary non-Buddhist company in believing it (Wasserman 2021).

The candle analogy raises other interesting questions, some of which are discussed in Chapters 39, 41, and 42. The analogy, recall, was that one survives from day to day, throughout one's life or even beyond, by being like a candle's flame. This seems palatable until one considers some of the implications this seems to have for survival. We tend to think of reincarnation as a case in which one person passes away but is born again in a different body. The candle analogy is supposed to show how this might be possible without unchanging selves existing. But it might be troubling that, when a candle passes its flame to another, the first candle needn't go out—it usually doesn't. Now consider the analogous case: your relevant mental features (memories, personality, etc.) are incarnated in a distinct body while you are still alive, with your own mental states left intact. Most of us would not feel that we have been doubly incarnated. You're in one of those bodies, and someone with a frighteningly similar psychology is in the other body (see Chapter 39). A similar problem occurs because it seems possible for a candle to light three or four other candles at once. In the analogous case, then, your psychological characteristics (or whatever characteristics are supposed to pass between lives) are passed into three or four different bodies. We're not tempted to say that there are now five of you. Each of these people is different from the other—they could go on to have different experiences and know nothing of each other—and none of them seem to be you, the candle that lit them all.

RECOMMENDED READING

CANONICAL PRESENTATION

The Milinda Pañha. Trans. T. W. Rhys Davids. Loshberg: Jazzybee Verlag.

OVERVIEW

Siderits, Mark. 2021. *Buddhism as Philosophy*, second edition. Indianapolis: Hackett. (See Chapters 3 and 6.)

ADDITIONAL DISCUSSIONS

Albahari, Miri. 2006. *Analytical Buddhism: The Two-Tiered Illusion of Self*. Basingstoke: Palgrave Macmillan.
Collins, Steven. 1982. *Selfless Persons*. Cambridge: Cambridge University Press.
Merricks, T. 2001. *Objects and Persons*. Oxford: Oxford University Press.
Parfit, Derek. 1984. *Reasons and Persons*. Oxford: Oxford University Press.
Quine, Willard van Orman. 1969. "Ontological Relativity." In *Ontological Relativity and Other Essays*. New York: Columbia University Press.
Thomasson, Amie. 2007. *Ordinary Objects*. Oxford: Oxford University Press.
Unger, Peter. 1979. "There Are No Ordinary Things." *Synthese* 41 (2): 117–54.
Van Inwagen, Peter. 1990. *Material Beings*. Ithaca, NY: Cornell University Press.
Wasserman, Ryan. 2021. "Material Constitution." *The Stanford Encyclopedia of Philosophy* (Fall 2021 Edition), Edward N. Zalta (ed.), URL = <https://plato.stanford.edu/archives/fall2021/entries/material-constitution/>.

THE BODY-SWAP PUZZLE

BACKGROUND

As we saw in our discussion of the Prince and the Cobbler in Chapter 39, body-swap cases are often invoked in discussions of personal identity time (see also the brain transplant cases discussed in Shoemaker 1963). In everyday life, facts about psychological continuity and bodily continuity tend to go together. Typically, if there is physical continuity between a person P1 on Monday and a person P2 on Tuesday, then there will also be psychological continuity between P1 and P2. The reverse is also true: Typically, if there is psychological continuity between P1 on Monday and P2 on Tuesday, then there will also be physical continuity between P1 and P2. In body-swap cases, when the consciousness associated with one person is transferred into the body associated with another person, psychological continuity and physical continuity come apart. When considering such cases, most people tend to think that the psychological facts have primary importance in determining personal identity. As this is sometimes put, we tend to think that *a person goes where their psychology goes*. Body-swap cases thus play a big role in supporting psychological theories of personal identity—that is, theories which claim that a person's identity over time consist in facts about psychological connectedness and psychological continuity. In the puzzle that we will discuss in this chapter, Bernard Williams tries to show that our intuitions about body-swap cases are much more ambiguous than is usually thought.

THE CASE

Williams raises his puzzle by asking us to compare two different cases.

Case 1. Imagine that scientists invent a machine designed to be used during brain surgery. The machine extracts all of the mental content from a person's brain, places it into a storage device for the duration of the surgery, and then restores it to the brain once the surgery is complete. The scientists then discover that the mental content extracted need not be restored to the original brain from which it was taken; they can transfer the mental content from X's brain into Y's brain, and likewise they can transfer the mental content from Y's brain into X's brain. Call this *the ET process* (for extraction/transfer).

Now imagine that we run a contest where two lucky finalists will have a 50% shot at a $1,000,000 prize. (When Williams proposed the thought experiment in 1970, the amount was $100,000, but we're adjusting it for inflation!) The downside is that the finalists will also have a 50% shot at being subjected to painful torture. Among the folks who sign up for the contest, we select two, A and B, as the finalists. We explain the ET process to A and B, and then we ask them to vote for who should get the reward afterwards. Should it be the A-body-person (whose brain now contains all of the mental content from B's brain and none of the mental content from A's brain) or the B-body-person (whose brain now has all the mental content from A's brain and none of the mental content from B's brain)? Assuming that the participants want to vote with their own self-interests in mind, how should A vote? How would you vote if you were A? Remember your answer.

Case 2. Imagine that an evil scientist kidnaps you and imprisons you in their secret lair. The scientist tells you that he is going to subject you to painful torture. Naturally, you feel scared. Now the scientist tells you that, when the time comes for the torture to start, something will happen to make you forget ever having been told about the torture. This probably doesn't make you feel any better; it doesn't change the fact that the torture is going to happen. But now the scientist tells you that your forgetting the torture will actually be part of a more dramatic memory change: At the moment of the torture you will have lost all of your memories and all of your mental content. Furthermore, you will somehow acquire an entirely new and different set of memories and mental content. Does any of this make you feel any better, or are you still just as fearful of the torture? Remember your answer here too.

By putting these two cases together, Williams can now motivate his puzzle. The key point is that Case 2 is really just one side of the scenario of Case 1, just differently presented. Recall your answer to the question asked at the end of Case 1. When hearing the thought experiment, many people think that A should vote for the B-body to get the money. Since A's memories will be in the B-body, it seems plausible that the B-body person is really A. A might feel sad that the A-body gets tortured, perhaps because of a sentimental attachment to their former body, but A won't regard the A-body as who (or where) they are. But now recall your answer to the question asked at the end of Case 2. Many people report that they would still fear the torture, that they would still be inclined to think that it was happening to them, even when they know that the person being tortured won't have any of their memories and, more generally, mental content—and in fact their mental content will be completely different. Williams concludes that our intuitions about body-swap cases are not to be trusted.

DISCUSSION

If Williams succeeds in showing that our intuitions about body-swap cases are unreliable, then he would have thereby undermined support for psychological theories of personal identity. On Williams' view, personal identity requires identity of the body. In addition to the puzzle that we're discussing in this chapter, Williams (1957, 1960) has offered other reasons in support of this claim. For example, he has argued that we cannot really make sense of the concept of a particular personality entirely independently of the body—that is, that the notion of personality and body are more intertwined than the body-swap cases allow. Let's reconsider the case of the prince and the cobbler discussed in Chapter 39. In that thought experiment, we're meant to imagine that the prince and the cobbler have undergone a body swap, and that the personality of the prince now inhabits the body of the cobbler. Williams asks us to suppose that the prince has a particularly arrogant manner and that the cobbler has a high-pitched squeaky voice and a naturally cheery face. He then argues that it seems implausible that the prince's haughtiness could be conveyed by that voice and that face.

In line with Williams' puzzle, a number of other philosophers have raised worries about the reliance on thought experiments in the debate about personal identity (see, e.g., Gendler 1998). Arguing that the thought experiments invoked in the debate about personal identity are bizarre and inconclusive, Kathleen Wilkes (1988) has suggested that we would do better to consider real-life cases instead. For example, we might consider cases of dissociative identity disorder, of amnesia and dementia, or of "split brains"—that is, cases involving the surgical severing of the corpus callosum (see Chapter 44). All of these actually occurring conditions allow us to explore what happens when psychological continuity and physical continuity diverge.

That said, many other philosophers continue to find the body-swap cases to be compelling, and they defend their reliance of thought experiments like these against Williams' criticisms. Many such defenses attempt to point out disanalogies between Case 1 and Case 2. For example, one disanalogy arises from the fact that Case 1, but not Case 2, is described in the third person—a disanalogy that Williams himself explicitly acknowledges. According to this line of response, the fact that Case 2 has been made personal twists our intuitions, and thereby corrupts our ability to trust our judgments.

Another disanalogy arises from the fact that in Case 1, but not in Case 2, one's memories end up in another body. In Case 2 the fact that one's memories disappear entirely means that there is no alternative person with which one can identify, and so that makes one more inclined to identify with the memory-less body. One way to put this point is that we are often inclined to identify ourselves with the individual who is our "closest continuer," and whether a given individual counts as one's closest continuer depends on what other continuers are around (see Nozick 1981).

The significance of the first of these disanalogies was explored via some empirical studies conducted by Shaun Nichols and Michael Bruno (2010). Drawing on earlier work by Blok et al. (2005), Nichols and Bruno tested whether people's intuitions about Case 2 changed when it was described in a second-person way (along the lines of "You will be tortured …") vs. a third-person way ("Jerry, the kidnapped person, will be tortured …"). They found no statistically significant difference between these two cases—people responded in the same way whichever way Case 2 was described. That said, when summarizing the results of their studies, Nichols and Bruno found that individuals' intuitions favoring the psychological theory are remarkably resilient. Even when they are presented with an example like Case 2 that generates some intuitions that run against the psychological theory of personal identity, individuals tend to hold on to their overall view that psychological factors are what matter for identity over time.

RECOMMENDED READING

CANONICAL PRESENTATION

Williams, Bernard. 1970. "The Self and the Future." *Philosophical Review* 79 (2): 161–80.

OVERVIEW

Kind, Amy. 2015. *Persons and Personal Identity*. Cambridge: Polity Press. (See Chapter 4, "The Physical Approach to Personal Identity," and especially section 4.1.)

ADDITIONAL DISCUSSIONS

Blok, S., Newman, G., and Rips, L. J. 2005. "Individuals and Their Concepts." In W.-k. Ahn, R. L. Goldstone, B. C. Love, A. B. Markman, and P. Wolff (eds.) *Categorization Inside and Outside The Laboratory: Essays in Honor of Douglas L. Medin*. Washington, DC: American Psychological Association: 127–49.
Gendler, Tamar. 1998. "Exceptional Persons: On the Limits of Imaginary Cases." *Journal of Consciousness Studies* 5 (5–6): 592–610.
Nichols, Shaun. 2008. "Imagination and the I." *Mind and Language* 23 (5): 518–35.
Nichols, Shaun, and Bruno, Michael. 2010. "Intuitions about Personal Identity: An Empirical Study." *Philosophical Psychology* 23 (3): 293–312.
Ninan, Dilip. 2022. "Williams on the Self and the Future." *Analytic Philosophy* 63 (2): 147–55. https://doi-org.ccl.idm.oclc.org/10.1111/phib.12229.
Nozick, Robert. 1981. *Philosophical Explanations*. Cambridge, MA: Harvard University Press. (See Chapter 1, "The Identity of the Self.")
Parfit, Derek. 1984. *Reasons and Persons*. Oxford: Oxford University Press.

Shoemaker, Sydney. 1963. *Self-Knowledge and Self-Identity*. Ithaca, NY: Cornell University Press.
Thomson, Judith Jarvis. 1997. "People and Their Bodies." In Jonathan Dancy (ed.) *Reading Parfit*. Oxford: Blackwell: 202–29.
Wilkes, Kathleen. 1988. *Real People: Personal Identity without Thought Experiments*. Oxford: Oxford University Press.
Williams, Bernard. 1957. "Personal Identity and Individuation." *Proceedings of the Aristotelian Society* 57: 229–52.
Williams, Bernard. 1960. "Personal Identity and Bodily Continuity: A Reply." *Analysis* 21: 43–8.

MIND UPLOADING

BACKGROUND

In previous chapters (see especially Chapters 39 and 41), we considered body-swap cases where the consciousness of one individual is transferred to another individual's body, and vice versa. But could one's consciousness also be transferred to a non-biological machine? This chapter considers that possibility, one often explored in works of science fiction. In fact, our description below is based loosely on the scenario presented in Robert Sawyer's science fiction novel, *Mindscan* (2005). Sawyer's example is also discussed at length by Susan Schneider (2019). We might imagine the uploading so that it occurs gradually over time. This kind of uploading is usually imagined by way of an information-transfer process involving nanobots. First, a single nanobot might be introduced into one's neural system to take the place of a single neuron. The process might then be repeated with a second nanobot, and then a third, until eventually there is no biological matter left and the whole "brain" is simply a collection of nanobots. In the case considered in this chapter, we imagine the uploading to occur all at once. Whichever way we imagine the case, it raises interesting questions about personal identity over time—that is, about what makes it the case that A at time t1 is identical to B at time t2.

As we mentioned in Chapter 39, philosophers working on personal identity tend to divide into three camps. Those who defend the soul theory suggest that a person's identity over time consists in the continued existence of the same soul. Those who defend the psychological theory suggest that a person's identity over time consists in psychological facts, such as memory connections. Those who defend the physical theory suggest that a person's identity over time consists in physical facts, such as having the same body. The upload scenario is often proposed as support for the psychological theory. But, as we will see, it also raises a deep problem for such theories in virtue of the fact that the same upload process can be run multiple times at once, producing multiple manifestations of the original person.

At present, mind uploading remains confined to the realm of science fiction. But some researchers think it is only a matter of time before it will be technologically feasible. The inventor and futurist Ray Kurzweil (2005) predicts that we will be able to upload the brain to a computer or android body via a straightforward scan-and-transfer procedure sometime in the late 2030s. One promising avenue of research into mind uploading involves a process called *whole brain emulation* or WBE. As philosophers Anders Sandberg and Nick Bostrom have suggested (2008, p. 5), though WBE "represents a formidable engineering and research problem," it appears to be an attainable goal; given currently existing technology, achieving WBE looks to be a matter just of additional extrapolation. Suppose, for example, that we had a "connectome"—a wiring diagram that maps out all of the neural connections in the brain (see Mandelbaum 2022). We would then have the kind of detail needed to create a software model of the brain; and, from there, the prospect of uploading capability does not seem far off.

THE CASE

Imagine Bhavith, a middle-aged man living in the near future. Recently he's been feeling sluggish and out of breath, and he's even been having intermittent chest pain. He decides to see his cardiologist, who examines him and does extensive lab work and tests. Shortly thereafter Bhavith gets a call that he needs to come back in for a follow-up visit as soon as possible. On his arrival, the doctor greets Bhavith with a grave demeanor. "I'm afraid I have some bad news," she says. "The tests we did revealed that you have an incurable and untreatable heart defect. Based on similar cases like yours, we expect that you have only months to live." As Bhavith struggles to absorb this news, he realizes that the doctor is still speaking. "Even though there is no treatment or cure, I do have one possible option for you," she says.

> An interesting procedure has been developed by an interdisciplinary research team working at the Humans of Tomorrow Institute. They'd scan your brain and body and make a record of your mental and physical configuration. When the scan is complete, they'll design an android body based on your own current body and then upload your mind pattern to a computer that operates the android body. They'll dispose of the old biological shell, and you'll be able to continue on just as before with the new body. Given that these android bodies last a very long time and can be easily replaced if they ever do wear out or suffer damage, this procedure lets you live on indefinitely, even forever if you'd like. This procedure hasn't yet been made available to the general public, since the Institute is still trying to get the insurance companies to cover patient costs. I have some connections and could get you an appointment. I know this is a lot to take in, but I think it's a really great option for you. My understanding is that it's worked very well so far. All my patients who have undergone the scanning and uploading procedure have been very happy with the results. It's expensive, but I'm pretty sure it's well within your means. So, what do you say? Shall I give them a call?

Bhavith is understandably freaked out by the news, and he is hesitant to make any big decisions on the spot. He goes home and talks things over with his spouse and family. Ultimately, he decides to go through with it. He schedules an appointment for the mindscan and uploading for two weeks later. During the procedure he is sedated. When he finds himself beginning to wake up, he isn't sure whether the procedure has even finished yet; but, as he opens his eyes, he realizes that he has a brand-new body—similar to his old one, but revitalized and stronger. And he feels just like himself. "It works just as they promised," he thinks with a sigh of relief.

We could stop the thought experiment there, but let's add one twist. Moments after Bhavith wakes up, there is a knock at his door. When the person comes in, Bhavith is startled to realize that it's ... Bhavith. It turns out that the facility's BDU (biological disposal unit) is currently malfunctioning, and so the team wasn't able to dispose of the biological body as they usually do. But, since they could tell that the biological heart was only days away from giving out, they decided to just let Bhavith live on in the biological body until he died a natural death, while also letting him live on in the android body. Staring at one another, neither Bhavith knows quite what to think.

DISCUSSION

If it is possible to upload one's consciousness to a computer and retain one's personal identity, then it looks like some version of the psychological theory of personal identity must be correct. Since there is no physical continuity between the individual pre-upload and post-upload—no continuity of brain and no continuity of body—successful uploading would render the physical theory of personal identity false. The question of whether uploading is compatible with the truth of the soul theory is less straightforward, since it might be that one's soul ends up being transferred to the machine along with one's consciousness. But, even if there is no contradiction between the upload scenario and the soul theory, the upload scenario does not mesh very well with the way that soul theorists tend to think about souls. For example, souls are usually thought to be indivisible, so it's unclear how a gradual transfer would work. Moreover, given that the upload procedure proceeds by way of a data transfer—with nothing really moving from one body to another—it's not clear when exactly the soul would "hop" over from one body to another, or why should we think that it would; and this unclarity arises even in cases where the data process is not gradual but takes place all at once.

When we stop the thought experiment before the final twist, before the person beginning to wake up hears the knock at his door, many people share that person's own initial assessment of the situation: The upload worked to preserve Bhavith's personal identity. He, the person in the bed with the android body, is Bhavith. But, just like the case of teletransportation mentioned in Chapter 39, the upload scenario raises a problem of reduplication, as we see in the final twist when Bhavith comes face to face with himself. The two Bhaviths share consciousness up to the moment of the upload; but, at that moment, their consciousnesses diverge. Bhavith-in-the-biological-body—or *bio-Bhavith*—awakens from the scanning procedure before *android-Bhavith* does, and so has memories of a period of time that android-Bhavith does not. Moreover, at the present moment, they are each having different thoughts: "Hey I'm looking at myself in the doorway" and "Hey I'm looking at myself in the bed." Since bio-Bhavith and android-Bhavith are not identical to one another, they cannot both be identical to the Bhavith who elected for the procedure, old-Bhavith (identity is transitive: if x = y and y = z, then x = z). Prior to the appearance of bio-Bhavith, it looked like android-Bhavith could be identified with old-Bhavith. But now that bio-Bhavith is on the scene, that identification is called into question. Still, one might be puzzled as to how the existence of bio-Bhavith could change who android-Bhavith is. And it seems weird to think that neither of them is identical to old-Bhavith. As Derek Parfit (1984) has asked, how could double success be a failure? After all, both bio-Bhavith and android-Bhavith seem to have successfully survived. They are both alive and well.

In recent philosophical discussion of uploading, philosophers tend to divide into two camps: the optimists and the pessimists. Surveying various upload possibilities, David Chalmers (2010) notes reason for optimism about gradual uploading. If only one of his neurons were replaced by a nanobot, the resulting person would still be him. A system with only 1% replaced by nanobots, call it $Dave_1$, would still be identical to the original him. And $Dave_2$, after replacement of another 1%, would surely be identical to $Dave_1$, and so on and so on, all the way up to $Dave_{100}$. So, by transitivity of identity, Dave is identical to $Dave_{100}$. Interestingly, once we embrace optimism about gradual uploading, we might use that to argue for optimism about the kind of instant uploading we saw in Bhavith's case. Instant uploading can be understood as gradual uploading in an expedited fashion, and it is hard to see how speeding up a process could change its metaphysical effects. So, if we accept gradual uploading, it looks like we should embrace instant uploading as well.

Many pessimists point to worries about reduplication to make their case against uploading. But there are other reasons offered for pessimism as well. Corabi and Schneider note that, even during a very fast upload, the upload process cannot be instantaneous: "Since information is being uploaded, the information has to be processed and reassembled in the computer host before anything like a functional duplicate of the original brain can be obtained" (2012, p. 35). So, we would have a situation in which at one moment a person exists in a biological body, then there is a brief period (perhaps very brief) in which the person does not exist, and then a moment in which a person exists again in a computer—a gap in their continued existence. Many philosophers reject the claim that entities (including persons) can have such a "gappy" existence. Things don't pop in and out of existence. If this is right, then we have further reason for pessimism that the person survives the upload process.

To mount a different kind of case for pessimism, Nicholas Agar (2016) proposes a thought experiment involving extraterrestrial scientists from the star Betelgeuse. These scientists are fascinated by humans, and, unbeknownst to any of us on Earth, they use long-range scanning technology to create blueprints of some of the humans they observe. They then use these blueprints to make human copies on their own planet. If you were one of the humans scanned by the scientists, would the copy they recreate on Betelgeuse be identical to you? Agar predicts that most of us would have the very strong intuition that the answer is no. As he goes on to argue, machine uploading parallels this kind of copying case.

Alternatively, some pessimists deny that an upload could even be a conscious being, let alone the conscious being that is you (see Hauskeller 2012, Mandelbaum 2022). The upload scenario seems to presuppose functionalism—that is, it seems to presuppose that mental states are functional states. Insofar as we have reason to doubt that functional duplicates of conscious beings really have qualia (see Chapters 7 and 16), we would have reason to doubt that uploads are conscious.

Finally, some philosophers take a position that is in one sense a kind of pessimism but perhaps is better seen as a way of rejecting this whole way of approaching the issue. According to Parfit (1984), *identity is not what matters to us in survival*. Because identity is a one-to-one relation, you are not identical to your upload in cases of nondestructive uploading—that is, cases in which your consciousness is retained in your biological body while also being uploaded into a machine. But, even if your upload is not identical to you, the upload has just about everything we care about in survival. When thinking about your future, then, Parfit suggests that you shouldn't focus on whether some future being is identical to you, but rather whether and to what extent you are related in relevant ways to some future being. Such relevant ways might include relating to that future being by memory and/or other psychological features. Whatever the relevant features are, in Parfit's view, personal identity is not one of them. Contrary to what is often assumed, personal identity is *not* what we should care about when thinking about our futures.

RECOMMENDED READING

CANONICAL PRESENTATION

Schneider, Susan. 2019. *Artificial You: AI and the Future of Your Mind*. Princeton: Princeton University Press. (See Chapter 6.)

OVERVIEW

Chalmers, David J. 2010. "The Singularity: A Philosophical Analysis." *Journal of Consciousness Studies* 17: 7–65.

ADDITIONAL DISCUSSIONS

Agar, Nicholas. 2016. "Enhancement, Mind-Uploading, and Personal Identity." In Steve Clarke (ed.) *The Ethics of Human Enhancement: Understanding the Debate.* Oxford: Oxford University Press: 184–97.

Corabi, Joseph, and Schneider, Susan. 2012. "Metaphysics of Uploading." *Journal of Consciousness Studies* 19 (1–2): 26–44.

Dainton, Barry. 2012. "On Singularities and Simulations." *Journal of Consciousness Studies* 19 (1–2): 42–85.

Goldwater, Jonah. 2021. "Uploads, Faxes, and You: Can Personal Identity Be Transmitted?" *American Philosophical Quarterly* 58 (3): 233–50.

Hauskeller, Michael. 2012. "My Brain, My Mind, and I: Some Philosophical Assumptions of Mind-Uploading." *International Journal of Machine Consciousness* 4 (1): 187–200.

Kurzweil, Ray. 2005. *The Singularity Is Near: When Humans Transcend Biology*. New York: Penguin.

Mandelbaum, Eric. 2022. "Everything and More: The Prospects of Whole Brain Emulation." *Journal of Philosophy* 119: 444–59.

Parfit, Derek. 1984. *Reasons and Persons*. Oxford: Oxford University Press.

Pigliucci, Massimo. 2014. "Mind Uploading: A Philosophical Counter-Analysis." In Russell Blackford and Damien Broderick (eds.) *Intelligence Unbound: The Future of Uploaded and Machine Minds*. Malden, MA: Wiley Blackwell: 119–30.

Sandberg, Anders, and Bostrom, Nick. 2008. *Whole Brain Emulation: A Roadmap*. Oxford: Future of Humanity Institute.

Sawyer, Robert. 2005. *Mindscan*. New York: Tor Books.

THE PUZZLE OF TOO MANY MINDS

BACKGROUND

What am I? More specifically, what is the relationship between me and my body? According to one view, famously held by Plato and Descartes, I am something immaterial—a soul, perhaps—that "resides in" or "occupies" a body. The nature of this residency is somewhat tricky, but on this dualist view one thing at least is clear: I am not identical to my body. This is also true on the psychological theory of personal identity (see Chapters 39, 41, and 42), according to which what I am from time to time is a matter of there being certain psychological connections, such as memory connections, between my past and future selves. According to this theory, whether I'm a soul or body is less relevant than whether these connections exist. Not all views place such an emphasis on psychology, however. According to physical theories of personal identity (see Chapter 41), one's identity over time consists in certain physical facts. According to Eric Olson's physical theory, called *animalism*, people are biological creatures: I, for example, am identical to a human animal. This view can seem extremely natural, but many philosophers—even those not tempted by dualism—resist it. On the animalist view, for example, if my brain is transplanted into a different body, I am still the brainless body (assuming the body is alive) even if the new body has all my memories, traits, and so on. For some, the animalist view seems to detach personhood from psychology in an implausible way. Some philosophers, therefore, adopt a different kind of physical theory of personal identity, according to which a person is not *identical* with a human animal but is nonetheless *constituted* by it.

THE CASE

How many things are sitting in your chair right now? The intuitive answer is one. But if we take a psychological view of personal identity, then we can't give that answer and we're presented with a puzzle. To see how the puzzle arises, consider *the thinking animal argument*:

1. Presently sitting in your chair is a human animal.
2. The human animal sitting in your chair is thinking.
3. You are the thinking being sitting in your chair.
4. Therefore, the human animal sitting in the chair is you.

All of these premises are compelling—assuming you are sitting in a chair, of course—and they seem to entail the conclusion in a straightforward manner. Suppose, though, that one was inclined to say "Yes, there is a human animal here, but I am also a person. And being a person is not the same as being a human animal!" That sounds plausible enough, but it sounds like it results in there being too many thinking things in your chair. There is the human animal thinking and then there is you, the person. Unless the animalist is right and those two things are identical, there are too many thinking things in the chair. The best response, says the animalist, is to accept that human persons such as ourselves are simply human animals.

DISCUSSION

Many philosophers think this argument for animalism moves a little too quickly. This can be seen by considering a corollary to the thinking animal argument that generates too many minds for the animalist.

Call the space occupied by you sitting in your chair the *chairspace*. Now consider the following argument:

1. There is a brain in the chairspace.
2. The brain in the chairspace is thinking.
3. The brain is not identical to the human animal.
4. The human animal is in the chairspace.
5. There are not two things thinking in the chairspace—that would be too many minds!
6. Therefore, the human animal is not thinking.

This argument seems to turn the animalist's reasoning against itself. The premises seem plausible, and, given their similarity to the animalist's own premises, it seems any response to the argument can be adjusted to be used as a response to the thinking animal argument as well.

While some philosophers opposed to animalism are substance dualists, believing that a person is identical with a soul, many are not. These philosophers, many of whom adopt a psychological view of personal identity (see Chapters 39, 41, and 42), think that, though we are material beings, we are nonetheless not identical with human animals. It seems, for example, that if my body is in a vegetative state with no consciousness, though the animal lives, I'm not there anymore. My identity over time seems to be more closely related to my psychological continuity than to bodily continuity. If somehow my brain (and therefore my psychology) were transplanted into a different human animal, I would be in that new body. How can the materialist say this without running into the problem of too many minds?

Lynne Rudder Baker (2000) attempts to thread the needle by appealing to a classic puzzle in metaphysics: the statue and the clay. Suppose an artist molds a lump of clay into a statue of the Buddha. What is the relation between the statue and the clay? It is natural to say the statue is identical with the clay. But there are problems with that answer. It seems the clay existed before the statue. Moreover, if the statue is smushed, the clay remains but the statue is gone. If the Buddha's left ear breaks off and another piece of clay—or even some other material—is molded to replace it, the statue remains though the original lump of clay doesn't. If the statue is identical to the clay, how can either one exist without the other? If they're not identical, there seem to be two distinct entities in the same place at the same time. Here there is no temptation to say that the statue is some shadowy, supernatural entity, related in some way to the clay. But if the statue and the clay are distinct, what is the statue if not the clay, and what is the relationship between these two entities?

A number of philosophers argue that, though the statue is not identical to the clay, it is *constituted* by it. Before the artist made the statue, the clay did not constitute a statue, and after some clay was removed and then replaced, something different—a different bunch of clay—constitutes the statue. Baker argues we should say something similar for the relationship between persons and their bodies. I am not identical to my body, just as the statue is not identical to the clay. Nevertheless, I am constituted by a particular physical body. If my body survives in a vegetative state, the body, the human animal, is there but it no longer constitutes a person—it is like a lump of clay no longer constituting a statue.

How does the constitution view respond to the animalist argument? The natural response is to say that the conclusion is true: you are the human animal in the chair. But this doesn't mean you are *identical* with that human animal; instead, you are *constituted* by it. Are there now too many minds—my mind and the mind of the human animal? No. That would be double counting. Compare: the statue weighs 10 pounds and the clay it is made of weighs 10 pounds. Since the statue and the clay are distinct entities, do they together weigh 20 pounds? No, the clay's weight just is the statue's weight, because the clay constitutes the statue. Similarly, the human animal's mind just is the person's mind, because the human animal constitutes the person.

Another response is to embrace the multiplicity of thinkers while denying that this is a problem. For example, C. S. Sutton (2014) argues that properties of objects related in a certain way are *nonsummative*—essentially, they don't "add up" in the way you would otherwise expect. So, in his example, if your body weighs 150 pounds and your arm weighs 9, you wouldn't expect the scale to read 159 pounds when you stepped on it—even though your body and your arm are both being weighed. The 9 pounds of your arm is part of the 150 pounds of your body. The same is true of the many minds in my chair. Perhaps they aren't identical. But they are made up of the same stuff, and so their properties—the number of thoughts, for example—are non-summative. As Luke Roelofs (2022) points out, this does have the consequence that two thinkers can share thoughts. While this might seem to conflict with the privacy of the mental, perhaps this isn't so worrisome given the overlapping nature of the subjects in question.

RECOMMENDED READING

CANONICAL PRESENTATIONS

Baker, Lynne Rudder. 2000. *Persons and Bodies: A Constitution View.* Cambridge: Cambridge University Press.

Olson, Eric T. 1997. *The Human Animal: Personal Identity without Psychology.* New York: Oxford University Press.

Snowdon, Paul F. 1990. "Persons, Animals, and Ourselves." In Christopher Gill (ed.) *The Person and the Human Mind: Issues in Ancient and Modern Philosophy.* Oxford: Clarendon: 83–107.

OVERVIEWS

Bailey, Andrew. 2015. "Animalism." *Philosophy Compass* 10 (12): 867–83.

Blatti, Stephan. 2020. "Animalism." *The Stanford Encyclopedia of Philosophy* (Fall 2020 Edition), Edward N. Zalta (ed.), URL = <https://plato.stanford.edu/archives/fall2020/entries/animalism/>.

ADDITIONAL DISCUSSIONS

Blatti, Stephan, and Snowdon, Paul F. (eds.). 2016. *Animalism: New Essays on Persons, Animals, and Identity.* Oxford: Oxford University Press.

Johnston, Mark. 2007. "'Human Beings' Revisited: My Body Is Not an Animal." In Dean W. Zimmerman (ed.) *Oxford Studies in Metaphysics*, volume 3. Oxford: Oxford University Press: 33–74.

Roelofs, Luke. 2022. "No Such Thing as Too Many Minds." *Australasian Journal of Philosophy*: 1–16. doi:10.1080/00048402.2022.2084758.

Shoemaker, Sidney. 2008. "Persons, Animals, and Identity." *Synthese* 162 (3): 313–24.

Sutton, C. S. 2014. "The Supervenience Solution to the Too-Many-Thinkers Problem." *Philosophical Quarterly* 64 (257): 619–39.

SPLIT BRAINS AND THE UNITY PUZZLE

BACKGROUND

The brains of all mammals are divided into two hemispheres. In placental mammals (as opposed to egg-laying mammals like monotremes or pouch-rearing mammals like marsupials), the hemispheres are connected via a brain structure known as the corpus callosum—a wide, C-shaped tract of nerve fibers approximately 10 centimeters long. In 1952, scientists performed an operation on a cat that severed the corpus callosum, and thus prevented communication between the two brain hemispheres. The cat's optic chiasm (the part of the brain where the optic nerves cross) was also severed, so that visual information provided directly to one of the cat's eyes went only to the corresponding brain hemisphere. Study of the split-brain cat showed that its two brain hemispheres could function independently of one another. For example, the cat was successfully taught a particular stimulus–response task via only one eye. When that eye was covered and the same task was presented to the cat via the other eye, it could no longer complete the task. In the early 1960s, subsequent studies with monkeys revealed similar results. In 1965, doctors treating patients with life-threatening epilepsy decided to perform the same kind of surgery (called a *commissurotomy*) on several human patients. By disconnecting the two hemispheres from one another, the doctors hoped to prevent the seizures from spreading across the whole brain. These surgeries were extremely successful. Seizure activity was not just confined but virtually eliminated.

The puzzle that we will discuss in this chapter arises from psychological studies that were conducted on the split-brain patients following the surgeries. Although in everyday life these patients were able to function normally, the studies revealed a similar kind of divided consciousness as had been detected in cats and monkeys. Understanding the results of these studies and how they give rise to a puzzle requires a little more background on human brains and hemispheric functioning. First, visual and tactile input is delivered contralaterally—that is, information from the right side of the visual field or from the right hand goes to the left hemisphere; and, likewise, information from the left side of the visual field or from the left hand goes to the right hemisphere. Second, the two hemispheres tend to have different specializations. (In fact, much of what we know about hemispheric specialization owes to research done on split-brain subjects.) One specialization will prove especially significant to the discussion of this chapter: While the left hemisphere tends to have the ability to generate spoken language, the right hemisphere does not.

THE CASE

Consider a typical split-brain subject that we'll call *Twain*. Suppose that Twain has his left hand underneath a table, where it cannot be seen, and that we give him an object to hold, like a phone. Since the hemisphere responsible for speech does not have any access to the information about what the left hand is holding, when we now ask Twain what he's holding, he'll respond by saying something like "I don't know." But now suppose that we take the phone away (still keeping it out of sight) and we give him a box with a bunch of different objects in it, including the phone. When we ask him to retrieve it, he can do so. Or if we give him a pencil (held in his left hand) and ask him to draw what he was just holding, he will produce a picture of a phone. One natural way to describe the case is to say that the right hemisphere knows something that the left hemisphere does not.

Other experiments with Twain reinforce the assessment that his two hemispheres are functioning independently of one another. Suppose we divide his visual fields and flash the word "heart" on a screen such that the letters "he" present only to the left half of the visual field (and thus to the right hemisphere) and the letters "art" present only to the right half of the visual field (and thus to the left hemisphere). If we ask Twain aloud what word he has seen, he will say "art." But if we hold up two cards, one of which has the word "he" written on it and the other of which has the word "art" written on it, and we ask Twain to point with his left hand to the word that he has seen, he will point to the card containing the word "he." Again, a natural way to describe the case would be to say that each hemisphere knows something that the other does not.

In ordinary situations, however, Twain functions more or less normally. And this generates a puzzle: Is Twain a single person with a single mind, as he appears to be in day-to-day interactions, or he is two persons each with their own minds, as he appears to be in the experimental situations? And, if the latter, when did this split happen? All the operation did was to sever a connection. When conjoined twins undergo an operation to sever the connection between them, the surgeons don't bring a new person into existence; rather, the surgeons separate two persons who already existed. So, was Twain two persons all along? If so, what does that say about the rest of us? After all, setting aside his epilepsy, Twain's brain was no different from any of ours prior to his commissurotomy. We too have two different hemispheres that could be separated from one another.

Following Elizabeth Schechter (2018), we can refer to the puzzle generated by split-brain cases as *the unity puzzle*. As she describes it, the unity puzzle consists of three claims that are each independently plausible but that jointly result in a contradiction. The three claims making up the inconsistent triad are as follows: (1) A split-brain subject has two minds. (2) A split-brain subject is a single person. (3) Each person has exactly one mind. (See also Wilkes 1988, pp. 141–3.)

DISCUSSION

Let's start by explaining why each claim in the inconsistent triad seems plausible.

In support of claim 1, that a split-brain subject like Twain has two minds, we might invoke considerations relating to the unity of consciousness. Generally speaking, we take a subject of conscious experience to be a single unified entity. If a subject is consciously experiencing an itch on their back and a pain in their right knee, then these two experiences get integrated as aspects of their overall conscious experience. This is not true of the split-brain patient, as when Twain's simultaneous visual experiences of "he" and "art" are not integrated with one another. Relatedly, if a subject is consciously having experiences, these should be accessible via introspection. But this does not seem to be true in the case of Twain, as there seems to be no single subject who can introspectively access both the visual experience of "he" and "art." Finally, the conscious mental states of a single subject would typically be internally consistent. While any of us might suffer from occasional irrationality, as a general matter a single conscious subject cannot consciously think "there is a phone in my left hand" and "there is not a phone in my left hand" simultaneously as Twain seems to be able to do.

In support of claim 2, that a split-brain subject like Twain is a single person, we might first point to the fact that this is how they seem to think of themself. They don't describe themself as having more than one mind, or like a part of themself is hidden to themself. We might also point to the behavioral integration that they exhibit in ordinary day-to-day life. Split-brain patients are able to tie their shoes, to play the piano, and to swim—activities that require coordination between both sides of the body. Disunity arises only in artificially induced conditions and is temporary. As Kathleen Wilkes notes, when someone experiences temporary disunity as a result of a post-hypnotic suggestion, or because of a fugue state involving memory loss, we don't take that to count against the claim that they have a single mind. So why should the temporary disunity exhibited by a split-brain subject be treated any differently?

As for claim 3, that each person has exactly one mind, this seems to be at the heart of our thinking about persons. For example, according to John Locke's influential account of personhood (1689/1974), a person is a thinking, intelligent being that has reason and reflection and can reflect on itself as itself (see Chapter 39). This account seems to presuppose that each person has only a single mind. A person with two minds would not be able to reflect fully on itself as itself, since each mind would not be able to reflect on the contents of the other mind, and there is no way to reflect on the contents of both together.

Philosophers have offered various responses to this puzzle. One common response tries to reject claim 1, that a split-brain has two minds. But there are different ways of rejecting this claim. Tim Bayne (2008) has suggested that a proper understanding of the notion of unity of consciousness allows us to attribute unity to split-brain patients. On his view, the split-brain patient's stream of consciousness is realized serially by the two hemispheres, sometimes by one and then sometimes by the other. The switching happens very fast, however, and this accounts for the appearance that split-brain patients have two minds.

Though Nagel (1971) agrees that we should not say that the split-brain subject has two minds, his reasoning is different from Bayne's. Rather than motivating the denial of claim 1 with the thought that a split-brain subject has only one mind, Nagel suggests that we should not try to assign a whole number of individual minds to the split-brain subject. The answer to the question "How many minds do they have?" is neither one nor two. While there is a strong temptation to think that we must be able to answer this question with some whole number or other, Nagel urges us to resist the temptation. Yes, we can attribute conscious mental activity to a split-brain subject. But this assignment does not entail that there is a mind associated with this mental activity. Granted, in ordinary cases, we do not see mental activity that cannot be assigned to one unified mind or another; but Nagel suggests that we should not be surprised that an extraordinary phenomenon such as the split-brain patients would present us with something that can't be described in normal terms.

In her discussion of the case, Wilkes goes even farther than Nagel. On her view, we should question whether the notion of a unified mind is even a coherent one. Even in our own cases, we may just be under an illusion that there is a unity of consciousness. Like the split-brain patients, we too may just be a system that happens to be more or less integrated, and there just happens to be a lot of cooperation in our own cases.

Other philosophers have attempted to deny claim 2, that the split-brain subject is a single person. One particularly radical defense of this claim is given by Roland Puccetti (1981). On Puccetti's view, not only are the split-brain subjects two persons, but all of us are really two persons—even those of us whose hemispheres are connected. (For a related view, which is developed independent of the split-brain cases, see Lewis 1976.)

Denial of the second claim also resonates with a line of argumentation offered by Derek Parfit (1984, 1987) in support of the claim that we shouldn't think that personal identity is what matters in our continued survival through time (see Chapter 42). If there is not a single person post-commissurotomy, then there is no person existing who is identical to the person pre-commissurotomy. The two persons post-commissurotomy are not identical to one another, so the person pre-commissurotomy cannot be identical to them both, and there are no grounds to identify the person with one rather than the other. But, even if personal identity is lost, we can say that the person prior to the commissurotomy *survives* as both people; and, on Parfit's view, this kind of survival supports everything that matters to us in thinking about our futures.

Attempts to resolve the puzzle by rejecting claim 3, the one-mind-per-person principle, have been relatively rare. But Schechter (2018) has recently mounted an extended defense of this option. While recognizing that her approach may seem initially to be deeply revisionary of our notion of persons, she suggests that the denial of this principle is more in line with other things that we believe about persons than we might expect. Central to Schechter's argument is the notion of self-consciousness. On her view, once we properly understand the way that self-consciousness operates in the split-brain subject where there are two minds, we will see that it is not so very different from the way that self-consciousness operates in more ordinary cases, suggesting that there might be two minds there as well.

RECOMMENDED READING

CANONICAL PRESENTATIONS

Gazzaniga, Michael S. 1967. "The Split Brain in Man." *Scientific American* 21 7(2): 24–9.

Nagel, Thomas. 1971. "Brain Bisection and the Unity of Consciousness." *Synthese* 22: 396–413.

OVERVIEWS

Schechter, Elizabeth. 2017. "Split Brains." In *Routledge Encyclopedia of Philosophy Online*. Taylor and Francis. https://www.rep.routledge.com/articles/thematic/split-brains/v-2. doi:10.4324/0123456789-W042-2.

Trevarthen, Colwyn. 2015. "Split Brains and Human Consciousness." In James D. Wright (ed.) *International Encyclopedia of the Social and Behavioral Sciences*, second edition. Oxford: Elsevier: 291–8.

ADDITIONAL DISCUSSIONS

Alter, Torin. 2010. "A Defense of the Necessary Unity of Phenomenal Consciousness." *Pacific Philosophical Quarterly* 91 (1): 19–37.

Bayne, Tim. 2008. "The Unity of Consciousness and the Split-Brain Syndrome." *Journal of Philosophy* 105 (6): 277–300.

Bayne, Timothy J., and Chalmers, David J. 2003. "What Is the Unity of Consciousness?" In Axel Cleeremans (ed.) *The Unity of Consciousness*. Oxford: Oxford University Press: 23–58.

Lewis, David K. 1976. "Survival and Identity." In Amélie Oksenberg Rorty (ed.) *The Identities of Persons*. Los Angeles: University of California Press: 17–40.

Parfit, Derek. 1984. *Reasons and Persons*. Oxford: Oxford University Press.

Parfit, Derek. 1987. "Divided Minds and the Nature of Persons." In Colin Blakemore and Susan A. Greenfield (eds.) *Mindwaves*. Oxford: Blackwell: 19–26.

Puccetti, Roland. 1981. "The Case for Mental Duality: Evidence from Split-Brain Data and Other Considerations." *Behavioral and Brain Sciences* 4: 93–123.

Schechter, Elizabeth. 2018. *Self-Consciousness and "Split" Brains: The Mind's I*. Oxford: Oxford University Press.

Tye, Michael. 2003. *Consciousness and Persons: Unity and Identity*. Cambridge, MA: MIT Press.

Wilkes, Kathleen. 1988. *Real People: Personal Identity without Thought Experiments*. Oxford: Oxford University Press. (See Chapter 5, "Being in Two Minds.")

OTHER REFERENCE

Locke, John. 1689/1974. "Of Identity and Diversity." In *An Essay Concerning Human Understanding*, edited with an introduction by A. D. Woozley. New York: New American Library: 206–20.

SHARING FEELINGS, COMBINING MINDS

BACKGROUND

When we empathize with someone, we might say "I feel your pain." But that's a figure of speech. We can't actually feel someone else's particular pain, can we? Thoughts and conscious states are *private*, in the sense that only subjects who have them can be aware of them in a certain way. Suppose you get a pain in your finger whenever your twin cuts himself dicing carrots. Do you feel his pain? Not really. Instead, it seems you are having pain when he has pain, perhaps mysteriously caused by his feeling pain or by his finger being cut. It's not literally his pain. Although his thoughts and feelings are of the same *type* as yours, his are his and yours are yours. As it is sometimes put, his thought *tokens* are different from your thought *tokens*. His pain could stop and yours doesn't, or vice versa. But is this how we *have to* think of things? Is there anything incoherent in the idea that two subjects or selves have to be in one and the same token conscious state?

The privacy of the mental is closely tied to what might be called *the independence of minds*, the idea that two minds cannot combine to form another mind. No matter how closely you and your twin work together and "share" thoughts, there are still two minds there, each with their separate (even if exactly similar) streams of consciousness. Moreover, it is difficult to understand how two distinct minds can also combine to form a further mind. This idea was motivated by the case proposed by Williams James (1890) that we consider in this chapter.

THE CASE

Consider a group of 26 subjects. Each of them is asked to think of a different letter of the alphabet—the first thinks of "A," the second thinks of "B," and so on. No matter how closely related the subjects are, no matter how close they stand together or how much they talk to one another, there is no 27th subject composed of them all—no further subject that holds the entire alphabet in mind. Minds do not compose other minds in this way. My mind is my mind, your mind is yours, and no matter how much we put our heads together, these two minds do not compose a third mind; nor can their contents in any way merge.

DISCUSSION

The independence of minds and the privacy of their contents might seem to be challenged by the thought experiments of science fiction such as the "mind meld" from *Star Trek*. The alien species the Vulcans can perform mind melds by way of a special form of contact with another individual: If the Vulcan puts their hand on another creature's face in a certain position, they can somehow become directly aware of that other creature's thoughts and conscious states—that is, they can know the contents of the other creature's mind the same way they know the contents of their own minds.

Unraveling the issues here requires a closer look at the metaphysics of thoughts. In particular, the privacy of thoughts is not like the privacy of a hand in poker. Even when the cards in your hand are known only to you, those cards—those very same token pieces of paper—could easily have been in your opponent's hand; and, before they were dealt, they existed without being in anyone's hand at all. Mental states aren't this way. They can't exist mind-independently. Pains don't just float around unfelt until they bother somebody.

One tempting path is to think of them as modifications of the self, rather than independent objects a particular subject happens to glimpse. Having a thought or feeling a pain is more like dancing a jig than holding an ace of spades. When one dances a jig, the jig is not some separate thing that is the object of the dance. It is inseparable from the dance and the dancer. You can't dance my (token) jig, but not because I'm protective of my jigs. Rather, it would be a different jig if you danced it. You might well dance the same *type* of jig, just as you might have the same type of thought as I do. But you wouldn't be dancing the very same token jig or thinking the very same token thought. We might say that the jig is a way of dancing, or the pain is a way of feeling. These "ways" are properties, not objects on their own, and as such they are *individuated by* the things that have them. That is, they are the specific token properties they are in part because of the subjects that have them.

On this view, token thoughts and token conscious states cannot be shared by distinct subjects. The Vulcan mind meld is not a counterexample. A Vulcan doesn't really feel anyone else's token thoughts. Rather, they are having thoughts of the same type caused by the thoughts of another. Although the Vulcan and the subject of the mind meld are intimately connected, their thoughts are their own.

On other views, token thoughts can be shared. Such a possibility might seem to be ruled out by the privacy of thoughts and conscious states. But that is not so clear. Privacy as defined above says that *only subjects who have thoughts or conscious states can be aware of them in a certain way*. That claim doesn't rule out the possibility that two subjects can each have the same token thought, perhaps by sharing a mind or by being partially overlapping subjects. Take the jig case again. Although you can't dance my jig, suppose I have a conjoined twin with whom I share a leg. If we dance a jig, there seems to be a situation in which we are dancing the very same jig—not just the same *type* of jig, but the same token jig. Now suppose my twin and I are joined at the skull and share some brain matter, as seems to be the case with some craniopagus twins (conjoined twins with a fusion of the skull). Suppose we share a region that is the neural correlate for a particular pain. "Ow!" we both say at once. Can we be said to be having the same token pain? This is a tricky case, but the jig analogy suggests that, even if pains are individuated by their bearers, two subjects of this sort who overlap in a peculiar way might well share a token pain. Maybe minds can combine after all.

This can be resisted, though, and probably depends upon additional metaphysical issues concerning the nature of subjects and their relationship to conscious states. If one is both a substance dualist and a property dualist, for example, one might well say that, while two non-physical subjects can have states caused by the same brain, the states are themselves still distinct. While a physicalist cannot say this, exactly, they still typically distinguish between what some philosophers call *the core realizer* of a token pain and its *total realizer* (Shoemaker 1981). Suppose a certain region of the brain, which we'll call *the phi region*, is activated when a person has a specific token pain experience. Call this the pain's *narrow realizer*. It is doubtful that if that piece of neural tissue were activated in a petri dish there would be pain there. It needs to be integrated in a working brain—the total realizer for the painful mental state. Given this distinction, the physicalist could maintain that, in the case of the craniopagus twins, there is only one narrow realizer for the pain, but there are two token feelings of pain. Each of those feelings is individuated by different *total* realizers. Pains on this view are still unlike playing cards—even if there is a shared physical base that "lights up" when a subject is in pain, there are two pains.

Though the question of sharing conscious states and minds is plenty interesting in itself, it also has bearing on a problem that is often raised for panpsychism. According to panpsychism, at least a substantial amount of fundamental—or, if not fundamental, very basic—features of the universe are mental. Panpsychists do not usually hold that quarks are popping around with fully developed conscious fields like yours. But they do hold that things like quarks nonetheless have some conscious properties. Far from appearing only when there are creatures with particularly sophisticated brains, consciousness is pervasive, appearing even at the microphysical level.

Odd as this view might sound, it has recently received an increasing amount of attention and shouldn't be dismissed simply because it sounds weird. Almost any story about consciousness will probably involve some weirdness (Goff et al. 2022). The motivation for the view is that there must be some consciousness on the microphysical level to explain how consciousness exists at the macrophysical level. The view does face a challenge, however, concerning how these little conscious states add up to compose conscious minds like ours. Suppose with the panpsychist there are conscious states at the most fundamental microphysical level. Conscious states there are presumably like conscious states anywhere—they have to be had by something. So, wherever there is a conscious state, there is a subject of that state. This means that, for the panpsychist, the world is filled with micro-subjects. But how do these micro-subjects combine in such a way to produce macro-subjects such as ourselves (Goff 2006)? Recall James' example—putting a group of subjects together does not create a new subject, but only a collection of subjects. If this is the case, panpsychism cannot explain part of what it meant to explain: the existence of conscious experience in subjects like ourselves. This is a version of what is known as *the combination problem* (Seager 1995).

A number of solutions have been proposed for this combination problem. According to one, just because some subjects don't combine in certain ways doesn't mean that no subjects, including those on the micro-level, can combine. True, you don't get a single mind by lining up a group of people thinking about letters of the alphabet. But it doesn't follow that there is no way to combine subjects. It is possible, for example, that some fundamental physical relations are such that, when two micro-subjects stand in those relations, they compose a further subject that contains the conscious states of both. It's also an option to deny James' intuition. The 26 subjects do compose a further subject, and it only appears otherwise because none of us are that subject; we just don't have access to the combined experience. The 27th subject is itself not likely to be integrated enough to do complex tasks like survey its own experiences and report on them, so there is a difference between subjects 1–26 and the 27th subject. But it is a difference in degree, not a difference in kind.

RECOMMENDED READING

CANONICAL PRESENTATION

James, William. 1890. *The Principles of Psychology, Vol. 1*. London: Dover: 158–62.

OVERVIEW

Goff, Philip, Seager, William, and Allen-Hermanson, Sean. 2022. "Panpsychism." *The Stanford Encyclopedia of Philosophy* (Summer 2022 Edition), Edward N. Zalta (ed.), URL = <https://plato.stanford.edu/archives/sum2022/entries/panpsychism/>.

ADDITIONAL DISCUSSIONS

Bayne, Tim. 2010. *The Unity of Consciousness*. Oxford: Oxford University Press.

Chalmers, David. 2016. "The Combination Problem for Panpsychism." In Godehard Brüntrup and Ludwig Jaskolla (eds.) *Panpsychism: Contemporary Perspectives*. New York: Oxford University Press: 179–214.

Goff, Philip. 2006. "Experiences Don't Sum." *Journal of Consciousness Studies* 13 (10–11): 53–61.

Hirstein, William. 2012. *Mindmelding: Consciousness, Neuroscience, and the Mind's Privacy*. Oxford: Oxford University Press.

Roelofs, Luke. 2019. *Combining Minds: How to Think about Composite Subjectivity*. New York: Oxford University Press.

Seager, William E. 1995. "Consciousness, Information, and Panpsychism," *Journal of Consciousness Studies* 2 (3): 272–88.

Shoemaker, S. 1981. "Some Varieties of Functionalism." *Philosophical Topics* 12: 83–118.

THE ELUSIVE SELF

BACKGROUND

It is natural to think that each of us has, or is, a self. There are not only our thoughts, feelings, and experiential states; there is also something that has those states. This doesn't seem to be just a random assumption: we seem certain of its truth. In the western tradition, Descartes insists that even given radical doubt about the existence of the external world—including doubt that we have bodies—each of us can nonetheless be certain that we exist. *Cogito ergo sum*: I think therefore I am. On the face of it, my knowledge that I exist doesn't depend upon my knowledge about the external world. And, whatever else my existence might involve, it involves the existence of *me*—that is, my *self*. It seems natural to think that we know about this self via introspection. But Hume (1739/1978), and long before him the Buddha, questioned this claim. In their view, the self is in fact particularly elusive.

THE CASE

Take a second and survey what you find in experience. Perhaps close your eyes and draw up an inventory of what you find. You're likely to find your thoughts, for example, a thought such as "This is a weird exercise." Perhaps you'll notice some bodily sensations like a pain in the back and a tickling in the nose. Maybe you'll also find auditory experiences of the sounds from the cars outside or the internal melody of an earworm. But do you find anything that is *you*? Do you find the thing *having* these conscious states? Both the Buddha and Hume think not. There is nothing found but conscious experiences. The thing that has them—the self, or the subject of those experiences—eludes introspection.

This point about elusiveness is primarily epistemological or experiential. It concerns what we can introspect or experience. But Hume and the Buddha both also draw metaphysical conclusions. The Buddhists adopt the doctrine of *no-self*. Though there is a conventional sense in which there is a self or person—so words like "I" or names like "Ananda" aren't meaningless—the deeper metaphysical truth is that there is no such thing (see Chapter 40). Hume seems to take a different path, adopting the view that the self just is the bundle of experiences. There is some chance that the difference in these views is merely verbal. Hume's bundle could just be the conventional referent of "I"; but since it is not an unchanging thing, persisting unaltered throughout a person's existence, it wouldn't count as a real (non-conventional) self for the Buddhists.

DISCUSSION

The claim that the self is elusive can be glossed as the claim that we do not have inner perception of the self. To determine whether this is true, and indeed to understand the view itself, we need to be clear about what is involved in this sort of perception. According to one view, to perceive an object is to perceive the properties of that object. When we perceive a desk, we perceive it by perceiving its shape and its color. If this view is true, then there is a clear sense in which we do in fact perceive the self. Thoughts and conscious states are properties of the self. They are not free-range experiences; they belong to the subject of experience and are modifications of it. Our awareness of these properties, then, just is perception of the self, in the same way that our awareness of the desk's shape and color just is perception of the desk.

Though it's true there is a sense in which one perceives something by perceiving its properties, questions remain. Suppose you are sitting in a coffee shop and hear music playing. You believe there must be a beatnik with a guitar, playing on the patio. In fact, a record is playing. Are you perceiving the record? You are plausibly perceiving some of its properties—the sound it contains, etc. But the record itself is elusive. The defender of the elusiveness thesis could say the same thing about the self—one is perceiving the properties of the self, but those properties don't make the subject itself a salient object of perception (Howell 2023).

Turning from the epistemological claim to the metaphysical one, could it really be that there is no self? One might argue that there simply cannot be experiences without something that has those experiences. Experiences have to be had by something; there cannot be a thought without a thinker. While this is compelling to many, others are suspicious. In the early 19th century, Lichtenberg claimed that when Descartes gave his *cogito, ergo sum* argument, he was not justified in concluding there is an I—a thing that thinks (2012). All we can conclude based on introspection is that *there are thoughts*—not that there is a thing thinking those thoughts. Here Lichtenberg invokes an analogy. Just as we can say "It is raining" without there being a thing that is doing the raining, we can say "There is thinking" without concluding there is a thing that is thinking.

It is not clear that Lichtenberg's challenge succeeds. As Roderick Chisholm (1969) argues, it would seem that the selfless view is committed to thinking that we can substitute "There is" for "I"—that is, we can translate I-sentences into impersonal sentences. There is a problem with this, however. When I say "I have a headache" and you say "I do not have a headache," we can both be right—these claims do not contradict one another. If you translate them into the impersonal, though, they do: if I am saying "There is a headache" and you are saying "There is not a headache," then one of us must be wrong. Impersonal reports are thus not equivalent to first-personal reports. Since it can certainly be the case that I have a headache and you don't, the selfless reports must leave something out. And it is evident what is missing from the selfless reports: *who* has the headache.

Putting the point in terms of language and impersonal versus personal thoughts might seem to invite a Buddhist response: though Chisholm's point shows that first-personal sentences are not equivalent in meaning to impersonal sentences, it doesn't follow that sentences or thoughts using "I" refer to a real self. They might just refer to the conventional self of the sort the Buddhists can accept. This might be a little quick, however. The point can be put in metaphysical terms instead. You can have a headache when I don't because there is a certain natural unity to each of our conscious states. The itch in my back and the pain in my knee occur together—in the same mental space, as it were—and they don't occur in the same mental space with your headache. My mental states are mine, and yours are yours. This doesn't appear to be a merely conventional matter. If someone adopted a convention to refer to "Torambert" as that self that combined the conscious states of the three authors of this book, that convention wouldn't change the metaphysical facts—Torin's headache is not unified with Amy's imaginings or the music playing in Robert's head. According to some philosophers, the self is just that which explains this *unity of consciousness* (Peacocke 2014, Howell 2023; see also Chapters 44 and 45).

Whether or not this argument from the unity of consciousness is convincing as an argument for the self, it seems clear that it is too quick to conclude from the elusiveness of the self to introspection that there is no self. Sometimes there are good reasons to believe in things even if they don't appear in perception—e.g., to explain what we do perceive. For instance, there is good reason to believe in quarks, which we can't see directly, because they explain various observations. Similarly, there might be good reasons to believe in the self even if we do not directly perceive it—e.g., to explain the unity of consciousness. Perhaps there is something about the self that requires it to be salient to introspection if it exists. But showing that would require further argument.

RECOMMENDED READING

CANONICAL PRESENTATIONS

Bodhi, Bhikkhu. 1995. *The Middle Length Discourses of the Buddha: A Translation of the Majjhima Nikāya.* Translated by Bhikkhu Ñāṇamoli and Bhikkhu Bodhi. Somerville, MA: Wisdom. (Chapters 35 and 36.)

Hume, David. 1739/1978. *A Treatise of Human Nature.* Edited by L. A. Selby-Bigge. Oxford: Oxford University Press. (Book I, Section vi.)

OVERVIEWS

Gertler, Brie. 2011. *Self-Knowledge*. Abingdon: Routledge. (Chapter 7.)
Howell, Robert J. 2023. *Self-Awareness and the Elusive Subject*. Oxford: Oxford University Press.

ADDITIONAL DISCUSSIONS

Albahari, Miri. 2006. *Analytical Buddhism: The Two-Tiered Illusion of Self*. Basingstoke: Palgrave Macmillan.
Chisholm, Roderick M. 1969. "On the Observability of the Self." *Philosophy and Phenomenological Research* 30: 7–21.
Duncan, Matt. 2015. "We Are Acquainted with Ourselves." *Philosophical Studies* 172 (9): 2531–49.
Lichtenberg, G. C. 2012. *Philosophical Writings*. Translated and annotated by S. Tester. Albany: State University of New York Press.
Musholt, Kristina. 2015. *Thinking about Oneself*. Cambridge, MA: MIT Press.
Nida-Rümelin, Martine. 2017. "Self Awareness." *Review of Philosophy and Psychology* 8 (1): 55–82.
Peacocke, Christopher. 2014. *The Mirror of the World: Subjects, Consciousness, and Self-Consciousness*. Oxford: Oxford University Press.
Sartre, Jean-Paul. 1957/1993. *The Transcendence of the Ego: An Existentialist Theory of Consciousness*. New York: Octagon.
Shoemaker, Sydney. 1996. *The First-Person Perspective and Other Essays*. Cambridge: Cambridge University Press.

THE ESSENTIAL INDEXICAL

BACKGROUND

Some expressions refer to the same thing, whether said by you or me, at whatever time we speak. If someone says "The Eiffel Tower is made of iron," we don't need to know who said it or when in order to know what they are talking about. Other expressions are more sensitive to context. The words "I," "here," and "now," for example, refer to different people, places, and times depending on their context of utterance. When you say "I am standing" and I say "I am standing," we're saying different things despite using the same words in the same ways. Though this sounds like a merely linguistic issue, there seem to be *indexical thoughts* as well: You and I can both have the belief that we would each express by saying "I am standing," and we'd be thinking different things. What is the nature of indexical thoughts?

Issues surrounding indexical thought bear on two interesting issues in the philosophy of mind. The first has to do with whether the world can be completely grasped from the objective perspective: Does the "view from nowhere" (from no particular perspective; see Nagel 1986) leave something out? The second has to do with the issue of self-awareness. Descartes thought that "I am thinking" is one of the most certain pieces of knowledge that there is. This is an indexical thought, however, so understanding the nature of this certain

DOI: 10.4324/9781003179191-53

piece of knowledge—and consequently understanding the nature of self-awareness—requires understanding indexical thought.

THE CASES

Suppose you are pushing your cart through the grocery store and come upon a trail of sugar. Good Samaritan that you are, you follow the trail so you can let the hapless shopper know that they have a leaky bag. You wind up going in circles through the aisles, never catching up to the shopper, until you notice that at each pass the trail is thickening. You have the realization "I am the leaky shopper!" (Perry 1979).

At the moment you come to realize that you are the one leaking the sugar, you gain an important belief with some interesting properties. We can call it an *I-belief*. When you gain this I-belief you gain a belief about yourself, but it's not easy to explain the exact nature of the belief. You already had a belief about yourself—since you believed that the shopper with the leaky bag was spilling sugar, and you were the shopper with the leaky bag, you believed that you were spilling sugar. But that belief doesn't generate the important realization you get when you realize "I am the shopper with the leaky bag." It doesn't lead you to act in the way the I-belief does: only when you have the I-belief do you look down and seal the bag of sugar. The puzzle is that this indexical belief doesn't appear to receive any clear explanation in non-indexical terms: the indexical component is essential and cannot be eliminated.

Consider two further cases:

Lingens in the Library: Rudolf Lingens is an amnesiac locked in the Stanford library. While in the library Lingens reads many books, including his own biography which describes his life down to the smallest detail. Nevertheless, he is missing something crucial: he doesn't know that he is Rudolf Lingens (Frege 1956).

The Two Gods: Imagine that in some world there are two gods. One sits on the world's tallest mountain and the other sits on the world's coldest mountain. Each of them is omniscient with respect to the non-indexical facts about the world. They know there are two gods, that they are located on these different mountains, and all other non-indexical facts about the world. Though they are, we might say, omniscient about the objective facts about the world, they can still fail to know which god they are. Until they learn "I am the god on the tallest mountain" or "I am the God on the coldest mountain," they will lack important knowledge about the world (Lewis 1979).

Both Lingens in the Library and The Two Gods contain a similar moral: indexical knowledge—which includes I-beliefs, but also here-beliefs and now-beliefs—cannot be derived from non-indexical knowledge. Indexical knowledge is, in a sense, *situated knowledge* in that it cannot be attained from a completely objective, detached perspective. Indexical belief also seems to have further interesting properties. First, it seems particularly connected with action. I can know the man with the axe is about to leap out at the boy in the garden maze, but that won't lead to action—or fear, or planning to act—unless I know *I* am the boy in the garden maze (or that the man with the axe is in front of *me*!) Second, indexical belief can involve a higher degree of certainty than other contingent truths. This is most obvious in Descartes' *cogito*. I am certain *that I* am thinking. I cannot be certain that *the author of this chapter* is thinking—even if I am the author of this chapter. I could be fooled that I have authored this chapter. All of these are puzzling characteristics that seem to demand an explanation in terms of the nature of indexical concepts and thoughts.

DISCUSSION

In his classic essay "The Thought: A Logical Inquiry," Gottlob Frege kicks off the discussion by claiming that "everyone is presented to himself in a particular and primitive way, in which he is presented to no-one else" (1956, p. 298). This can suggest several different possibilities. One is that each person has a self-concept at the heart of their I-thoughts—a concept that is completely unique to them. Gottlob Frege is presented in an irreducible *GF-ish* way to himself, and John Perry is presented in a *JP-ish* way to himself. Perhaps this is because Frege has an unshareable concept and Perry has his own unshareable concept. Or perhaps this is because each is self-acquainted—directly aware of themselves without conceptual mediation—and no one can be acquainted with anyone other than themselves. There is also a third possibility (though perhaps not consistent with some of Frege's views), according to which there is a single primitive indexical concept, which we each have but which refers to me when I use it and you when you use it. When GF uses that concept he refers to GF, and when JP uses that same concept he refers to JP.

According to David Kaplan (1989) and John Perry (1979), indexical beliefs have both a *content* and a *character*. The content of Descartes' belief he would express as "I am thinking" is simply the proposition *Descartes is thinking*, where Descartes himself is a constituent of the proposition. When Frege thinks the same sort of I-thought, he is thinking something completely different, namely *Frege is thinking*. But there is also something in common between their two thoughts—the character. The character is, roughly, *the way that the content is thought*. The character of I-thoughts just picks out the thinker of that thought. Indexicals on this view don't figure into the content of thoughts at all, but only into the way those contents are thought.

Roderick Chisholm (1981) and David K. Lewis (1979) suggest a different theory. One way to put their theory is that, instead of treating I-beliefs as an odd case that requires tweaks to our picture of certain thoughts, they treat these I-beliefs as the foundations for *all* thought— in some sense, all thought is I-thought. To put it in Lewis' terms, all belief is *self-ascriptive* in the sense that when I believe something— whether it's a belief I would express using "I" or not—I am attributing a property to myself. When Perry believes he is spilling the sugar, he self-ascribes the property of spilling sugar. When Perry believes that the sky is blue, he self-ascribes the property of being such that the sky is blue (or, to put it another way, he self-ascribes the property of being in a world where the sky is blue).

Finally, there are descriptivist theories (Howell 2006, 2023). On these theories, when we have I-thoughts we are thinking of ourselves indirectly, as bearers of certain properties. On one view, for example, in I-thoughts we think of ourselves as the subjects of the conscious states of which we are directly aware. This view thus takes a page from the acquaintance view, which allows that we have direct access to certain subjective things, but, instead of being self-acquainted, we are acquainted with our conscious states (see Chapter 46).

RECOMMENDED READING

CANONICAL PRESENTATIONS

Castañeda, Hector-Neri. 1966. "'He': A Study in the Logic of Self-Consciousness." *Ratio* 8: 130–57.
Frege, Gottlob. 1956. "The Thought: A Logical Inquiry." *Mind* 65 (259): 289–311.

Kaplan, David. 1989. "Demonstratives: An Essay on the Semantics, Logic, Metaphysics and Epistemology of Demonstratives and Other Indexicals." In Joseph Almog, John Perry, and Howard Wettstein (eds.) *Themes from Kaplan*. New York: Oxford University Press: 481–563.

Perry, John. 1979. "The Problem of the Essential Indexical." *Noûs* 13 (1): 3–21.

OVERVIEWS

Braun, David. 2017. "Indexicals." *The Stanford Encyclopedia of Philosophy* (Summer 2017 Edition), Edward N. Zalta (ed.), URL = <https://plato.stanford.edu/archives/sum2017/entries/indexicals/>.

Torre, Stephan. 2016. "*De Se* Thought and Communication: An Introduction." In Manuel García-Carpintero and Stephan Torre (eds.) *About Oneself: De Se Thought and Communication*. Oxford: Oxford University Press: 1–21.

ADDITIONAL DISCUSSIONS

Cappelen, Herman, and Dever, Josh. 2013. *The Inessential Indexical: On the Philosophical Insignificance of Perspective and the First Person*. New York: Oxford University Press.

Castañeda, Hector-Neri. 1967. "Indicators and Quasi-Indicators." *American Philosophical Quarterly* 4: 85–100.

Chisholm, Roderick. 1981. *The First Person: An Essay on Reference and Intentionality*. Minneapolis: University of Minnesota Press.

Howell, Robert J. 2006. "Self-Knowledge and Self-Reference." *Philosophy and Phenomenological Research* 72 (1): 44–70.

Howell, Robert J. 2023. *Self-Awareness and the Elusive Subject*. Oxford: Oxford University Press.

Lewis, David K. 1979. "Attitudes *De Dicto* and *De Se*." *Philosophical Review* 88 (4): 513–43.

Millikan, Ruth. 1990. "The Myth of the Essential Indexical." *Noûs* 24: 723–34.

Perry, John. 1977. "Frege on Demonstratives." *Philosophical Review* 86: 474–97.

Stalnaker, Robert. 1981. "Indexical Belief." *Synthese* 49: 129–51.

OTHER REFERENCE

Nagel, Thomas. 1986. *The View from Nowhere*. Oxford: Oxford University Press.

THE QUEEN AND THE GAMETES

BACKGROUND

An object's *necessary* (or *essential*) properties are those without which it could not have existed. A traditional philosophical view, dating back at least to Aristotle, is that objects have both necessary properties and contingent (or inessential) properties. Consider a table t that consists of a square wooden top attached to four wooden legs. Suppose its top is painted blue. Intuitively, blueness is a contingent property of t. For example, t might have existed even if its top had been painted green instead of blue. That is something we can easily imagine. By contrast, having a certain shape might be a necessary property of t. Perhaps t's shape could have been slightly different. For example, the carpenter might have decided to make its top rectangular instead of square. But could t have existed if it were spherical or cylindrical? Or compressed into a tiny lump no bigger than a grain of sand? That seems doubtful. Intuitively, if the wood from which t was actually made instead constituted a wooden sphere or a large cylinder, those entities would not have been t. What about ourselves? Which properties of individual human beings are contingent, and which are necessary?

THE CASE

Consider Queen Elizabeth. Must she have been born of royal blood (Sprigge 1962, pp. 202–3)? Reflecting on this case, Saul Kripke (1972/1980) suggests that it seems doubtful that having royal blood was one of her necessary properties, for, if it were, then it would have to be necessary that at some point her family acquired royal power. And that her family acquired royal power is a contingent fact of history; her family might never have come to power. What about her biological origins? Are those necessary or contingent? Elizabeth originated from a certain set of gametes (sperm and egg) g, that came from her actual biological parents—the previous king and queen. Could she have existed if she had not originated from that particular pair of gametes? Could she have originated from a different set of gametes $g\star$, which came instead from Harry and Bess Truman?

Initially, that possibility might seem easy to imagine. For example, imagine reading a news headline: "Unsealed secret records reveal that Queen Elizabeth was born to the Trumans and then adopted by the English king and queen!" Such a revelation may be unlikely, but is it impossible? Surely not, it might seem.

But that reasoning is dubious. Granted, we do not know with certainty that the imaginary headline's claim isn't true. But that's irrelevant. When we asked "Could the Queen have existed without having originated from g?," we weren't asking a question about knowledge or certainty. Our question was rather this: Given that the Queen actually originated from g, is there a possible world—a way history could have gone but didn't—in which she existed but didn't originate from g? Here the issue of whether she did in fact originate from g is not up for grabs. Instead, we are assuming that she did and asking whether there is a different way the world could have gone such that she did not.

It should also be granted that we can imagine a woman who looks, acts, feels, etc. just as Queen Elizabeth does but who originated from $g\star$ rather than g. Such a thing is possible; such a woman might have existed. But, for present purposes, that too can be set aside. Our question was about a specific individual, Queen Elizabeth. With respect to that question, it is irrelevant that there could have been a *different* woman—one who didn't originate from g but had many of Elizabeth's other properties.

So, to imagine the Queen failing to originate from g is not as easy as one might have initially thought. But is that scenario possible? According to Kripke (1972/1980, p. 113), the answer is *no*: "It seems to me that anything coming from a different origin would not be this object."

DISCUSSION

Kripke's discussion of the Queen and her biological origins occurs in the context of his defense of the existence of *a posteriori* necessities: necessary truths (that is, truths that must be the case) that we cannot discover without empirical investigation. Prior to the early 1970s, when Kripke raised these issues, it had been widely thought that all necessary truths can be known *a priori*, by conceptual reflection alone. For example, one can know that all squares are rectangular just by reflecting on the concepts of squareness and rectangularity. What goes for "all squares are rectangular" was thought to hold for all necessary truths: they are *a priori* knowable. Kripke rejected that view. His most widely discussed examples of *a posteriori* necessities concern chemistry and physics—e.g., water is necessarily H_2O, lightning is necessarily electric discharge, and heat is necessarily mean molecular kinetic energy. Discovering those truths required empirical investigation. Nevertheless, according to Kripke, they are necessary. What is more, they are necessary in a non-relative sense. They are true in *all* possible worlds, rather than only in some subset of possible worlds such as worlds with the same natural laws as those that obtain in the actual world.

If Kripke is correct about the Queen and the gametes, then we have another *a posteriori* necessary truth: the truth that if the Queen exists, then she originated from g. But this case is unusual. In the cases of water and H_2O, lightning and electrical discharge, etc., the necessity primarily concerns *types* of phenomena. By contrast, the Queen case concerns a necessary connection between what are arguably distinct individual objects: the Queen and g. Kripke's conclusion, that the Queen must have originated from g, might therefore threaten a doctrine associated with David Hume (1738/1978) that some consider a fundamental metaphysical principle: there are no necessary connections between distinct existences (Wilson 2010). For example, suppose a cue ball's motion causes the eight-ball to move. Because those two events are distinct events, it's in principle possible for one to occur without the other. But the Queen and g are distinct existences no less than those two billiard-ball movements are. So, if the Humean principle is true, the Queen and g are not connected by necessity. Yet they are, if Kripke is right. Kripke's conclusion has further interesting consequences. For example, it seems to conflict with a familiar view on which one's essence is mental and one's connection to any physical body, let alone any set of gametes, is contingent (see Chapters 39, 41, and 42).

Kripke's conclusion is thus consequential. Do his reflections establish it? As he emphasizes, his conclusion is not refuted by the possibility of someone who did not originate from g having many of the Queen's properties. But establishing his conclusion requires more than the observation that it is hard to imagine the Queen herself not originating from g. Perhaps we are simply unimaginative. And, even if were impossible for us to imagine the Queen not originating from g, it would not immediately follow that such a thing could not have happened (Gendler and Hawthorne 2002).

Kripke connects his discussion of the Queen with another example, and others have followed him in doing so. He considers a wooden table t and asks whether it could have been made from a completely different block of wood b—or even from "water cleverly hardened into ice" (1972/1980, p. 113). His answer is *no*, and his reasoning parallels what he says about the Queen and the gametes. For example, he notes that, although we can imagine a table not made from b that has many of t's properties, that does not show that t itself could have failed to have been made from b. Taking this one step further, Kripke uses both the Queen example and the table example in support of a general principle that we might call *the essentiality of origins principle*: "If a material object has its origin from a certain hunk of matter, it could not have had its origin in any other matter" (1972/1980, p. 114, fn. 56). As Kripke remarks, the general principle just stated probably requires qualification—e.g., concerning the vagueness of the notion of a "hunk of matter." Also, whether the Queen (or any person) is a material object is controversial (see Chapters 1, 39, 41, and 42). But the Queen, the table, and the latter principle are usually discussed in tandem.

Several different arguments for the essentiality of origins principle have been developed. Colin McGinn (1976), Nathan Salmon (1981), Graham Forbes (1985), and others develop arguments based on *sufficiency* principles—principles detailing conditions for being a particular object (t or the Queen, say) in any possible world. J. L. Mackie (1974) and Penelope Mackie (1998) instead appeal to a *branching-times model of necessity*. On that model, they argue, the only possibilities concerning t itself, rather than a distinct (even if similar) table, emerge only *after* t is produced from b. And Guy Rohrbaugh and Louis deRosset (2004) show how one could derive the essentiality of origins principle from a principle concerning the sorts of factors that could prevent the production of a particular material object from a particular hunk of raw material. Such factors, they argue, must be *local*. In the case of table t and block b, such factors would have to affect b or other elements of the process by which t actually emerged (e.g., the tools, the artisan, etc.). The scenario in which t does not originate from b would, Rohrbaugh and deRosset argue, violate the latter principle. Likewise, they suggest, for a scenario in which the Queen does not originate from g. None of those arguments have gone unchallenged. Thus, whether the Queen could have existed without having originated from g—and, likewise, whether our own biological origins are essential to us as persons—remains unresolved.

RECOMMENDED READING

CANONICAL PRESENTATION

Kripke, Saul. 1972. "Naming and Necessity." In D. Davidson and G. Harman (eds.) *Semantics of Natural Language*. Dordrecht: Reidel: 253–355. Reprinted as *Naming and Necessity*. Cambridge, MA: Harvard University Press, 1980. (Citations in this chapter are from the latter edition.)

OVERVIEW

Roca-Royes, Sonia. 2011. "Essential Properties and Individual Essences." *Philosophy Compass* 6 (1): 65–77.

ADDITIONAL DISCUSSIONS

Cameron, Ross. 2005. "A Note on Kripke's Footnote 56 Argument for the Essentiality of Origin." *Ratio* 18: 262–75.
Forbes, Graham. 1985. *The Metaphysics of Modality*. Oxford: Clarendon.
Gendler, Tamar Szabó, and Hawthorne, John (eds.). 2002. *Conceivability and Possibility*. New York: Oxford University Press.

Hawthorne, John, and Szabó Gendler, Tamar. 2000. "Origin Essentialism: The Arguments Reconsidered." *Mind* 109: 285–98.

Hume, David. 1738/1978. *A Treatise of Human Nature*. Oxford: Oxford University Press.

Mackie, J. L. 1974. "*De* What *Re* is *De Re* Modality?" *Journal of Philosophy* 71: 551–61.

Mackie, Penelope. 1998. "Identity, Time and Necessity." *Proceedings of the Aristotelian Society* 98: 59–78.

McGinn, Colin. 1976. "On the Necessity of Origins." *Journal of Philosophy* 73: 127–35.

Quine, Willard V. O. 1960. *Word and Object*. Cambridge, MA: MIT Press.

Robertson, Teresa. 1998. "Possibilities and the Arguments for Origin Essentialism." *Mind* 107: 729–49.

Robertson, Teresa, and Forbes, Graham. 2006. "Does the New Route Reach its Destination?" *Mind* 115: 367–74.

Rohrbaugh, Guy, and deRosset, Louis. 2004. "A New Route to the Necessity of Origin." *Mind* 113: 705–25.

Salmon, Nathan, 1981. *Reference and Essence*. Princeton: Princeton University Press.

Sprigge, Timothy. 1962. "Internal and External Properties." *Mind* 71: 197–212.

Wilson, Jessica. 2010. "What is Hume's Dictum, and Why Believe It?" *Philosophy and Phenomenological Research* 80 (3): 595–637.

THE TREKKIE, MR. OREO, AND NARRATIVE CONCEPTIONS OF THE SELF

BACKGROUND

The philosophical problem of personal identity is best seen as a cluster of problems. One problem concerns identification: What makes a given being a person? A second problem concerns reidentification: What makes a given being at one time the same person as a being at a later time? A third problem concerns characterization: What makes a given person the person that they are—that is, which are the characteristics that go towards making that person the person they are (see Schechtman 1996)? Thought experiments like the Prince and the Cobbler (Chapter 39) and other body-swap cases (Chapter 41) concern the reidentification question. In this chapter, we turn from issues concerning reidentification to issues concerning characterization. Facts about reidentification don't seem to capture all that's salient about our identity. For example, when it comes to our racial identity or gender identity, or the way that our selves are shaped by traumatic events and transformative experiences (see Chapter 50), the notion of personal identity in question does not seem to be one that's primarily concerned with identity over time.

In addressing the characterization question, many philosophers have suggested that the constitution of self-identities involves the construction of a narrative. Usually narratives are dynamic rather than static: they depict events that take place over time. They are also selective: they need not incorporate everything that has ever happened. In this way, certain personal characteristics can be highlighted as especially salient. Narratives also help situate the particular incidents and events of one's life in a larger context. But how do such narratives get developed? Are they constructed by the individual themself or by others? And what constraints are there on which characteristics, incidents, and events get incorporated into a narrative? To answer these questions, philosophers have often reflected on a variety of cases, both hypothetical and real, several of which we consider here.

THE CASES

We'll start with a case drawn from real life. Barbara Adams is a die-hard *Star Trek* fan. She is committed to living her life according to the ideals espoused by the show. She is very active in a local *Star Trek* fan club, where she has attained the rank of Commander. She asks others, even outside the fan club, to use this title when addressing her. Employed by a local printing company, Barbara heads to work each day wearing a Starfleet uniform and carrying a plastic phaser and tricorder. As she notes in a letter posted to the website Trekdoc.com:

> I've been a Star Trek fan as long as I can remember. ... The positive future, our planet working with a league of other planets, and the intelligence and ideals that Gene Roddenberry and crew cleverly weaved into the plots ... made it something that I could embrace for our future.

The Adams case suggests that narratives are something that individuals construct for themselves. Barbara has deliberately and self-consciously developed a self-narrative organized around her love of *Star Trek*. She is not deluded. She recognizes that she is not actually a member of Starfleet, and that *Star Trek* is a fictional television show. Nonetheless, her fandom not only deeply affects how she lives her life but also her sense of who she is.

What about individuals who *are* deluded, that is, who have constructed self-narratives that seem disconnected from the actual facts of their life? Let's take a hypothetical case: Avery is a Wall Street banker who for years has been working 80-hour weeks in determined pursuit of career advancement and personal wealth. She acts competitively and even ruthlessly towards her colleagues. But when she thinks about herself and her life, these facts do not play a big role. Avery is not deliberately trying to misrepresent herself. Rather, she simply engages in a selective attention in the weaving of her story. She focuses on the birthday presents she's bought rather than the birthday parties she failed to attend; she remembers clapping loudly at her son's performance in the school play but manages to ignore the fact that she'd arrived late to the show; her recollection of the family vacation in Hawaii excludes the fact that she spent most of the trip either on the phone or on her laptop. Overall, she thinks of herself as fundamentally a compassionate woman who has been an attentive mother to her kids. Avery's self-narrative is thus out of step with the truth about who she really is. So, what should we say about the constitution of her identity?

Finally, consider a thought experiment developed by Charles Mills (1998) involving a man he calls *Mr. Oreo*. (While Mills himself uses the case to probe questions about the metaphysics of race, it also works nicely to probe questions about narrative identity.) Mr. Oreo is dark-skinned, has distinctively African features, and has known African ancestry. But he is unhappy being considered black. Thus, when he is asked to provide demographic information about himself, he checks the box for "white" rather than for "black"; he thinks of himself as white, and he shies away from customs, music, and food that are typically associated with black culture. Even so, he has trouble getting other people to accept his own self-characterization. To address this, Mr. Oreo invents a machine that can completely transform his skin, hair, and facial features so that he will present as white. Because his invention was inspired by a similar device described in the book *Black No More* by George Schuyler, he calls it *the Schuyler machine*. After undergoing his cosmetic transformation, his physical appearance is more in line with his sense of himself, and he begins to be treated by others as white. What should we say about the constitution of his identity?

DISCUSSION

Many of the philosophers who offer narrative views in response to the characterization question have taken the relevant narratives to be first-personal in nature (Schechtman 1996, Lindemann 2001, DeGrazia 2005). Call this *the self-narrative view*. The decision to focus on first-person narratives rather than third-person narratives can be motivated by the sense that individuals are typically authoritative about their own identities. On the self-narrative view, individuals engage in an active process of construction and unification when constituting their narrative. Though the narrative may fall short of perfect consistency, the very process of bringing disparate events together serves to impose a degree of coherence and intelligibility on them. In constituting one's self in line with a first-person narrative, an individual comes to understand and interpret their life's experiences against the background of an overall story that serves to imbue those experiences with overall significance. The process of developing such stories varies from individual to individual along many different dimensions—e.g., how explicit they are, how detailed they are, how aspirational they are, and so on. Moreover, narratives will differ in terms of which properties and factors play an organizing role. In some cases it might be gender and race. In some cases it might be political affiliation or career. And in some cases—as with Barbara Adams—it may have to do with hobbies.

Self-narrative theories differ in terms of how they treat outside influences on a person's self-narrative—that is, how much other people's narratives about an individual can impact or override that individual's self-narrative. While some argue strongly that other people's stories cannot override an individual's own story about herself (DeGrazia 2005, p. 87), others allow for more impact and influence (Lindemann 2001, Plantikow 2008). How self-narrative theorists come down on this issue will also affect their assessment of cases like Avery. To deal with cases like this, where an individual seems to be in some sense deluded, some self-narrative theorists incorporate constraints on an individual's narrative about themself. For example, one might impose a *reality constraint* according to which narratives must cohere with reality in fundamental ways, even if it contains minor inaccuracies along the way (Schechtman 1996, p. 119). Unfortunately, it's left fairly vague how to determine what counts as *fundamental coherence with reality*. For example, it is not clear how exactly to assess the case of Mr. Oreo in light of the reality constraint.

Many philosophers working on issues relating to gender and racial identity explicitly adopt a narrative framework. In a discussion of transitions from one sex or gender to another, Christine Overall argues that we develop our gender identities "by, in effect, creating the continuing narrative of our lives" (2009, p. 21). Françoise Baylis makes the connection to narrativity explicit in talking about her own racial identity: "My life is a collection of stories (mine and those of significant others) that tells me where I am from, where I have been and where I am going" (2003, p. 145). Interestingly, Baylis herself can be seen as a reverse case from that of Mr. Oreo. Though Baylis has very light skin, and is generally taken to be white, she considers herself black. As she notes, from a very young age, she deliberately incorporated her racial identity into her own self-narrative, something that wasn't always easy: "Building a Black identity is hard work when you have white skin" (2003, p. 144). A narrative framework also works well in discussion of online identities. One's narrative about oneself might blend facts from one's real life in the (physical) world and one's virtual life through an avatar in an online world (Schechtman 2012).

Despite the merits of the narrative view, it has faced criticism along various dimensions. One significant challenge comes from the existence of people who don't view their lives in narrative terms. Calling himself an "episodic" person, Galen Strawson denies that his own life exhibits narrativity—rather, it is just a series of relatively disconnected episodes. As he describes it:

> I have a past, like any human being, and I know perfectly well that I have a past. I have a respectable amount of factual knowledge about it, and I also remember some of my past experiences "from the inside," as philosophers say. And yet I have absolutely no sense of my life as a narrative with form, or indeed as a narrative without form. Absolutely none.
>
> (Strawson 2004, p. 433)

Other critics of the narrative view claim that it's fairly rare that individuals engage in the kind of sustained self-reflection that would count as organizing one's life in a narrative way. According to those critics, though we might have moments where we take an introspective turn, we rarely take the time to pause and take up the project of giving our lives some kind of overall form and coherence (Vice 2003). Such claims challenge versions of the narrative view that are intended to apply to all or most persons. But whether all narrative views have that ambition is not entirely clear. Nor is it entirely clear that the truth of the narrative view requires it to be the case that all or most people consciously and deliberately construct their own narratives. But what the narrative view looks like in light of those responses is also less than entirely clear.

RECOMMENDED READING

CANONICAL PRESENTATIONS

Mills, Charles. 1998. "But What Are You Really? The Metaphysics of Race." In *Blackness Visible: Essays on Philosophy and Race*. Ithaca, NY: Cornell University Press: 41–66.

Schechtman, Marya. 1996. *The Constitution of Selves*. Ithaca, NY: Cornell University Press.

OVERVIEW

Kind, Amy. 2015. *Persons and Personal Identity*. Cambridge: Polity Press. (See especially Chapters 5 and 6.)

ADDITIONAL DISCUSSIONS

Baylis, Françoise. 2003. "Black As Me: Narrative Identity." *Developing World Bioethics* 3 (2): 142–50.

Christman, John P. 2004. "Narrative Unity As a Condition of Personhood." *Metaphilosophy* 35: 695–713.

DeGrazia, David. 2005. *Human Identity and Bioethics*. Cambridge: Cambridge University Press.

Lindemann, Hilde. 2001. *Damaged Identities, Narrative Repair*. Ithaca, NY: Cornell University Press. (Originally published under the name "Hilde Lindemann Nelson.")

Overall, Christine. 2009. "Sex/Gender Transitions and Life-Changing Aspirations." In Laurie J. Shrage (ed.) *"You've Changed": Sex Reassignment and Personal Identity*. Oxford: Oxford University Press: 11–27.

Plantikow, Thane. 2008. "Surviving Personal Identity Theory: Recovering Interpretability." *Hypatia* 23: 90–109.

Schechtman, Marya. 2012. "The Story of My (Second) Life: Virtual Worlds and Narrative Identity." *Philosophy & Technology* 25: 329–43.

Strawson, Galen. 2004. "Against Narrativity." *Ratio* 17: 428–52.

Vice, Samantha. 2003. "Literature and the Narrative Self." *Philosophy* 78: 93–108.

THE PUZZLE OF TRANSFORMATIVE CHOICE

BACKGROUND

When we make decisions about our futures, whether routine decisions about what to have for dinner or more monumental decisions about what career path to pursue, our decisions are guided by our beliefs and desires. Normative decision theory proposes a framework for judging the rationality of an agent's decisions in light of these beliefs and desires—that is, in telling us what choice an agent should make given the beliefs and desires that they have. Since there are various elements of uncertainty in most cases of decision-making—e.g., we might not be sure whether the vegetables in the fridge are still fresh or whether there will still be a demand for accountants in 10 years' time—decision theory aims to provide an adequate model for how to deal with this uncertainty. Although different theories spell out the details in varying ways, generally speaking the model will involve the notion of *expected value*. An agent choosing between Option A and Option B makes a calculation about what value A is expected to have, a calculation about what value B is expected to have, and compares the two. The rational decision will favor the option with the higher expected value. Calculating expected value will often be difficult. But, as the cases of transformative experience we'll consider in this chapter bring into focus, sometimes it seems not just difficult but impossible. So, the possibility of making a rational decision is threatened. Moreover, knowing expected values seems important not just for our decisions to be rational but for them to be authentic—that is, for ensuring that we are able to stay true to ourselves. Thus, as we'll see, the puzzle of transformative choice raises a threat not just about rationality but about our ability to shape ourselves into the kinds of future selves that we want to be.

THE CASE

Consider Blythe, a woman who is about to travel to Malaysia for the first time. When talking with her friends about what she should do while she is there, one of them suggests trying durian, a local fruit. This suggestion proves extremely divisive. While they all agree that it smells awful, about half of them say that the taste is sublime and shouldn't be missed, while the other half say that it's absolutely terrible. When Blythe does some research, she finds that it's not just her friends who are split on the matter. She comes across an essay from Alfred Russel Wallace that describes the durian as having an exquisite flavor unparalleled by other fruit; according to Wallace, eating it offers "a new sensation worth a voyage to the East to experience." But, on the other hand, Blythe also reads a post from a travel blogger who describes the smell as a blend of onion and sweaty socks, and goes on to say that "the durian tasted how it smelled, only worse. I was done." When Blythe finally encounters durian at a local market, she's not sure whether to try it or not. Though she has read lots of descriptions of its flavor, she still doesn't know what tasting durian is like, and so she doesn't know what she'd be getting into. So, what should she do? How should she decide?

The durian case is fairly low stakes. But now consider a much higher-stakes case. When she returns from Malaysia, Blythe finds herself thinking a lot about parenthood. Though she is currently childless, her biological clock is ticking, and she realizes she needs to decide whether or not to have a biological child. She's done some babysitting before, but she's been told that watching someone else's child for a short period of time is really nothing like being a parent. She has read various parenting guides and books about the experience, but those seem to fall short of teaching her what it would be like to be a parent. She has also talked about parenthood with friends and siblings who have kids, but this also falls short, in part because the different reports conflict in various ways with one another. Although most of those people are wildly enthusiastic about the experience, they also have various complaints, and a few seem to have some regrets about their decision to have kids. In all cases, however, it's clear that the individuals' lives have been dramatically changed as a result of becoming parents. They also find themselves having radically different preferences from the ones they had before. For example, some who were die-hard night owls have now happily become early risers. Most all of them have given up old hobbies and taken up new ones. As Blythe tries to make her decision, she finds that she really doesn't know what she'd be getting into—just like in the durian case, although now with a lot more on the line. So, what should she do? How should she decide?

Whether to become a parent is just one of many big life decisions that present this problem. Edna Ullmann-Margalit (2006, p. 160) suggests many other examples, such as decisions about whether to get married, whether to migrate to a new country, what career path to choose, or whether to quit one's job to explore a longtime passion. She refers to these kinds of cases as *big decisions*, and they involve what L. A. Paul (2014) calls *transformative experiences*. For Paul, transformative experiences have both an epistemic dimension and a personal dimension. When an experience is *epistemically transformative*, the experiencer learns something that is in principle epistemically inaccessible to them absent that experience. When an experience is *personally transformative*, the experiencer undergoes changes to their individual point of view and personal preferences that are not fully predictable in advance. As described by Ullmann-Margalit, in these kinds of cases one emerges after the decision as a different person.

All of this seems to make the calculation of expected value impossible. Someone facing one of these decisions doesn't know what the experience is like, and it looks like they can't trust their imaginings of what the experience is like. So, they can't do the sort of cognitive modeling that one might normally do in a decision-making context, the kind of modeling where one imaginatively projects oneself into each situation and compares the two. Hence, we have the puzzle of transformative choice: In cases involving transformative experience, it appears to be impossible for us to make decisions that are both rational and authentic.

DISCUSSION

In addressing the puzzle of transformative choice, some philosophers offer what we might think of as skeptical solutions. People who adopt this strategy accept that in cases of transformative choice we can't make rational and authentic decisions in the usual way. There is no direct solution to the puzzle. But they think there are other ways that we might handle decision-making in these cases, and thus that we can give indirect solutions. For example, Paul herself suggests that cases of transformative experience present us with situations in which we have to make "a leap into the unknown" (2020, p. 26). Insofar as we are people who like to make that sort of leap, we can rationally and authentically opt for the new experiences. Return to the low-stakes durian case. Here one might decide to try the durian not because of what this new experience will be like, but simply for the sake of having a new experience. Adapting this solution to a high-stakes case like parenthood, Paul suggests that when we choose whether to become a parent, we should do so partly on the grounds of whether or not we want to discover new experiences and preferences. Since we can't know what the experience will be like, our choice should be based partly on the value we place on discovery and revelation.

A different skeptical solution is offered by Marcus Arvan, who suggests that we should approach transformative experience not in terms of revelation but in terms of resilience. People who don't over-plan but instead accept life as it comes, people who are psychologically resilient, are better positioned to handle transformative experiences. From this, Arvan concludes that the most rational way to approach transformative experience would be to shape our lives such that we develop such attitudes and become resilient people. In fact, he sees resilience as "an adaptive tool *specifically* for dealing with transformative experience" (2015, p. 1200).

But many other philosophers adopt a non-skeptical strategy for dealing with the puzzle. Rather than accepting that the best we can hope for is an indirect solution, they instead try to dissolve the puzzle.

Often this involves what we might think of as a partial dissolution. Such philosophers grant that there might be cases of transformative experience in which we can't make such choices rationally and authentically, but they argue that there are many kinds of cases in which we can. For example, Rachel McKinnon (2015) argues that someone who has come to know that they are trans and is deciding whether to undergo a gender transition might not be able to know exactly what such a transition would be like; but they might be able to know based on the information they presently have that it can't be worse than what life would be like if they didn't transition. Even if they can't assign a precise expected value to the option of transitioning, given how low the expected value of not transitioning is, they don't need to be able to do an exact calculation. Moreover, even if they can't predict exactly the ways in which the transition will allow for authenticity, they can also be certain that a future in which they don't transition is worse since, in that future, there is no possibility of authenticity. In such cases, then, the choice to transition can be made both rationally and authentically.

Focusing on the parenthood case, Elizabeth Barnes (2015b) offers a related line of argument. Pointing to people (herself included) who have never had any desire to have children, she argues that their choice not to become parents can be rational even if they can't know what having children is like. As Barnes notes, Paul herself admits that one can rationally choose not to be attacked by a shark even if one doesn't know exactly what it's like to be attacked by a shark. In Barnes' view, the decision of whether to become a parent has more in common with the shark-attack case than Paul thinks. Granted, there are differences. Even people who in advance didn't want to be attacked by a shark don't report afterwards that they are so glad they did so anyhow, whereas many people who in advance didn't want to have children do report afterwards that they are glad they did so anyhow. But that gladness results, in part, from various fairly dramatic changes in character. Sometimes, one can be rational in knowing that one wouldn't want one's character to change in such dramatic ways—ways that would be alien to one's current sense of self. Valuing the way that one is at present, and engaging in character planning in line with that, can be rational. So, in some cases at least, one can rationally decide not to have children even without knowing what the experience is like.

Finally, some have suggested that the puzzle arises in large part due to a mistaken or overly pessimistic picture of imagination and its role in decision-making (see, e.g., Campbell 2015). Arguing that imagination is a skill, Amy Kind (2020) notes that some people are much better at imagining than others, just like some people are much better than others at juggling, ballroom dancing, or solving crossword puzzles. Perhaps many, even most, people are unable to imagine what it's like to be a parent prior to having the experience. But that does not mean that no one can. People with skilled imaginations are better able to leverage the experiences that they have already had to extrapolate to new experiences. Moreover, even people who are not skilled imaginers can work to become better at imagining, just as people can work to become better jugglers, ballroom dancers, or crossword-puzzle solvers.

RECOMMENDED READING

CANONICAL PRESENTATIONS

Paul, L.A. 2014. *Transformative Experience*. New York: Oxford University Press.
Paul, L. A. 2015a. "What You Can't Expect When You're Expecting." *Res Philosophica* 92 (2): 149–70.
Ullmann-Margalit, Edna. 2006. "Big Decisions: Opting, Converting, Drifting." *Royal Institute of Philosophy Supplement* 58: 157–72.

OVERVIEWS

Paul, L.A. 2015. "Précis of *Transformative Experience*." *Philosophy and Phenomenological Research* 91 (3): 760–65.
Schwenkler, John, and Lambert, Enoch. 2020. "Editor's Introduction." In John Schwenkler and Enoch Lambert (eds.) *Becoming Someone New: Essays on Transformative Experience, Choice, and Change*. Oxford: Oxford University Press: 1–15.

ADDITIONAL DISCUSSIONS

Arvan, Marcus. 2015. "How to Rationally Approach Life's Transformative Experiences." *Philosophical Psychology* 28 (8): 1199–218.
Barnes, Elizabeth. 2015a. "Social Identities and Transformative Experience." *Res Philosophica* 92 (2): 171–87.
Barnes, Elizabeth. 2015b. "What You Can Expect When You Don't Want to be Expecting." *Philosophy and Phenomenological Research* 91 (3): 775–86.

Campbell, John. 2015. "L.A. Paul's *Transformative Experience*." *Philosophy and Phenomenological Research* 91 (3): 787–93.

Chang, Ruth. 2015. "Transformative Choices." *Res Philosophica* 92 (2): 237–82.

Kauppinen, Antti. 2015. "What's So Great about Experience?" *Res Philosophica* 92 (2): 371–88.

Kind, Amy. 2020. "What Imagination Teaches." In John Schwenkler and Enoch Lambert (eds.) *Becoming Someone New: Essays on Transformative Experience, Choice, and Change*. Oxford: Oxford University Press: 133–46.

McKinnon, Rachel. 2015. "Trans*formative Experiences." *Res Philosophica* 92 (2): 419–40.

Paul, L. A. 2015b. "Transformative Choices: Discussion and Replies." *Res Philosophica* 92 (2): 473–545.

Paul, L.A. 2020. "Who Will I Become?" In John Schwenkler and Enoch Lambert (eds.) *Becoming Someone New: Essays on Transformative Experience, Choice, and Change*. Oxford: Oxford University Press: 16–36.

GLOSSARY

A posteriori knowledge Knowledge that depends, for its justification, on sense experience. For example, one can know that water is H_2O only a posteriori. *See also* a priori knowledge.

A priori knowledge Knowledge that does not depend, for its justification, on sense experience. For example, one might know a priori that $5 + 7 = 12$. *See also* a posteriori knowledge.

Animalism The theory of personal identity that says that a person is fundamentally a physical organism (a human animal), and thus that a person's continued survival through time consists in facts about the survival of the human animal.

Anti-individualism *see* externalism.

Behaviorism Behaviorism is the theory that explains the mental in terms of behavior or behavioral dispositions. For example, the mental state of belief is explained in terms of behavior such as assenting to a proposition; the belief that snow is white might be explained in terms of such dispositions as being disposed to say "Yes" when asked "Is snow white?" Methodological behaviorism is a theory about how to study the mind scientifically: one should study the mind by studying behavior. Philosophical behaviorism is a theory about the nature of mental phenomena: mental phenomena are behavioral phenomena.

Blind spot Area where a person's view is obstructed. Normally sighted humans have an anatomical blind spot corresponding to the place where the optic nerve is attached to the retina.

Constitution A thing's constitution is what makes it up. For example, a diamond is constituted by a lattice of carbon atoms; a statue is constituted by the clay from which it is made, perhaps together with certain other features, such as the clay's shape.

Content What is represented as being the case. For example, the content of the belief that Biden is the president of the United States in 2023 is the proposition that Biden is the president of the United States in 2023. One can hold different attitudes toward that same proposition. For example, one could not only believe that Biden is the president of the United States in 2023 but also desire that Biden is the president of the United States in 2023. *See also* proposition, propositional attitude.

Contingent A proposition is contingent if it need not have been the case. For example, the claim that all frogs are happy is contingent. Even if all frogs happen to be happy, this is not a necessary truth; it might have been the case that not all frogs are happy. By contrast, the claim that all frogs are frogs is necessary—that is, not contingent.

Disposition A tendency to do something or to behave in a certain way. For example, salt has the disposition to dissolve in water.

Dualism The theory that the mental and the physical are fundamentally distinct. *See also* property dualism, substance dualism.

Epiphenomenalism The theory that mental states or properties are by-products (effects) of physical phenomena but do not themselves have any effects on the physical world.

Epistemic Epistemological—that is, concerning knowledge and related phenomena, such as belief and evidence.

Epistemology The part of philosophy that concerns knowledge and related phenomena, such as belief and evidence. Examples of epistemological (or, equivalently, epistemic) questions include: How can we know anything? What is the nature of knowledge? Is knowledge the same as justified, true belief?

Essence That which makes something what it is, and that it cannot exist without. For example, on some views the essence of water is its chemical composition, H_2O. On this view, the fact that water is composed of H_2O molecules is what makes water what it is. Also, on this view, water cannot exist without being so composed.

Extended substance An entity that exists in three-dimensional space. Descartes defines "body" in terms of being extended.

Externalism The theory that the content of some mental states depends constitutively on features of a subject's environment. For example, according to this theory, a molecule-for-molecule duplicate of you might have different belief contents if, in their environment, there were no water but instead a substance that looks, feels, and tastes like H_2O but has a different chemical composition.

Extrinsic feature Relational property. For example, that a baseball is larger than a table tennis ball is an extrinsic feature of the baseball. By contrast, a baseball's spherical shape is an intrinsic feature of the baseball. *See also* intrinsic feature.

Folk psychology The implicit theory behind the way people ordinarily (in everyday life) think of psychological states and psychological categories. For example, according to folk psychology, *belief* and *desire* are distinct mental states, and beliefs and desires often cause people to act in certain ways—as when my desire to beat an opponent at Scrabble and my belief that playing defensively will help me win causes me to play defensively. Folk psychology is a "theory" in the sense that it might turn out to be false; but it is not an explicit theory in the science of psychology.

Functionalism The theory that mental states are functional states. Functional states are states consisting of (i) environmental stimuli, (ii) behavioral responses, and (iii) relations among mental states. For example, according to functionalism, human pain is that mental state that (very roughly) is typically (i) caused by damage to the body, (ii) causes wincing and saying things such as "ouch," and (iii) combines with other mental states (such as the desire to avoid the state and the belief that aspirin will help one do that) to cause one to take aspirin. Human pain, on this theory, is whatever state plays that role in humans, e.g., a certain brain state. However, functionalism is not a theory about what realizes or implements mental states in humans. Just as a functional description of a hammer (e.g., as a tool for banging in nails) does not tell you what actual hammers are made of, functionalism does not tell you whether in humans the mind is realized by a brain or an immaterial soul. Nevertheless, functionalists are often physicalists, who say that all mental phenomena are realized by physical phenomena.

Idealism The theory that all concrete phenomena are fundamentally mental. For example, on Berkeley's idealism, rocks are composed of ideas, such as the idea of solidity, the idea of having a certain shape, etc.

Immaterial Not made of matter. The claim that immaterial things exist is incompatible with physicalism. For example, according to Cartesian dualism, the mind is immaterial: it can exist without the body. *See also* substance dualism, extended substance.

Individualism *see* internalism.

Infallible Incapable of being incorrect. For example, according to Descartes, his knowledge of his own existence is infallible.

Intentional content *see* content. *See also* intentionality.

Intentionalism *see* representationalism.

Intentionality The property in virtue of which things are about or represent other things. For example, beliefs are considered intentional states because they have representational content: they represent the world as being a certain way. In other words, they have *accuracy conditions*—that is, they are more or less accurate depending on how the world is. Your belief that snow is white is accurate to the extent that snow is, in fact, white.

Internalism The theory that the content of any mental state depends constitutively only on internal features of a subject rather than on features of their environment. *See also* externalism.

Intrinsic feature A feature of a thing itself, rather than a feature it has in virtue of its relation to other things. For example, a baseball's spherical shape is an intrinsic feature of the baseball. By contrast, that the baseball is larger than a table tennis ball is an extrinsic (or relational) feature.

Introspection The distinctive and direct process by which one can acquire knowledge of one's own mental life. For example, right now I know by introspection that I'm thinking about an old friend. Though I might come to know that you are also thinking about an old friend (perhaps because you tell me that you are), I cannot have introspective access to your mental life.

Irreducible Not reducible.

Materialism *see* physicalism.

Memory theory of personal identity The theory that a person's identity through time consists in connections of memory. This theory is typically attributed to John Locke.

Mental state State of the mind. Some examples: beliefs, desire, visual experiences, and pains.

Metaphysical necessity A proposition is metaphysically necessary if it is necessary without qualification. For example, on some views it is metaphysically necessary that everything is identical to itself. By contrast, perhaps it is a *physical necessity* that there is no stable cubic mile of uranium-235; the laws of physics entail that such a thing would be unstable. But arguably the physical laws could have been different from what they are. If they were different, perhaps there could be such a mass of uranium-235. *See also* necessity.

Metaphysics The part of philosophy that concerns existence and identity. Examples of metaphysical questions include: Do souls exist? Is the mind identical to the brain? Is a statue identical to the clay of which it is composed? What, if anything, makes you the same person from one time to the next?

Natural kind A kind of thing found in nature. For example, *water* is widely considered a natural kind. So is the species *tiger*. Contrast *water* and *tiger* with the kind *being a zoo animal*. *Being a zoo animal* is a kind of thing, but it's not unified and natural in the way that *water* and *tiger* are. Natural kinds also contrast with artifactual kinds, such as *table*. Unlike water and tigers, tables are artifacts—human creations.

Naturalism This term is sometimes used for the theory that everything that exists is part of nature—that is, that nothing is supernatural. Proponents of this theory typically reject views about the mind such as Descartes', on which the mind is an immaterial soul that exists in a non-physical realm. "Naturalism" is also sometimes used for a methodological theory: the theory that the best way to understand the natural world is through natural science. According to a naturalistic perspective on the mind, the best way to understand the mind's nature is through the empirical methods, such as those employed by cognitive psychology.

Necessity A proposition is necessary if it must be the case. For example, the claim that all frogs are frogs is necessary. By contrast, the claim that all frogs are happy is not necessary—that is, contingent. Even if all frogs happen to be happy, this is not a necessary truth; it might have been the case that not all frogs are happy.

Numerical identity Being the same individual thing. Numerical identity contrasts with similarity, even exact similarity. Two identical twins are numerically distinct, no matter how similar they might be.

Panpsychism The theory that mentality is everywhere. On some versions of this theory, at least some of the fundamental features of the concrete world (e.g., quarks) are or have phenomenal properties.

Phenomenal concept A concept of conscious experience in the "what it's like" sense. For example, those who have seen colors usually have a concept of what it's like to have that sort of experience, and those who have not usually lack (or at least do not well understand) that concept. *See also* phenomenal consciousness, phenomenal property/qualia.

Phenomenal consciousness Consciousness in the "what it's like" sense. For example, there is something it's like to feel pain or see red. For a person to be phenomenally conscious is for there to something it is like to be that person. For a mental state to be phenomenally conscious is for there to be something it is like to have that mental state.

Phenomenal property/qualia Property of conscious experience in the "what it's like" sense. For example, the distinctive way it feels to experience pain. *See also* phenomenal consciousness.

Physical necessity A proposition is physically necessary if it is necessary relative to physical phenomena such as physical laws. For example, arguably it is *physically necessary* that there is no stable cubic mile of uranium-235; the laws of physics entail that such a thing would be unstable. *See also* necessity, metaphysical necessity.

Physical theory of personal identity The theory of personal identity that holds that a person's identity over time consists in various physical facts, such as facts about the brain and/or body.

Physicalism/materialism The theory that all concrete phenomena, including mental phenomena, are fundamentally physical.

Possibility A proposition is possible if it might be, or might have been, the case. For example, you might have not ever read a philosophy book; and you might one day write a philosophy book. Both propositions are possible. *See also* necessity.

Possible world A way the world could have been. For example, although Chen Meng won the 2021 gold medal for women's singles in table tennis, there is a possible world in which Chen Meng lost and Mima Ito won.

Property dualism The theory that mental properties and physical properties are fundamentally distinct. For example, consider the mental property of feeling pain. In humans, pain is at least caused by brain processes. According to property dualism, however, the property of feeling pain is distinct from any neural property. This view does *not* say that the mind—the thing that *has* mental properties—is distinct from the brain. But it does say that mental *properties*—features of the mind—are distinct from physical (and in particular neural) properties. *See also* dualism, substance dualism.

Proposition Something that is either true or false, and that is expressible by a "that"-clause, such as "that snow is white."

Propositional attitude An attitude toward a proposition, such as belief, hope, or desire. For example, one can believe that snow is white, hope that snow is white, or desire that snow is white. *See also* proposition.

Psychological theory of personal identity The theory of personal identity that holds that a person's identity over time consists in the continuity and connectedness of various psychological states, such as memory and intention, as well as various psychological character traits. *See also* memory theory of personal identity.

Qualia *see* phenomenal property. *See also* phenomenal consciousness.

Realization How a feature is implemented or constituted. For example, consider the feature *being a hammer*. That feature can be realized by an object made of metal and wood. It can also be realized by an object made of plastic. Likewise, on some philosophical theories, the feature *pain* can be experienced by creatures with biological brains such as ours *and* by creatures with non-biological "brains," such as robots.

Reducible Minimally, the relationship that holds between two features A and B when A is nothing more than B. Usually the term "reducible" implies something stronger than the "nothing more than" relation. For example, the claim that mental properties are reducible to physical properties often means that every mental property is identical to a physical property, such as a specific sort of neutral property. *See also* constitution.

Representation *see* content.

Representationalism The theory that phenomenal properties are just representational properties—that is, properties of representing that something is the case. For example, according to this theory, the property of being phenomenally red is just the property of representing something, in a certain way, as being red. *See also* content.

Self-awareness Awareness of oneself. Many philosophers have held that each of us is aware of oneself, and/or one's own mental states, in a distinctive way. For example, according to this theory, I am aware of my own existence, and of the contents of my mind, in a far more direct way, and with far more justification, than you are aware of those things.

Structural truths Truths that concern how things relate to one another, as opposed to how things are in themselves. According to some philosophers, the truths in theoretical physics are structural. That is because those truths concern abstract relations among entities that are themselves described in terms of how they interact with each other. Basic particles, for example, are described in terms of their propensity to interact with other particles. Mass is described in terms of a propensity to be accelerated by certain forces.

Substance dualism The theory that the mind and the body are fundamentally distinct substances, where substances are things rather than properties of things. The best-known version of substance dualism is the version developed by Descartes, known as Cartesian dualism. According to Descartes, a *substance* is something that exists independently of other things. So, according to Cartesian dualism, the mind and the body are things that can exist independently of each other. *See also* dualism, property dualism.

Supervenience Supervenience is a relation of dependency. If A supervenes on B, then A cannot vary without B varying. For example, suppose a statue supervenes on the clay out of which it is composed. In that case, there can be no change in the statue without a change in the clay. Physicalism is usually thought to entail that the mental supervenes on the physical: there cannot be any variation in a mental state without variation in the physical state in which the mental state consists.

Transitivity A relation R is transitive if and only if the following is true: If x stands in relation R to y, and y stands in relation R to z, then x stands in relation R to z. For example, identity is transitive: if $x = y$ and $y = z$, then $x = z$.

Types and tokens Types are kinds of things, and tokens are individual things. For example, consider the word "book." How many letters does that word contain? If you count by letter types, then the answer is three. If you count by letter tokens, then the answer is four. Philosophers of mind often apply this distinction to mental states. For example, they distinguish pain as a type of mental state from token pains. Andy's headache and Barbara's headache are states of the same type, but their token headaches are distinct from each other.

INDEX

absent qualia argument 94
access consciousness 231–233
accuracy conditions 212
Adams, Barbara 302, 304
Agar, Nicholas 265
AI Consciousness Test (ACT) 102
Akins, Kathleen 29
aliefs 184, 209–210
all-mental and all-physical world (MPW) 130
Alzheimer's disease 162
analytic functionalism 88–90
animalism: background on 267–268; case overview 268; discussion 268–271
Anscombe, Elizabeth 178–181
Antarean antheads 96
aphantasia 198–199
a posteriori necessary truth 297
Aristotle 5, 185
Arnauld, Antoine 15
Arthritis-man case 153–158
Artificial General Intelligence 99–100

Artificial Intelligence (AI) 98–102, 104–108
Arvan, Marcus 310
attention: introduction to 2, 183–184; representationalism and 110–114
autonomy 73, 79–80
Avicenna (Ibn Sina) 3, 5; floating man argument 5–7; self-awareness 6–7

Baars, Bernard 20
Ball, Derek 155
Balog, Katalin 44–47
Barnes, Elizabeth 310
bat echolocation experiences: background on 26; case overview 26–27; discussion 27–29; physicalism and 26–29
Baylis, Françoise 305
behavioral responses 82–85, 87, 96, 115
behaviorism: mental states and 197–198; neobehaviorism 85; philosophical behaviorism 82–84;

physicalism and 68; in research psychology 82, 84
beliefs: functionalist account of 179–180; here-beliefs 292; I-belief 291–292; informationally integrated beliefs 165; now-beliefs 292; perception, imagination, and attention 183–184; standing beliefs 164–165
blindness 185–188; inattentional 225–226; see also change blindness
blindsight: access consciousness 231–233; background on 184, 230; case overview 230–232; discussion 232–234; mongrel concept 230
Blockhead argument: background on 92–93; case overview 93–94; discussion 94–96; homunculi and 94
Block, Ned 53, 119, 228, 231–232
body-swap cases: background on 254–255; discussion 256–258; overview 255–256; reidentification and 301
Boethius 238
Bostrom, Nick 261
brain in a vat (BiV) thought experiment: background on 167–168; case overview 168–169; discussion 169–171
brain processes 19, 21, 87, 108
brain states 2, 14, 45–47, 72–73, 90, 117–119, 147, 158
branching-times model of necessity 299
Broad, C. D. 63–64
Brown, Christopher Devlin 130–131
Bruno, Michael 257–258
Buddhism 238, 247–253
Burge, Tyler 161

Campbell, John 187
candle analogy in identity 247, 249, 252–253

causal connection 74, 169, 249
causal co-variation 116, 120, 150
causal theory of reference 169–170
ceteris paribus 150
Chalmers, David J.: consciousness 18, 19, 20, 21–22; externalism and 161; hard problem of consciousness 19–23, 55, 57–58; Inverted Mary 35; mind uploading case 264; standing beliefs 164–165; virtual experiences 170; yogis argument 46; zombie argument 38, 46
change blindness: background on 224; case overview 224–226; discussion 226–228
characterization question 301–306
chariot analogy in identity 247–253
ChatGPT 100
Cheselden, William 187
China Nation case see Blockhead argument
Chinese Room thought experiment: background on 104; case overview 104–106; discussion 106–108; Luminous Room argument and 107–108; Robot Reply 107; Systems Reply 107
chip test 102
Chisholm, Roderick 287–288, 293
Chomsky, Noam 141–142
chromesthesia 217–218
Churchland, Patricia 22–23, 55, 57–59, 107–108
Churchland, Paul 107–108
Church–Turing thesis 98
Clark, Andy 161, 164–165
coffee tasters argument: background on 49–50; case overview 50–52; Dennett on 49–50, 52; discussion 52–53
cogito, ergo sum argument 285, 287
cognition/cognitive states: background on 161–162; case overview

162–163; discussion 163–165; externalism and 161–165; Otto's notebook case 161–165; standing beliefs 162, 164–165
cognitive ability 19
cognitive function 19–20, 22
cognitive science 18–20
colored hearing see synesthesia
color swatches argument 200–202
common sensibles 185
completeness of physics 72–74
conceivability argument: Descartes and 15–16, 40; epistemic gap and 61; slugs and the tiles argument 61–64; zombie argument and 40, 44
concept of pain 16, 83, 89, 192; see also pain/pain experience
conscious experience 4, 11, 20–23, 26–29, 39, 68, 119, 148, 228, 275, 283–285
consciousness: access consciousness 231–233; background on 18–19; Chalmers on 18, 19, 20, 21–22; Descartes on 3–4, 18; discussion 21–23; hard problem of 19–23, 55, 57–58; introduction to 2–4; introspection and 50; mind uploading case 260–266; nature of 1–2, 15, 28–29, 61, 183; non-physical and 21; perceptual consciousness 225–226; physicalism and 21, 26, 38–40; physical phenomena and 21, 64; physical theory and 28; temporary disunity 275–276; unity of 238–239, 275–277, 288; what-it's-like aspect of 20; see also phenomenal consciousness
content of thoughts 135–138
counterfactual situation 155–156
Currie, Greg 210
Cyrillic text case 213–214
Cytowic, Richard 219

Davidson, Donald 143–144, 146–150
decision-making cases 307–312
Dennett, Daniel C. 23, 33; coffee tasters argument 49–50, 52; Mary case 33, 35; qualia, defined 50; quining, defined 49; third-person perspective of 23
deRosset, Louis 299
Descartes, René: cogito, ergo sum argument 285, 287; conceivability arguments and 15–16, 40; consciousness 3–4, 18; external experiences and 167; imagination and 184; imagining chiliagons 195–199; indexical thought 290, 293; mind-body dualism 13, 18, 67–68, 157; physicalism and 68–69, 122; self/selfhood 238; substance dualism 3–4, 70; thought experiments of 167–168
descriptivist theories 293
Diderot, Denis 186
disembodied pain argument: absent qualia argument 94; background on 13; case overview of 13–14; conceivability arguments 15–16; debate over 7; discussion 14–16; Gertler on 4, 13, 15, 16
disembodiment 5, 13–15
Dretske, Fred 227–228
dualism see mind-body dualism; specific dualisms

echolocation see bat echolocation experiences
economics, law of 78–79
eliminativism 52–53
Elisabeth of Bohemia 67–68, 70–71
Eloise and the tree representationalism: background on 110; case overview 111; discussion 111–114

elusive self: background on 285; case overview 285–286; discussion 286–288
environmental stimuli 82, 87
epiphenomenalist property dualism 32–33
epistemically transformative experiences 309
epistemology: Descartes on 167; elusiveness and 286–287; Floating Man argument 6–7; gap in conceivability argument 61; introduction to 1–6; introspection and 202; inverted qualia and 116; of perception 200–204; physicalism and 29; special sciences and 78
essentiality of origins principle 298–299
Evans, Gareth 187
Evil Demon argument 157
exclusion problem: background on 70–71; case overview 71–72; discussion 72–75
expected value 307–309, 311
Experienced Mary 35
experiences: conscious experience 4, 11, 20–23, 26–29, 39, 68, 119, 148, 228, 275, 283–285; of imagination 148; intrinsic properties of 112; nature of 29, 34; olfactory 112; subjective 19; transparency of 111–112; virtual 170; visual experience 19, 111–112, 116–117, 187, 212–213, 219, 225, 275; see also bat echolocation experiences; pain/pain experience
experiential perspective-taking 198
explanatory gap 20–21
extended minds 137
extended mind thesis 162

externalism: cognition/cognitive states and 161–165; defined 137; in mental states 153–158, 161
external stimuli 85, 115, 139, 142

floating man argument: background on 3, 5; case overview of 5–6; discussion 6–7
Fodor, Jerry 78–79
folk physics 52
folk psychology 52, 206
4E (embodied, embedded, enactive, extended) Cognition program 162
Frege, Gottlob 173–174, 292–293
French, Robert 100
functionalism: analytic functionalism 88–90; Blockhead argument 92–96; defined 68; neobehaviorism as 85; qualia and 115–120; synesthesia and 221; see also physicalism
functionally definable 19

Galton, Francis 218
Galton, Frank 198
gender identity 302–303
Gendler, Tamar 208–209
Gertler, Brie: conceivability arguments 16; disembodied pain argument 4, 13, 15, 16; internalism vs. externalism 157; standing beliefs 165
God 13, 168
Grand Canyon Skywalk case: background on 206–207; case overview 207–209; discussion 209–210

hallucinations 200–201, 212, 218
Hardin, C. L. 118
hard problem of consciousness 19–23, 55, 57–58

Harman, Gilbert 111
Hart, W. D. 14–15
Hempel, Carl 122–126
Hempel's dilemma: background on 122; case overview 122–123; physicalism and 122–126
here-beliefs 292
heterophenomenology 23
hidden essence 16
Hobbes, Thomas 9
hornswoggle argument: background on 55–56; case overview 56–57; discussion 57–59
Hume, David: imagination and 183–184; metaphysical principles 297–298; missing shade of blue case 190–192
Humean compatibilism 123

I-beliefs 291–292
Ichino, Anna 210
identity: animalism and 268–271; candle analogy in 247, 249, 252–253; chariot analogy in 247–253; gender 302–303; identification and reidentification 301–306; introduction to 2, 237–239; mind uploading case 260–266; physical theory and 238, 240–241, 261, 263; racial 302–303; transitivity of 201, 243, 264
identity theory 87–88, 158
illusionism 52–53
imagination: access consciousness and 232; beliefs 183–184; Descartes and 184; experience of 148; Hume and 183–184; introduction to 2, 183–184; mental imagery in 198–199; mental states and 208–210; as philosophical tool 195; pure understanding and 195–196; as skill 193

imagining chiliagons: background on 195; case overview 196; discussion 196–199
imitation game: background on 98; case overview 98–99; discussion 99–102
inattentional blindness 225–226
independence of minds 279–283
indeterminacy of translation 141–143
indexical thoughts: background on 290–291; case overview 291–292; discussion 292–293
individualism see internalism
informationally integrated beliefs 165
inner states 19, 46, 68, 84–85
intentionality/intentionalism: Eloise and the tree representationalism 110; general question 136; introduction to 135–138; mental states and 135–138, 148; particular question 136; Swampman case 146–150
interactionist dualism 33
internalism (individualism) 153–157
introspectability 165
introspection: access to the self 239; bat echolocation experiences 29; Blockhead argument 95; consciousness, and 50; Eloise and the tree representationalism 111–113; elusive self case 285–288; narrative conceptions of self 305–306; Otto's notebook case 164–165; split-brain case 275; synesthesia and 221–222; theory of seemings 202
intuition pumps 49
Inverse Mary 35
Inverted Earth 119
Inverted Mary 35
inverted qualia: background on 115; case overview 116–117; discussion

118–120; functionalism and 115–120
inverted spectrum cases 118
involuntary mental imagery 199
I-thought 293

Jackson, Frank: intelligent sea slugs argument 63; Mary case 27, 31–35, 192–193; see also knowledge argument
Jackson, Magdalena Balcerak 198

Kaplan, David 292–293
Keeley, Brian 220
Kim, Jaegwon 71, 79–80
Kirk, Robert 38
know-how 34
knowledge argument 27, 31–35, 61–64
knowledge-that 34
Kripke, Saul 296–298
Kurzweil, Ray 261

law of economics 78–79
Leibniz, Gottfried Wilhelm 3–4, 9–11
Lewis, David K. 87–90, 293
linguistic meaning: background on 139; case overview 140–141; discussion 141–144
Locke, John: inverted qualia cases 116; materialism and 9; memory theory 238, 241–243; mind, as blank slate 190; Molyneux's problem and 183, 185–188; physical theory and 240–241; self/selfhood 237–238
logical possibility 14
Luminous Room argument 107–108

Macpherson, Fiona 222
mad pain and Martian pain argument: background on 87; case overview 88; discussion 88–90

Mandelbaum, Eric 209
Mary case: background on 31; case overview of 31–32, 192–193; discussion 32–35; epistemic gap in 61; Experienced Mary 35; Inverse Mary 35; Inverted Mary 35; RoboMary 35; Subliminal Mary 35; Swamp Mary 35
Masham, Damaris 9
materialism: case overview of 9–10; discussion 10–11; Leibniz on 9; Locke on 9; perceptual experiences and 9–11; phenomenal consciousness and 9; thinking/ thoughts and 9–11; types A, B, and C 22–23, 58; see also physicalism
Maxwell, James Clerk 107
McGinn, Colin 21
McGurk effect 220
McKinnon, Rachel 310
Melnyk, Andrew 123
memory connections 267–268
memory theory 238, 241–243
mental causation problem 71–75, 158
mental content: background on 146–147; case overview 147–149; discussion 149–150; introduction to 1–2; Swampman case 146–150; Twin Earth case 155–156
mental imagery 198–199
mental phenomena 4, 9, 68–69, 71, 75, 82, 87, 124, 129–131
mental states: aliefs 184, 209–210; behaviorism and 197–198; externalism and 153–158, 161; imagination and 208–210; internalism 153–157; inverted qualia and 115, 118, 120; representationalism and 148–149; Swampman case 146–150
Mercury's orbit 56–57
metaphysical possibility 14

metaphysics: nature of consciousness and 1–2, 15, 28–29, 61, 183; physicalist theories and 67–69; zombie argument and 41–42
Millian principle 173–174
Millikan, Ruth 147
Mill, John Stuart 173–174
Mills, Charles 302
mind-body dualism: causation and 67; Descartes on 13, 18, 67–68, 157; exclusion problem 70–75; interactionist dualism 33; introduction to 1–4; not fundamentally mental 125; property dualism 4, 28, 32–33, 71–75, 282; substance dualism 3–4, 70
mind uploading case: background on 260–261; case overview 261–263; discussion 263–266
misperceptions 200–201
missing shade of blue case: background on 190–191; case overview 191; discussion 191–193
Molyneux's problem: background on 185; case overview 185–186; discussion 186–188
Molyneux, William 183, 186
mongrel concept 230
Montero, Barbara Gail 129–130
Moore, G. E. 111
multiple realizability 90

Nagel, Thomas 21, 26–29, 276
naïve realism 215
narrative concept 302–306
Narrow (or Weak) Artificial Intelligence 99–100
narrow content 157
nature of consciousness 1–2, 15, 28–29, 61, 183
nature of experiences 29, 34
nature of mind 1–2, 183

necessary truths 297
neobehaviorism 85
neurons/neuron firing 55, 71–73, 88, 93–96, 136, 260, 264
Newtonian theories 56
Nichols, Shaun 257–258
Nida-Rümelin, Martine 35, 118
No Fundamental Mentality constraint 124, 129–130
No Low-Level Mentality constraint 130–132
non-physical consciousness 21
non-reductive physicalist 72–74
normative decision theory 307
no-self view 238–239, 247–248, 251, 286
now-beliefs 292

O'Callaghan, Casey 214
olfactory experience 112
Olson, Eric 268–271
Only Compositional Mentality constraint 130–131
Otto's notebook case 161–165

pain/pain experience: concept of 16, 83, 89, 192; independence of minds 279–283; mad pain and Martian pain argument 87–90; phenomenal quality of 45; as subjective 19; super-spartans argument 82–85; see also disembodied pain argument
panpsychism 124, 132, 282–283
Parfit, Derek 277
parity principle 164
Paul, L. A. 309–311
perception/perceptual experiences: color swatches argument 200–202; elusive self 286–288; introduction to 2, 183–184; materialism and 9–11; misperceptions 200–201; Molyneux's problem 185–188;

representational content of 212; speckled hen argument 202–204
perceptual consciousness 225–226
perihelion orbit 56
Perry, John 292–293
personal identity see identity
personally transformative experiences 309
phenomenal character 106, 110, 113, 120, 148, 221
phenomenal concepts 192–193, 201–204
phenomenal concept strategy 23, 34, 41–42, 46
phenomenal consciousness: access consciousness vs. 231–233; defined 19; materialism and 9; pain as 158; physicalist theories and 68; representationalism and 110; subjective nature of 26; Swampman case 148; zombie argument 42
phenomenal-contrast cases: background on 212–213; case overview 213–214; Cyrillic text case 213–214; discussion 214–215; pine trees case 213–214; Rich Content View 213–215
phenomenal experience 29, 112
phenomenal greenness 116
phenomenology 16, 23, 204
philosophical behaviorism 82–84
physical information 31–35
physicalism: background on 128–129; bat echolocation experiences 26–29; behaviorism and 68; case overview 129–130; consciousness and 21, 26, 38–40; defined 31; Descartes on 68–69, 122; discussion 130–132; Hempel's dilemma and 122–126; identity theory 87–88, 158; inverted qualia and 115–120; Leibniz rejection of 3–4; Mary case and 31–35; Nagel on 21, 26–29; physical phenomena and 128–130; positive characterization of 125; via negativa physicalism 125–126; zombie argument and 15, 38–42; see also functionalism; materialism
physicalist theories 1–2, 70–75
physical phenomena: consciousness and 21, 64; deferential strategy for defining 122–124; mad pain and Martian pain argument 87; metaphysics of mind 67–69; non-reductive physicalist 72–74; physicalism and 128–130; special sciences and 77–81; zombie argument 38–39
physical possibility 14
physical theory: animalism and 267–268; conscious experiences and 28; Hempel's dilemma 122–126; identity and 238, 240–241, 261, 263
physical truths 22, 31–32, 47, 61, 64, 193, 286
Pierre puzzle case: background 173–174; case overview 174–175; discussion 175–176
pine trees case 213–214
planetary orbits 56–57
Plato 5, 190
positive characterization of the physical 125
prince and cobbler case: background on 240–241; as body-swap case 256–257; case overview 241; discussion 241–245; memory theory 238, 241–243
Prinz, Jesse J. 35
Project Prakash 187
property dualism 4, 28, 32–33, 71–75, 282

propositional attitudes: background on 135, 153–154; case overview 154–156; counterfactual situation 155–156; discussion 156–158; Pierre puzzle case 173–174; Twin Earth case 154–158
psychological theory 240, 244–245, 254–258, 261, 263, 267
psychology, laws of 77–79
Puccetti, Roland 277
pure understanding 195–196
Putnam, Hilary 68, 82–83, 85, 95, 154, 161, 167–168
Pythagorean theorem 15, 40

qualia, defined 50, 112, 115; see also inverted qualia
queen and the gametes: background 295; case overview 296–297; essentiality of origins principle 298–299; necessary truths 297
Quine, Willard Van Orman 49, 136, 139–144
quining, defined 49

racial identity 302–303
rational perspective-taking 198
reality constraint 304–305
reductio ad absurdum 142
reduplication 244, 263–264
refrigerator-light illusion 226
reidentification 301–306
Reid, Thomas 242–243
reincarnation 247–252
relationalism 215
relativity of meaning and reference 143
reportability 19, 233
representationalism: Eloise and the tree 110–114; introduction to 135–138; inverted qualia and 115–120; mental states and 148–149; transparency and 111–112
response bias 233
retinal photoreceptors 118
Rich Content View 213–215
Rick case 35
RoboMary 35
Robot Reply 107
Roelofs, Luke 271
Rohrbaugh, Guy 299
Russell, Bertrand 22
Russellian monism 22, 75
Ryle, Gilbert 197

Sandberg, Anders 261
Sawyer, Robert 260
Schechter, Elizabeth 274, 277
Schneider, Susan 101–102
Schuyler, George 302
Schwitzgebel, Eric 96
Seagull Test 100–101
Searle, John 101, 104–108
seemings, theory of 201–204
self-awareness 6–7, 239, 290–291
self-narrative view 302–306
self/selfhood: background 247, 301–302; candle analogy 247, 249, 252–253; case overview 248–249; chariot analogy 247–253; discussion 249–253; elusive self 285–288; identification and reidentification of 301–306; introduction to 2, 237–239; no-self view 238–239, 247–248, 251, 286; reincarnation 247–252
shared feelings: background 279–280; case overview 280; discussion 280–283; independence of minds 279–283; panpsychism and 282–283
Shoemaker, Sydney 95

shopping list case: background 178; case overview 178–179; discussion 179–181
Siegel, Susanna 212–213, 215
Siewert, Charles 214
skepticism 57, 90, 137, 169, 191
slugs and the tiles argument: background on 61; case overview 62–63; discussion 63–64
Smith, Michael 179
soul: floating man argument and 5–6; identity and 261; immateriality and 267, 269; individualism and 242; nature of mind and 1–2; substance dualism and 70
soul theory 240, 261, 263
special sciences: background on 77; case overview 77–79; discussion 79–81
speckled hen argument 202–204
split brains: background on 272–273; case overview 273–274; discussion 274–277; temporary disunity 275–276
standing beliefs 162, 164–165
Star Trek case: background 301–302; case overview 302–303; discussion 303–306; narrative concept 302–306; self-narrative view 302–306
stellar composition 56–57
Stoljar, Daniel 21–22, 35, 61–64
Strawson, Galen 85, 305
strong AI 104, 106
strong transparency thesis 113–114
subjective experience 19
Subliminal Mary 35
substance dualism 3–4, 70
super-spartans argument: background on 82–83; case overview 83–84; discussion 84–85; pain experience 82–85; super-super-spartans 83–85
Sutton, C. S. 270

Swampman case 146–150
Swamp Mary 35
sympathetic magic 208
synesthesia: background on 217–218; case overview 218–220; chromesthesia 217–218; discussion 220–222
Systems Reply 107

that-clauses 135
theory of mind 52, 84, 88–90, 94–95, 106, 197
theory of seemings 201–204
thinking animal argument 268–269
thinking/thoughts: content of 135–138; indexical thoughts 290–293; introduction to 135–138; materialism and 9–11
transformative choice: background on 307–308; case overview 308–310; discussion 310–312; epistemically transformative 309; expected value 307–309, 311; personally transformative 309
transitivity of identity 201, 243, 264
transparency of experience 111–112
trauma 245, 301
Turing, Alan 99–102
Turing Test 99–102, 105
Twin Earth case 153–158
Tye, Michael 112, 227
type-A materialism 22, 58
type-B materialism 22–23, 58
type-C materialism 58

Ullmann-Margalit, Edna 309
unconsciousness 20, 95, 119, 227–228
unity of consciousness 238–239, 275–277, 288

Van Leeuwen, Neil 197–198
verificationist principle 84

via negativa physicalism 125–126
virtual experiences 170
visual experiences 19, 111–112, 116–117, 187, 212–213, 219, 225, 275; see also change blindness; synesthesia

weather watchers 85
whole brain emulation (WBE) 261
wide content 157
Wilkes, Kathleen 257, 275
Wilson, Jessica M. 124, 129

yogis argument: background on 44; case overview of 44–46; Chalmer on 46; discussion 46–47

zombie argument: background on 38; case overview of 38–40; Chalmers on 38, 46; conceivability argument and 15, 40, 44, 61; discussion 40–42; epistemic gap in 61; not fundamentally mental 125; proponents of 46; rejection of 44–46

For Product Safety Concerns and Information please contact our EU representative GPSR@taylorandfrancis.com
Taylor & Francis Verlag GmbH, Kaufingerstraße 24, 80331 München, Germany

www.ingramcontent.com/pod-product-compliance
Lightning Source LLC
Chambersburg PA
CBHW052012290426
44112CB00014B/2212